"I'm Still Aggravated But At Least I Didn't Kill Anybody!"

A HUMOROUS LOOK AT ANGER MANAGEMENT

JOHN KNIGHT

outskirtspress

DENVER, COLORADO

Outskirts Press, Inc.
http://www.outskirtspress.com

ISBN: 978-1-4327-8615-1

Outskirts Press and the "OP" logo are trademarks belonging to Outskirts Press, Inc.

PRINTED IN THE UNITED STATES OF AMERICA

ONE

We were on the ground and I glanced at my watch for the first time. I still had twenty-five minutes, plenty of time. That wasn't so bad. I don't know what I was worried about. That's when the plane came to a complete stop short of the gate. I'm not talking about slowing down. No we were stopped, not moving at all. Sometimes they do that, maybe the ground crew wasn't in position yet, no need to fear. When we were still not moving after a couple of minutes I started to suspect that there might be a problem. At this point in time I needed every possible minute if I was going to make my connection and here we were just sitting, going nowhere.

The Captain came over the intercom, "Ah, folks... There is a plane sitting at our gate. He should be out of there in the next three to five minutes and then we can go on in. Sorry for the inconvenience."

I looked at my watch. I should still have ten or fifteen minutes. If I run and my connecting gate isn't too far, I should still make it. It'll be close but I think I can do it. At least that's what I was trying to tell myself.

I was still feeling confident and there was no reason to get anxious, even though I was. I'll make it, don't panic... I kept telling myself over and over again in my head. Deep down I didn't believe a word of it but I was making a valid attempt.

That's when the Captain came back on the intercom, "I'm afraid I have some bad news folks. This flight ahead of us is having some issues. It's going to be at least another twenty minutes before we can get into the gate. I'll give you an update when we get more information. Again, sorry for the inconvenience."

OK, now we had a major problem, inconvenience my ass! The plane was on the ground, I had time to make my connection, and I can't get out of there! How could there not be a gate for us? We're late, we should have been on the ground half an hour ago and there's not a gate for us! What kind of bullshit airline are you operating here? I hate flying to begin with. It seems like it hardly ever goes smoothly. Making a connection is the worst. I think that every time I have to make a connecting flight my originating flight leaves behind schedule. Sometimes I think that they might just be screwing with me on purpose. I know that a major commercial airline is not going to throw their whole schedule out of whack just to mess with me, but thinking it seems to get me through the day.

As we were sitting there I tried to get one of the flight attendants to notice me. They were in that seat at the front of the plane that faces the passengers. I was only a few rows back so it shouldn't be hard to get their attention, at least that's what I thought. I started to wave my arm at them. The female attendant wouldn't even look at me. What's her problem? I guess she doesn't want to be bothered. I could see that the male attendant had to see me out of the corner of his eye. I know that he could see me. Come on, I'm not invisible here, look at me you fucking moron! Maybe he's already off of the clock when we landed and now it's every man, woman, and child for themselves. Look at me asshole! Come on, look at me you know I want something.

Ah, there it is, eye contact. I looked at my watch and then at him and said, "I have a connection that leaves in five minutes. It doesn't look like I'm going to make it." He just gave me a smirk and said, "Yeah, I don't know."

"Well I know! I'm not going to make it!" I must have been getting loud because the other passengers were beginning to look at me. Some of them looked worried like I was about to cause a scene. I never got that. Why do people get upset and begin to feel uncomfortable when somebody goes off the deep end and causes a commotion. It's free entertainment isn't it? Unfortunately I'm usually the one doing the entertaining.

The male flight attendant went right back into the conversation with the female attendant showing me that he didn't really give a dam about me. I didn't feel that our discussion was over.

"You know I was wondering if maybe you could let my connecting flight know that I was here. Maybe if they knew they could wait until we get to the gate. There are probably other people here that have connections as well." I figured I might as well take the initiative. Nobody else was speaking up.

He looked at me smugly and replied, "I'm sure that they are well aware that we are here." Then he gave me an arrogant stare. This really set me off.

"How the hell do they know that we're here? Apparently nobody else does. I mean we got in half an hour late and they still didn't have a gate for us! I don't think anybody was expecting us!"

Smartass didn't have an answer for that one. His smugness looked like it was giving way to confusion. His lips were kind of pursing like he was trying to say something but his brain just wouldn't cooperate. The Captain came back over the speaker, "OK...um, it looks like this plane in front of us isn't going anywhere. They're looking to find another gate for us. I will let you know as soon as I'm notified."

I really don't remember heading for the door of the plane. It was one of those blackout moments when you just react without thinking. I realize now that I should have really thought that one through. Do you know that when you try to let yourself out of an airplane before it reaches the gate that they call the authorities? I found that one out. They were waiting for me as soon as we finally reached the gate some twenty minutes later. I really felt that it was an over reaction on the part of the airline since I had stopped trying and gone back to my seat at least ten minutes before that.

They wouldn't listen to me though and as soon as the door was opened the police came on and escorted me off of the plane before anybody else was allowed to leave. I don't think that I had ever been the first person off the plane before so that was new to me. I just wish it had been under better circumstances. Being escorted through an airport by the police certainly draws attention. Anybody that witnessed it probably went home and told everyone that they had seen a terrorist. The worst part of everything was that as we passed the board showing the outgoing flights I noticed that my flight to Pittsburgh was delayed. I would have made it anyway.

I should be home right now. I really screwed up this time. My wife has been telling me for years that my temper was going to get me into trouble and now it really happened. I'm stuck in Las Vegas for I don't know how long. I'm sitting in the waiting room of some medical center waiting to be evaluated by a psychotherapist to see if I'm mentally stable. It's a real mess that I've gotten myself into. The day started off well enough yesterday. I was on my way home after ten days on the road and I was really looking forward to it. If everything had gone efficiently, none of this would have happened. Unfortunately it did not.

There was really no reason to get to the airport as early as I did. It's just that I'm not one of those people that expect everything to go smoothly. I'd been in Reno for the past week and I was flying home Monday. I woke up early, to get myself adjusted to east coast time, got in a workout, a shower, packed and really had nothing left to do around the hotel so I headed on over to the airport around one o'clock even though my flight wasn't until three-twenty. The airport in Reno is never too crowded but this is Thanksgiving week and I thought it was best to get to the airport a little early just in case. I never leave anything to chance. I always believe that anything that can go wrong probably will. It's my motto and I live by it.

After I checked my luggage I looked up at the monitor to see that my flight was going out on time. Of course I still had two hours for that to change. This is the biggest problem with getting to the airport early; it gives me more time to stress out. My flight out of Reno was scheduled to get into Las Vegas at four-thirty five and my connection into Pittsburgh was supposed to leave at five-twenty. I'm never comfortable with less than an hour between flights. It's just been my experience that if either of the flights is going to be delayed it's always the first one.

When I arrived at the airport I could see that it wasn't overly crowded so I decided to grab something to eat and make a few phone calls before I got on the plane. Around two-thirty I decided to start up to my gate, of course that's after passing through security, which now involves removing shoes, belts, metal of any kind, and cell phones. Laptops have to be removed from their cases, all liquids and gels must be put into plastic baggies which I presume work as some kind of deterrent to keep them from exploding. It all seems like a bunch of bullshit that we have to go through just to give us the feeling that they are really "keeping us safe"!

The thing is that the lunatic terrorists keep coming up with newer and crazier ways to cause mayhem. First it was the shoe bomber and then the underpants bomber. We've been lucky so far because they both turned out to be idiots. The shoe bomber couldn't get his matches to stay lit and there could have been a major catastrophe had he been intelligent enough to bring along a lighter instead. Then the underpants bomber did nothing but burn his balls. If one of these guys ever comes along with an IQ higher than twelve they may be able to get the job done.

With each new incident security has to come up with new and innovative ways to eliminate the threat. This would include the new screening machines that allow security to see passengers naked as they pass through. I wish I was making this up but they have developed monitors that can see right through our clothing! It's another improvement to keep us free while taking away another of our freedoms and for what, to stop a potential underpants bomber from setting his crotch on fire?

You have to wonder how far these morons are willing to go. What's the next step, the ass bomber? You won't be able to hide a bomb in your ass if they can see through your clothing because they'll be able to see the detonator hanging out of your crack. I think we can also expect a heavy increase in sexual predators applying for security jobs, but we'll be safe from the ass bombers.

When I got to my gate it was around quarter till three and the first thing that I always do is look to see if there's a plane parked there. At this time there was not a plane there or one moving toward it. We should have been getting ready to board and there was no plane. The sign at the gate still had the departure time at three-twenty, no need to worry.

At three o'clock with no plane in sight I began to feel the slightest bit of alarm and by slightest bit I mean I was thinking, "I'm fucked!" That's when I approached the gate agent for the first time. She was a blonde, probably around thirty-five, a little chunky with long blonde hair that hung down her back in curls and made her look like she was a time traveler from the distant past, maybe around the time of the American Revolution. She looked like she took off her bonnet and let her hair hang down.

"Excuse me, is this flight to Las Vegas going to be late?" I asked her.

"We're waiting for the flight to arrive, when it does we will be able to let the inbound passengers disembark and then we'll start to board." She replied.

Now that really didn't answer my question. "Do you know when it's coming in?" I asked.

"It should be any minute, then we'll let the passengers that aren't going to Las Vegas off and then we'll start to board." She said and I took it from my own experience that we would in fact be going out late. The question was how late?

It was ten after three when I approached for the second time. There was still no sign of a plane coming into our gate and since we were supposed to leave in ten minutes I was really getting a sense that there was no way in hell for that to happen.

As no one made any announcement to inform us what was going on it was up to me to find out on my own. "Do you have any idea what time this flight might be leaving?" I asked the gate agent.

"We can't do anything until the flight gets into the gate." She replied.

"Do you know when that might be?" I asked.

"It's in range so it should be any time now." She answered.

It's in range means that it's not even on the ground yet which means it could be another half an hour or so before it even gets to the gate. "I have a connection out of Las Vegas and I only have forty-five minutes between flights so I might be cutting it a bit close." I informed her.

"You should be all right," is all that she said through a forced smile and then she turned away.

I know that I can be a real pain in the ass sometimes but I was just trying to get an answer. Why would this woman give a shit about me? No matter where I end up tonight she's going to go home and sleep in her own bed. Once I'm out of here I would no longer be her problem and I can tell by the way she acted that it couldn't happen soon enough.

This is when the stress started coming on full force. I couldn't think of anything else except that I was going to miss my connecting flight, the last one going out of Las Vegas into Pittsburgh Monday night and since it was Thanksgiving week, the busiest travel week of the year, I could have a hard time getting another flight.

An announcement was finally made at twenty after three, which was supposed to be our departure time. "For those of you in the boarding area waiting for the flight to Las Vegas, that flight is now on the ground and heading for the gate. Once the incoming passengers are off we will begin the boarding process. The new time of departure is three-forty five. Thank you for your patience." The gate agent informed us. I don't know who the hell she was thanking for their patience, certainly not me, my patience was now shot. My forty-five minute window was now down to twenty minutes at best. That's if she's not full of shit and something else happens.

It was actually ten to four when we finally pulled back from the gate. Luckily the flight wasn't too full going out of Reno so it didn't take long to board. My connection time was now down to fifteen minutes if we didn't make up any time in travel. That was my best hope. Usually the airlines add extra time on to flight schedules.

That way if they actually make it on time they look like they're competent.

I decided not to look at my watch the whole flight. That's too nerve-wracking, knowing that if you don't land within the next five or ten minutes you're in big trouble. That's usually when the plane goes into a holding pattern and makes you totally freak out. I didn't want to do that. I just put on my ipod and sat back and tried to relax. Of course I couldn't really relax. All that I did was sit there through the whole flight thinking, "I wonder what time it is?"

When I could see the lights of Las Vegas below it didn't seem like we were in the air very long. I remember thinking to myself that we made pretty good time and that I wasn't going to have any problems making my connection. I actually began to relax. That was until I could no longer see the lights of Las Vegas below me. Son of a bitch, we flew right past it!

Las Vegas was shining like a beacon below me a minute ago and now there's nothing down there. We were in the middle of the desert and there sure as shit isn't anywhere to land there! What the hell was going on? Vegas must be backed up and now we have to take the long way around and wait our turn and I'm going to miss my connection and I never should have believed that I was going to make it in the first place! The Captain came on the intercom, "Flight Attendants, prepare for landing." I was going to make it, at least that what I thought for a brief moment before I found out about the gate situation.

TWO

I spent the night in the Las Vegas jail. They let me call my wife back at home to let her know that I wouldn't be arriving. She acted as is she was concerned about me but I could tell by her tone that when we have more time to talk there would be a lecture. I will have to just sit and listen, interrupting every now and then to say, "Yes, of course you're right, I know."

There was a tiny cot in the cell and I didn't think that there was a chance in hell that I would get any sleep but I did manage to pass out for an hour or two. It must have been from all of the anxiety. In the morning I had to go before judge Ackerman. With a name like Ackerman I was picturing him as some little guy with a receding hairline and a potbelly. I was wrong about that. When he walked in the judge looked like some cowboy out of the old west, the way they look right before they shoot you dead. He had slicked jet-black hair, a stern jaw and a look on his face like he didn't give a damn about anybody. As soon as I saw him I was sure that I was screwed. He'll probably give me the chair I was thinking. He actually turned out to be a decent guy. Because I had no prior record and I wasn't really making terrorist threats, he determined that I should probably be evaluated by a professional to make sure that I wasn't a danger to myself or those around me. After that I would come back to appear before him and he would decide my fate.

I've been sitting around this waiting room at the medical center for about an hour now and it's given me time to really worry. I was fine just sitting here in my own misery pretending to read a magazine. Unfortunately the guy next to me, some guy named Dave, wanted to talk. It seems he had a nervous breakdown at work. Dave was a blackjack dealer for seventeen years and one day it just got to him and he totally freaked out. They had to drag him out of the casino kicking and screaming. That was after he flipped over his black jack table, sending the cards and chips flying. I wish I could have been there for that. That's the kind of show I'm talking about! The hell with going to see one of the lavish bullshit production shows that they overcharge for in this town. I'll gladly pay big money to watch some poor bastard lose his mind and flip over a black jack table. I can only imagine the looks on the faces of those poor people from Middle America getting a glimpse of reality in the center of this charade in the desert. That's entertainment.

Dave has a dazed look about him that can only mean that he's been really beaten down by life or he's heavily medicated. I'm guessing a little of both. I can really sympathize with Dave. I don't know how he put up with it for seventeen years. If you've ever been in a casino you know of the constant noise, bells and whistles going off over and over again. Not to mention the crowds. Every day there are hundreds of thousands of people continuously walking around without a clue. They are looking at all the shiny lights and stopping to take photos in the middle of a busy walkway with little regard for anybody but themselves. Imagine that for eight, maybe ten hours a day for seventeen years. It's amazing that he only turned over a table and didn't show up for work one day packing a semi-automatic and picking people off. Maybe that kind of thing only happens at the post office.

The officer that escorted me here pops his head into the waiting room. I guess he's been standing guard outside to make sure that

I don't make a run for it. Believe me the thought has crossed my mind. If I wanted to I could probably slip out the back door without anybody noticing that I'm gone. I could spend the rest of my days on the lamb, living under an assumed name, staying one step ahead of the law. It just seems like a lot of work over a little fit that I threw on an airplane.

This cop doesn't seem too happy about the fact that I'm still sitting in the waiting room. He looks like the type that would rather be out busting heads or harassing the innocent. If you were casting the part of badass cop you couldn't do any better than this guy. He has a crew cut, thin frowning lips and black eyes that look right through you. He's wearing one of those leather jackets that always look like they are way too tight and the way that badge is shining he must polish it every night. I don't even know his name since he didn't say a single word to me on the ride over here. He wasn't very pleasant then and I imagine his mood will be even fouler on the way back since he doesn't seem to be overjoyed by this assignment.

"Mr. Knight."

I wasn't paying attention so I didn't notice the door open. There's a knock out brunette standing there that just called my name. I'm hoping that she's the one that's going to be evaluating me.

"Mr. Knight, Doctor Keller will see you now."

When she says this I realize that she's probably not going to be the one doing the analysis. That is unless she's one of those overly pretentious people that refer to themselves in the third person. Nah, that would be too weird. Can you imagine going to a psychotherapist that suffers from narcissism? Then again, this is Las Vegas after all.

I follow her through the door and down the hall. She is wearing tight black slacks that accentuate the shape of her ass. It's a great one too, not too big, not too small but just right and very shapely. Even though I know that it's wrong I stare at it the whole way. I may be under a lot of stress here but at least I'm not dead. We reach a door and she holds it open for me. She's wearing a white, low cut blouse and I try not to stare. Actually I guess that I'm trying to not get caught. My gaze goes right to the cleavage and it looks like she's had them done. Man, I was really trying not to look there. I try not to be obvious and take my eyes off when I notice that she sees me looking. I feel embarrassed but then I think, "Hey, if you don't want me to look they shouldn't be out on display like that." I don't know what the deal is with that, women wear a revealing outfit and when you take a gander they look at you like you're some kind of disgusting pig. At least that's the way that they seem to look at me.

As I enter the office she closes the door behind me. Dr. Keller leaps out of his chair behind his desk and rushes over to me with his hand out.

"John, nice to meet you, come in." He says as we shake hands.

The fact is I'm already in so you don't have to tell me to come in but I don't say anything. The thing really freaking me out is this guy is a giant. He looks to be at least six feet seven with long arms and a lanky build. He's just all arms and legs flopping all over the place. His skin is tan and he's got a full head of blonde hair that he probably dyes. I'm guessing that he's in his mid-forties but looks like he's had some touch up work. The skin around his eyes just doesn't look natural, like if he closed them too tight the back of his head would explode. I guess that's one of the advantages of working in a Medical building like this. He probably gave some free therapy to a plastic surgeon in exchange for an eye job and then had them throw in a set of breasts for his receptionist. Why the hell not I suppose.

"Yes, nice to meet you." I say even though it's really not. I don't mean that because he's an asshole or anything. It's just that I would rather not be meeting him, not under these circumstances anyway.

Dr. Keller waves his gangly arm toward a chair in the center of the room.

"Have a seat." He instructs.

I sit down and Dr. Keller sits in an identical chair directly across from me. His long legs seem to cross the room toward me with his bony knees sticking out like some kind of dangerous weapons.

"So I hear that there was a little incident on the plane yesterday." He says.

"Yes, that's why I'm here." I answer.

"Have you ever seen an analyst before?" He asks.

"No." I answer.

"Are you taking any medications for depression or stress?" He asks.

"No." I answer again.

"Have you had other instances when you let your emotions get out of control?" He asks.

I think about this one before answering. What's the best response for this situation? In other words which one is going to make things easier on me? Ah, what the hell. Let's tell the truth.

"Not like this." I say.

"But you have had other times when your rage may have gotten out of control?" He asks.

I have to be careful here, "Yes, I suppose that once or twice during my life I may have let my emotions get the best of me and I may have overreacted. Doesn't everybody?" I say.

"No." He replies.

He's just staring at me, waiting for me to give some kind of response to what he just said. I can't get over the fact that the chair that he is sitting in looks like it was made for a child. He just doesn't look like he fits. Dr. Keller then crosses his right leg over his left and twists his right foot behind his left leg. I've never seen anything like this before. This guy is all twisted up like a pretzel and it reminds me that I haven't eaten anything since around two o'clock yesterday. Some pretzels would really hit the spot right now.

He must realize that I'm not going to say anything because he says, "Let's talk about what happened to you."

And now he's just staring at me again. I guess he wants me to tell him what happened even though he's already been filled in.

"OK, here's what happened. I hate to even think about it because it was so aggravating. The flight was already late by half an hour coming in and I was cutting it very close to make my connecting flight. Now I'm trying not to pay attention to the time. In fact I never even looked at my watch until the wheels hit the ground in Vegas. When we left Reno I figured I had no shot at making my connection. Then we made it in with twenty minutes to spare and I felt relief, calm. I was going to make it" I tell him.

"So you had already determined that you weren't going to make your connecting flight in advance." He says.

"I just said that I was feeling calm because I was going to make it." I respond.

"Yes, but before you said that you made the statement that you felt that there wasn't any chance that you would make it." He says.

"Let's just say that I wasn't giving it much hope." I say.

"Wouldn't you consider that to be a pessimistic attitude?" He asks.

"More of a realist," I reply.

He just looks at me and then writes something down on his note pad. "Now, you say that you were feeling calm and relieved. What happened to change your state of emotion?" He asks.

"We got screwed, that's what happened! Because there was no gate for us, can you believe that? I mean we get in half an hour late to begin with and then there's no place for us to go! Nobody seemed to care." I say.

"When you say nobody cared, who are you referring to?" He asks.

"Well the flight attendants for one. They could care less when I told them that I was going to miss my connecting flight." I say.

"I don't know what you expected them to do. It's not up to the flight attendants to find a gate for the plane. At least I don't believe that's one of their jobs. You don't think that is one of their jobs do you?" He asks.

"No." I reply.

"Well then what did you expect them to do?" He asks.

"For one thing, I asked if they could let my other flight know that we were on the ground and what the situation was." I say.

"And how did they respond to that?" He asks.

"They said that they probably already knew that we were here." I say.

"But that wasn't a good enough answer for you?" He asks.

"Nobody checked!" I say.

Dr. Keller writes something else in his pad and then just sits there staring at me. It's kind of intimidating to have him looking down at me this way and I think that I would hate to be one of his regular patients. How can you make somebody feel better about themselves if you're constantly looking down at them?

"Were any of the other passengers concerned about making a connecting flight?" He asks.

"If they were nobody was saying anything," I say.

"And why do you suppose that was?" He asks.

"Because most people are afraid to say anything, they'll just sit there while they get taken advantage of and that's why the service we receive keeps getting worse. The airlines and all of the other big corporations just figure that they can treat us however they want. As long as nobody is saying anything it must be all right." I say.

"Did it occur to you that maybe there were others on the flight that were equally apprehensive about missing a connection? It's just that they were able to keep their emotion from getting the best of them." He says.

"Maybe they were just a bunch of wimps." I shoot back.

Again with the staring, I don't know if he's waiting for me to say something else or if he's searching for an answer or if this is just some kind of technique that he uses. Whatever it is it's starting to creep me out.

"Why do you keep staring at me like that?" I ask.

"I don't feel that I'm staring. I'm just paying attention to you. I'm interested in what you have to say." He replies.

"I was waiting for you to ask me another question." I say.

"Therapy isn't necessarily a question and answer session. It's about listening, about giving you the opportunity to express what is troubling you." He says and then he stares at me again.

"You're doing it again!" I say and I stand up and begin to pace around the room.

"Have you ever considered the fact that you may be suffering from paranoia?" He asks.

"What are you implying?" I ask as I try to avoid his judgmental watch.

"According to the information that I received about you, you're an entertainer. Are you telling me that when you're on stage you don't want the audience to pay attention to you?" He asks.

"Of course I do. I just don't like people staring at me other times." I say.

"Why is that?" He asks.

"I just don't like it." I answer.

"Do you ever find yourself staring at another person?" He asks.

When he says this I get the impression that somehow he is aware of the way that I was just ogling his receptionist.

"No." I reply.

"Really? You never find yourself looking at another person for an extended length of time?" He asks.

"Ok, yes maybe I do on occasion." I say.

"But, you don't like people looking at you?" He asks.

"I don't know. I guess not." I say as I sit back down across from him.

"Let me ask you this? Do you ever feel like you're being watched?" He asks.

"I don't want to say." I respond.

"Why don't you want to answer?" He asks.

"I just don't." I say.

"You realize that by not answering, you are actually telling me what I want to know." He says.

"OK, then you know." I say.

"Then you do feel like you are being watched?" He asks.

"Not as much now." I say.

"So who do you think was watching you?" He asks.

"I'd rather not say."

"That's you're choice and I have to respect it…"

I interrupt him. "Dick Cheney." I say.

"Who?" Dr. Keller asks.

"Dick Cheney. I felt like Dick Cheney was watching me." I respond.

"Dick Cheney? I'm sure that the Vice President of the United States had better things to do than to watch what you were doing." He says.

"But you can't guarantee that, can you? I mean look at the technology that's out there. Did you ever Google your house? You can go on the computer or your phone and put in your address and there's your house! They have satellites taking pictures of our homes without us even being aware they are doing it and then it's right there for anyone to look at. Then there are the GPS systems, they know exactly where you are all the time. We have caller ID, picture phones, face identification and these are just the things that we know about. The government can probably see right through your walls and listen in to any conversation you are having. If this is the case then how can you know that Dick Cheney was not spying on me?" I ask.

He begins to respond and then just shrugs his shoulders.

Dr. Keller sits back in his chair and folds his hands in front of his mouth as if he's searching for just the right thing to say.

"When you were on the plane and you were unable to get to the gate, did you at any time get the feeling that what was happening was directed entirely at you? In other words did you think the airline was messing with you and everybody else was in on it?" He asks.

What is this guy, some kind of mind reader? I know the thought did cross my mind but there's no reason for him to know that. I don't need to be dragged out of here in a straight jacket. It might be a good time to protest.

"What kind of a question is that? What kind of a lunatic do you think I am?" I respond.

"First of all we don't use words like lunatic. What I'm trying to do is determine where your hostility comes from. I need to determine if you have an underlying sense of paranoia that may lead you to irrational behavior." He says.

"Did you ever think maybe I might just be a guy that's sick of getting crappy service and lack of concern? Prices keep going up and we get less. Where does it end? If nobody is willing to take a stand and let these companies know that we are not satisfied they'll just keep taking away more and more until you have to kiss their ass just to have them spit in your face!" I respond.

"Did you ever consider a more civilized approach, perhaps sending a letter?" He asks.

"I would have had a hell of a time getting to a mail box when I was trapped on the plane." I reply.

"Ah! So you felt trapped, helpless. Could these feelings have led to your behavior?" He asks.

"I didn't feel trapped, I was trapped." I say.

"What did you hope to accomplish by going to the door?" He asks.

"I was going to accomplish getting out of there." I answer.

"Now let's just say that you were able to open the door. How then did you plan to go from there since you weren't at a gate?" He asks.

"I guess I would have jumped." I reply.

"That's a heck of a jump. Do you think you could have made it without injuring yourself?" He asks.

"I don't know. I suppose I hadn't really planned that far ahead. I just felt like I had to do something." I say.

"Has your erratic behavior ever caused you to hurt yourself or cause injury to somebody else?" He asks.

I think about the question and to the best of my recollection I haven't.

"No." I reply.

"Then you've been lucky. If you continue to behave in this manner it's just a matter of time. We've got to do something about this." He says.

He rises from his chair and towers over me. He walks over to his desk and pulls out a drawer, grabs a binder, and places it on top of the desk.

He looks at me and says, "Talking to you here, I get the impression that you need help dealing with your anger and to some extent paranoia. It will take some work but I hope that in time you will be able to control your temper. Understand of course that it's going to be up to you. You are going to have to want to change. We can't accomplish much here today so what I'm going to do is give you the name and contact information for somebody in your area that I think will be able to work with you. I'm going to tell the authorities that I recommend you receive counseling for anger management. Now I can't make you go through with this, but I'm fairly certain that you're being able to fly again will be determined by whether or not you do." He says.

"So if I don't go I won't be able to fly anymore?" I ask.

"I would assume that to be correct." He says.

He begins to look through the file on his desk.

"I'm going to find somebody in your area. I'll have to make a call to see if they are available and explain the situation. This could take a few minutes so why don't you have a seat in the waiting room and I'll have Jennifer bring it out to you." He says. I stand to exit and he follows me to the door. He holds out his giant hand to shake mine.

"Good luck with everything." He says.

"Thank you doctor," I say as I exit.

When I get to the waiting area I see Officer Chuckles is the only one in the room. He doesn't see me when I enter. He's too caught up in the magazine that he's reading. Oh man, its Cosmo! Probably reading "Ten ways to drive your man wild in the bedroom." I was thinking about reading that myself but I was too embarrassed. Now he notices me and lays down the magazine. The way he's looking at me tells me that I shouldn't say a word about it and don't dare laugh or even smile. Just pretend like it never happened. One wrong move here and he'll take me out back and beat me to a bloody pulp with his Billy club. Back at the station he'll just tell them I tried to make a run for it and nobody will ever believe that the real reason was because I laughed at him for reading a woman's magazine. No, I didn't see a thing.

Jennifer, the hot receptionist, comes into the waiting area and I can see the officer is practically drooling when he looks at her. Too bad she didn't get here before he put down the magazine. I would have liked to see how he acted then. It would have been amusing anyway. I can see him fumbling with the magazine acting like he picked it up by mistake. I can see her giving him a look to let him know that he wasn't getting away with anything. I can see myself getting a good laugh out of that one. Then I can see myself spending the rest of the evening trying to remove a copy of Cosmopolitan from my rectum.

"Here you go Mr. Knight," She says as she hands me a slip of paper. On it is an address, phone number, and a name. DR. AMILE JONAS.

The ride back to the station is a quiet one. This officer doesn't look like he wants to talk to me and I'm not about to push it. It's OK though; I doubt that we'd have a whole lot in common anyway. To tell the truth I can't even stand looking at the back of the jackass's head, although it's better than that hard ass look on his face. We haven't said a word to each other the whole time that we've been together and I could probably tell you all about him anyway. I would imagine that he's racist, homophobic, and votes Republican no matter who is running because he thinks liberals are out to destroy the country. He probably eats a lot of red meat, very little fiber, and is constipated which has a lot to do with his disposition. He probably has a tiny penis although I suspect if any woman has ever mentioned that to him she received a thorough thrashing. It's amazing how much you can tell by looking at the back of a person's head.

I'm just trying to take my mind away from my own thoughts because I really don't know what's going to happen to me right now. On the one hand Doctor Keller said that he was going to recommend that I receive therapy for anger management. Then again I don't know if the judge is going to go along with this or take away my right to fly forever. Of course, even if he does agree to the anger management thing, I still can't fly home. How am I going to get home? This is all very traumatic. I should have read the article in Cosmo and then the officer and I would have something to discuss to take my mind off of things.

Back at the station they give me the good news and the worst news. They are going to release me on my own recognizance as long as I don't leave town before I again appear before the judge. The bad news was that because it was a holiday week, this isn't going to happen until Monday. I'm not going to make it home for Thanksgiving. I don't even have the option of taking the bus. Not only that but it's going to cost me a fortune to stay in Vegas for another week. My wife has every right to be as pissed at me as she's about to be and the worst part is there's nothing that I can say about it. This is my fault. I really hate it when that happens.

THREE

I can tell you right now that if you think you can get a good rate on a hotel room in Vegas at the last minute on Thanksgiving weekend, you are sadly mistaken my friend. It would actually be less expensive to fly home, have Thanksgiving and come back for the trial on Monday. It's just that I was told not to leave town or I would be considered a fugitive and the fact that I'm not allowed to fly. Anyway you look at it I'm stuck here.

Even though I didn't make it home, my luggage did. I guess there just wasn't time to notify the luggage handlers that one of the passengers was being arrested and he wouldn't be making his connecting flight. I have my garment bag with me. That should give me enough clothes to get through the week. I also have some laundry in there, socks and underwear that I can wash. I wasn't planning on doing laundry, then again I wasn't planning on being arrested either. I don't think that's the kind of thing that you can ever set up in advance. "Yes, I'm scheduled to fly home on Monday but I may get myself arrested and have to stay an extra week for a hearing so I'd better pack some extra socks." Of course all of my toiletries were in my checked luggage because of the bullshit laws that only allow you to bring certain sizes of shaving creams and toothpaste. So now I have to buy all of these items again, even though I have almost completely full containers of each. It's just that they are in Pittsburgh right now.

So I'll be spending Thanksgiving in Las Vegas. I know it's not the worst thing I could be doing and I've done it a few other times, just under much better circumstances. It's one thing to make the choice to be here, planning a holiday weekend to drink, gamble, and really get down to the true meaning of Thanksgiving. I'm sure this is what the pilgrims had in mind when they sat down for that first Thanksgiving. Thankful they had survived the long dangerous journey across the Atlantic Ocean and praying they get through the harsh winter ahead; so that one day their ancestors could go for broke in some monstrous casino in the middle of the desert where life was never meant to survive anyway.

Of course the Indians at that first Thanksgiving were probably thinking about the casinos they themselves would someday establish across the country to take back as much of the wealth these new white settlers were about to steal from them. And on that day all were thankful. Thankful for the greed that would establish and rule this new world for centuries to come; until that greed would be its downfall and those left at the end would have to say to themselves, "If only we had been thankful for what we had instead of trying to always acquire more and more." That will be the last Thanksgiving, which could be any day now.

This Thanksgiving I will be spending in Las Vegas awaiting a hearing.. Because of this, I don't want to spend any more money than is absolutely necessary. If they decide I am going to have a trial, I'll have to take a second mortgage and get a lawyer. Either that or I could just have them give me the chair. Which do I choose, dealing with a lawyer or death? There's really not a good choice between the two. It's something that I can think about over the weekend and hopefully I won't have to make that decision.

I have friends in town and I'm sure that they wouldn't have a problem putting me up for a few days. Then again, maybe they would, it is Thanksgiving after all. Who wants to have to explain the extra setting at the table? "Oh, he's a friend of ours that can't get home to Pittsburgh because he has a hearing on Monday for going psycho on an airplane. Please pass the potatoes." Right now I don't even want to see anyone or discuss what happened yesterday. I just need a night or two alone to sort things out. Of course there is one person that I'm going to have to discuss this with, my wife. We really haven't had a chance to chat since this went down. I was able to give her the basics of what was happening. To the best of my knowledge she's established that I acted like a total asshole and the whole thing is my fault. Aside from that we haven't really discussed the matter.

The best rate I am able to get on a hotel room is a place about ten or fifteen minutes off the strip. It's just a hotel, no casino and that's what I need right now. No bells and whistles, no thousands of people yelling and drinking, no merriment of any kind. Just a bed, a TV, and a place to chill. That's fine; I don't need to be around all of these people. Not tonight anyway. I'm stressed out enough. I make the reservation through one of those Internet services that are supposed to get you the absolute best price, but I still feel like I'm getting ripped off.

In the cab on the way to the hotel I think about all the good times I've had in this town over the years. This, of course, is not one of them. The thing is you never really consider the fact that you might get arrested for something in Las Vegas. It's just the kind of place that seems to look the other way at whatever you do. That's where that slogan came from, "What happens in Vegas stays in Vegas!" Today that has a different meaning for me, "What happens in Vegas makes YOU stay in Vegas."

As I enter the small lobby of the hotel I'm overcome by the powerful smell of stale coffee. It must be coming from the stainless coffee machine in the corner. It was probably made some time last week and they just don't bother to make new until whatever's in there is completely gone. The young man behind the desk is dressed in the usual generic hotel garb, white shirt, black tie, and total blandness. It's the rest of him that doesn't look right. He looks to be around twenty, pudgy, freckles, and the thing that throws everything out of whack is his hair. Bright red hair that he has chosen to wear in dreadlocks, I guess that nobody has taken the time to tell him he looks ridiculous.

When I get to the counter I see he is on his cell phone, engaged in conversation and not really giving a damn that there is a customer standing here.

"Man bro, I was out wif my bitches last night, gettin down an shit and dis mo' fo' starts dissin on me. So I was like, bitch you ain't better be talkin to me an shit..."

And there we have it, the crowning touch, another white American youth skilled in the use of Ebonics.

"Excuse me. I'd like to check in." I say politely hoping to steer him away from his conversation at least long enough that I can get my room.

"Yo, bro...I'll be right wif you. I'm talkin to my homey." He says.

I'm thinking that I'd like to insert that phone permanently into his ear right now but that would be rude.

"Bro, I gotta go. I'll be talkin at you later." He says and then turns toward me.

I decide to initiate our conversation.

"Reservation for John Knight," I say.

He starts banging at the keyboard. He looks confused as he stares at the computer screen. He types some more, looks more confused and then looks toward me.

"Nope, ain't no reservation for John Knight." He says.

"Look, I made it earlier. I'm sure that it's in there." I say.

"Man, I be lookin an there ain't no John Knight. You sho you at the right crib?" He asks.

I assume that he wants to know if I'm at the correct hotel.

"Yes this is it." I tell him.

"Yo sho you be givin me the right name?" He asks.

Now I may not know everything that there is to know but I do know my own name.

"Yes, John Knight. It's the name I've been using my whole life." I tell him.

He takes another look.

"Nope," He says and just stares at me.

I remember that I wrote down my confirmation number. I dig the number out of my pocket and read it to him. He begins to punch the keyboard again and then a shocked look comes over his face.

"Yo, could this be it? K-N-I-G-H-T?" He asks.

"Yes, that's what I've been telling you." I reply.

"Man, you diddin tell me that you be spellin yo name all freaky an shit. I don never be hearin about no one be spellin night wif a K." He says.

"That's the standard spelling." I tell him.

"Man, I ain't never be hearin about nufin like dat. What the..."

He stops mid sentence before he drops an F bomb in front of me. I suppose that he doesn't want to offend me but we are way beyond offense. No, right now I am truly frightened, frightened that this person and I don't even think that we can call him a person because at this time he is just a pod occupying space on this planet. I think that there are certain criteria that should be met to qualify you as a person. Things like being able to function in society, communicate with others, or make some kind of contribution. I don't think that this creature is capable of any of those things. The best thing I could possibly do right now would be to strangle the son of a bitch before he becomes a burden to humanity.

"Gonna be needin yo credit card and ID." He tells me.

I hand him my credit card and driver's license and he takes a long hard look at them.

"Man, check dat out. You really be spellin night wif a K an shit. I ain't never be hearin nufin like dis."

He says shaking his head in disbelief as his red locks swing back and forth. I realize that looking at him I could just as well be looking at Howdy Doody with cornrows and it wouldn't be any more ludicrous. He hands back my credit card and driver's license and gives me a key.

"Room 227," he tells me and points to the elevator behind me. I pick up my bags and start toward the elevator. I should really just let it go but I can't resist.

I turn back toward him and say, "Excuse me, I hate to be the one to break this to you. It's something somebody probably should have told you a long time ago but the thing is that you're white."

His mouth drops open and I'm wondering if I could actually be the first one that broke the news to him. I enter the elevator and as the door closes I let out a good laugh.

When I enter the hotel room I realize that it's exactly what I thought it was going to be, a bed a small uncomfortable chair, a television and a bathroom. No luxuries here, but I guess it's better than a jail cell. I throw down my bag and take a seat in the chair and stare at the wall for what seems like at least an hour. I look at my watch and it's only been ten minutes, time moves slowly when you're not enjoying it. I guess I should call my wife. I've been putting it off.

Normally I look forward to talking to her, but not this time. It still all seems like a bad dream but I can't wake up from this one. The thing is that I know that I fucked up. I wouldn't be here if I didn't. It's just that I don't need her to remind me about it.

"Hello, it's me." I say.

"Where are you, are you on your way home?" She asks.

"No, I can't come home. I have to stay here until Monday and then go in front of the judge again. Not only that, but I'm not allowed to fly." I tell her.

"How are you going to get home?" She asks.

"I don't know, I guess I'll deal with that when it happens." I say.

"What about Thanksgiving?" She asks.

"It looks like I'm not going to make it." I say.

"What am I supposed to do?" She asks.

We were supposed to spend the holiday with my wife's sister and her husband, which is always a good time.

"I don't know, I guess you can go by yourself. There will be more food." I answer. From the quiet on the other end I'm guessing that wasn't the right answer.

I know what's coming and we might as well get it over with. And then there it is, I get the "I knew that eventually your temper and impatience would get you into trouble" speech. She really has it down. It doesn't sound like something that was being improvised. It didn't even sound like something she'd been working on since Monday. No, this was too precise. Each point was well thought out and perfectly executed. This had to be something she'd been working on for all the years we'd known each other and now she finally had the chance to use it! At least some good came from this.

My plan was to just sit in the room, maybe watch some television and get some much-needed rest. I never watch television and there is a reason for that. It sucks! I've gone through the dial twenty times and it's just shit, shit and more shit. "The Biggest Loser," for God's sake! A bunch of overweight people crowded into the same house and forced to lose weight to get a monetary prize at the end. Of course only one of them will walk away with the prize. The rest will be encouraged to back stab and vote off their fellow contestants in the meantime. It seems like it should be the kind of situation where everyone is helping and pulling for each other but who would watch that? No, you have to make it more like real life where everybody fucks each other over and one person gets to keep all of the money. Just like the CEO of one of our major corporations. What happened to television being entertaining? I'm sitting here watching some fat bastard cry his eyes out because he can't control his passion for sweets. Eat a donut and quit your whining you fat fuck!

The other choices are even worse, "Real Housewives that nobody should give a shit about," or something like that. Do people really watch this garbage? I don't know what started this downward trend in entertainment. These reality shows or big piles of shit as I like to call them. I realize that like everything else it's about putting out the least expensive product and dividing the profits among a select few, but this is really annoying. Just because it's cheaper than paying real actors and writers to maybe put on something entertaining to just get a group of lunkheads to show us how bad their lives are doesn't mean that I have to watch it. I turn off the television and stare into space.

I can't take it anymore and the walls seem to be closing in on me. I've been pacing for the last half hour and I feel like I'm going to lose my mind. I'm not going to be able to sleep feeling this way. This whole ordeal just keeps racing through my thoughts and I can't seem to concentrate on anything else. I need something to take my mind off things. The hotel here has a shuttle that goes over to the strip. I know that earlier I thought that I didn't want to be around all the people and noise tonight but now that doesn't seem like such a bad idea. I think that going out and just walking around and doing some people watching could help.

The shuttle stops in front of New York New York and I exit. I've got twenty dollars in my pocket so I'm hardly a high roller. I've never been much of a gambler, probably because I've never won. Maybe if I had hit big the first time I would have been hooked and spent the rest of my life chasing another huge payout. That's the way they get you. They let you win a little, get you feeling confident, and then trounce you. With me it's been one long losing streak. I've never lost more than I could afford but I can't help but think that it would have been nice to win at least once. I'm thinking that with all I've been through surely I'm due for a break. This is a dangerous way to think and I know it. I'm not going to lose the whole twenty. In fact I'm not planning on losing any. I'll throw five maybe ten dollars into a machine and if my luck is in fact going to change for the better I should hit right away. I enter the casino and begin to scout for the machine that is going to give me the big payout.

PUT IT ALL ON RED! It was a brilliant thought that occurred to me as I pass the roulette table. I could put the whole twenty on red. It can only come up black or red or the long shots zero or double zero green. It's almost fifty-fifty, just about the best odds in town. What's the worst that could happen? I lose the whole twenty on one spin and have to go back to stare at the walls in the hotel. If I win though, I've doubled my money. I'll have that extra twenty to play with which really wasn't mine to begin with. I could put the original twenty in my pocket and see what I can do with the casino's money. Maybe let it ride and before you know it I'm out of my financial hole. Hell, if it keeps coming up my way I could take the year off and to hell with flying. It's thoughts like these that built this town. How many of these bums panhandling up and down the strip were once upstanding citizens in their community? They came here to chase the dream and let it all slip away. I once watched a guy lose eight thousand at a black jack table trying to get his forty dollars back. How many of these hotels have added a tower just from the money they made from people trying to get even? That's the dream, getting even. "If I could just get even everything will be wonderful."

I decide to be cautious and not risk it all at once. The table has a ten-dollar minimum so I buy ten dollars in chips and put that on red. No sense in being greedy here. What I can do is take the ten that I win and put that into a slot machine, maybe one of the progressives where I can win millions on one spin. I can live with that. Aside from the fact that they'll have to take my picture and hang it on the wall for all to see it's not a bad thing really. I've got to think positive here. That's the key, thinking positive will bring good things to your life. I've heard that it really works. It's just that I've never tried it. This is the time to start thinking that good things are going to happen, here when I'm at what could possibly be the lowest point in my life. It's going to come up red. Just keep thinking it, red, red, red. The dealer spins the wheel, he releases the ball, it goes around and around, red, red, come on red, it begins to slow, and it's going to fall into the red. Look at it. I'm going to win! The ball falls into the slot, "Double Zero," the dealer yells out. What the hell was I thinking? Now I'm even more depressed. I should have just stuck to my original plan, to walk around in misery.

Now I'm trying to get all of the negative thoughts out of my head. I've never tried such a thing before but I hear that other people do it. I keep telling myself that "no matter how bad things seem right now they can only get better," even though I don't believe a word of it. People always say this, not realizing that it's nothing but a crock of shit! What if right now is only the beginning of a long downward spiral from which you can't escape? Someday I'll look back at this moment and think, "I wish I could be back there, back at that moment when things only started to suck. Back then I was almost even."

It's like the phrase, "No matter how bad things seem to you there is always somebody that is much worse off," as if that makes it any better. Do you realize that phrase works for everybody in the world except one person? Somewhere in the world is the person that has it worse than everybody else. He and I say he because it has to be a man, I can't imagine a woman letting herself get that low. But somewhere is the person who isn't doing better than anybody. They are at the bottom rung of the futility ladder. He probably lives under a bridge and his body is covered in festering boils. His whole family hates him and would never do anything to help. He has no hope and only dreams of when things were bad but not as bad as now and the realization that things will only keep getting worse. What do you say to that poor son of a bitch? "You know as bad as things seem to you right now. Oh, that's right. Things are pretty damn bad aren't they? Thank God I'm not you."

There are worse things than being stuck in Las Vegas with no money, a hearing hanging over your head in a few days and a wife back home that is really pissed at you, but at this moment I can't think of any! The worst part is watching all the happy people walking around with big smiles on their faces like they don't have a care in the world. Look at all of these giddy fuckers having a good time. They make me want to puke! God, you people suck, can't you contain your joy? There are unhappy people around here. Have some sympathy. I guess I'm not doing a real good job of getting the negative thoughts out of my head.

I guess this would be one of those times when it would be nice to be one of those people that just go with the flow, roll with the punches, and take it all in stride and all the other stupid sayings that apply. I have to be honest with you; I have never understood these people and I really feel that they don't have a clue. It looks like I was wrong, all the bells and whistles not to mention all these happy bastards walking around is really getting on my nerves! I should just go back to my room, maybe close the drapes and sulk in the dark. It's a plan anyway, no sense trying to sleep, I don't think that I'll be getting much of that this week.

Wednesday morning, the day before Thanksgiving, I slept off and on during the night. I don't think I was ever out for more than an hour at any one time. Then I'd toss and turn for I don't know how long and maybe pass out for another half hour or so. I haven't been able to get back to sleep since I saw the first ray of daylight creep through the drapes. It's eight AM now, no use trying anymore I may as well just get out of bed and face the day. The worst part is that I have nothing to do but kill time until Monday. I wish I could have slept all the way through until then. That would have been the best. Go to sleep on Tuesday night, wake up, and its Monday morning. Then I could go and get this damn hearing over with and find out what the hell is going to happen to me. Its eleven AM back east, my mother will be up now. I should probably call her and get it over with. She already knows the situation. My wife did me the huge favor of calling her yesterday and lying. Telling my mother I was too busy to call and I would get around to it. I'm really dreading this phone conversation. I think I'll go out and get some coffee first. It's nothing that can't wait for another hour or two.

My mother has a way of taking a bad situation and making it seem even worse. I know that she doesn't mean to be this way, it's just the way she is. She always looks for the worst possible scenario in a situation. I used to watch those mothers on television telling their children not to worry and that everything would be all right. To me this was always a fabrication. I couldn't believe anyone would actually ever say something like that to his or her children. I couldn't understand why they couldn't be more like real life, saying things like, "Oh God, what are you going to do now?" Well, my real life anyway.

There's a Starbucks a block from the hotel. Isn't there always one a block from anywhere you are? I grab a large coffee and decide to make the dreaded call on my walk back.

"Hello," my mother says on the other line.

"Yeah, it's me." I respond.

"What the hell is the matter with you?" She asks.

I guess I'm just a negative psychotic that always expects things to go horribly wrong for me and as a result of that I pushed things beyond reasonable boundaries. Now as a result of my attitude I'm in this trouble. Don't you know this? You're the one that raised me after all.

That's what I'd like to tell her but instead I just say, "I don't know."

"How are you going to get home?" She asks.

"I don't know." I answer.

"If you can't fly how are you going to be able to make a living?" She asks.

Again, "I don't know."

The thing is, I don't know the answers to these questions. Hopefully I will have a better understanding after Monday and I'm really trying not to think about it right now, but my mother would never allow me to do that.

When the conversation finally ends after what seems like an eternity, I feel worse than ever. Now I've had my morning coffee, read the newspaper, got a big guilt trip from my mother and it's only ten-thirty in the morning. What the hell am I supposed to do now? This is no different than being in prison with nothing to do aside from trying to pass the time away. It's funny but the days usually fly by so fast and the years keep going by so quickly they are gone before you realize it. Right now I feel as though I can actually see the seconds ticking away in front of me and they seem to be going in slow motion. It's only ten-thirty one in the morning. What the hell am I supposed to do now?

"Wednesday afternoon around four o'clock, I'm getting really tired of sitting around this hotel room and feeling sorry for myself. I decide to break down and call my friend Carl who lives in town. I'll tell him what happened and see if he might be hospitable enough to put me up until Monday. He has a good laugh about my little incident and feels that any reasonable person would have reacted the same way (He might make a good character witness if this thing ever goes to trial). It turns out that since he's a single guy whose family lives back east, he had no plans for Thanksgiving. He was very receptive to the idea of putting me up for the weekend, even if that meant harboring a possible terrorist.

"You can crash on the couch. Just give me time to clean up the place." He tells me.

The thing is that Carl is even more anal retentive than I am and I can't imagine his place to ever be in disarray, but I'll take his word that he wants to straighten up.

I've notified the front desk that I will be checking out and they tell me I will still have to pay for tonight since it's already past check out time. This is fine with me. I really don't care. I just have to get away from this place. Carl told me he would pick me up around six so I get my things together and head down to the lobby around ten till. There's a young black girl working behind the desk along with the red headed idiot.

"I'll be checking out now." I say to the young lady.

"Was everything all right during your stay with us?" She asks politely.

"Yes, fine." I say.

"It'll just be a moment while I print out your receipt." She explains.

I can't help but notice that the dread locked moron is giving me the cold shoulder. He won't even look my way. I'd like to point out to him how ironic it is that this black woman is speaking perfect English and conducting herself in a professional manner while he fancies himself to be some kind of gangsta rapper but in these politically correct times I'm afraid that it would make me look like some kind of a bigot. It's all so confusing these days.

He won't even look at me and I'm getting a real feeling of tension coming from him toward me. I can tell when somebody has a problem with me and this guy seems to have a real bug up his ass right now.

"Here you go sir." The girl says as she hands me my receipt. "You have a wonderful Thanksgiving." She tells me.

"You do the same." I say and I know with that I should just walk out the door and leave this place as a distant bad memory but I just can't let it go. "I can't help but notice that you seem to have an attitude toward me." I say to him.

"Man, you be checked out an shit, so why don't you just be gettin on wif yo life an shit." He says, letting me know that our little chat the other day didn't affect him in the least.

"Look, I was just pointing out to you that I didn't think you were conducting yourself in a very professional manner." I explain.

"Man, I don't see why you gotta be hatin like that." He says.

"I wasn't hate...I mean..." Now this idiot has me confused with proper English. "What I'm trying to say is that I wasn't being hateful. I felt that I was trying to give you a tip on grammar. Something useful that could help you in life." I say.

"Man, you didin be hafin to call me whitey an shit." He says.

"First of all, I didn't call you whitey and even if I did, the fact of the matter is that you are white. He is white isn't he?" I say to the black girl.

She seems very amused by all of this and just shakes her head in agreement with me.

"Man I don't know why you people gotta be dissin on me like this." He says and he walks away from the front desk into an office and slams the door behind him.

"Oh well, have a nice evening." I say to the girl as I grab my bag and walk toward the exit.

I gave it a shot, there's nothing I can do now. The kid is a lost cause. He has to go through life with this identity crisis. There is nothing that can't be fixed with a good old-fashioned ass kicking and I'm not the one to do that. That mission is up to his parents or some stranger he hasn't even met yet. It will probably be from some black guy that is offended by the way this moron has chosen to present himself. It's probably going to happen soon and it could be very devastating at first, but in the long run it will straighten him out. He won't realize it at the moment he is getting pummeled, but it will be the best thing that ever happened to him.

The night air has a chill as I walk outside to wait for Carl. Even though the temperature outside is probably warmer than the highs are at this time of year back east, there is something about the desert that makes it feel a lot colder. I should just forget about, it but for some reason I'm still aggravated by the imbecile at the hotel. I can see through the window that he's come back out from his little pouting incident. He's having a heated discussion with the girl in there. I have to imagine he's telling her what a jackass I am. He's got some nerve this kid. I try to help him out and he's in there talking shit about me. What I should do is go back in there, pull him over the counter, knock some sense into the idiot, and SPLASH! I wasn't paying attention to the puddle just off the curb where I'm standing. I don't know where in the hell a puddle came from anyway. There's been no rain for the three days I've been here and this has to be the only puddle in Las Vegas this evening, but some asshole has managed to drive through it and soak my pants!

I look up and see the culprit. It's a blue pick up truck with a rebel flag in the rear window. What would ever possess you to put a rebel flag in the window of a truck out here? Las Vegas is not a part of the old south. Hell, it didn't even exist during the civil war. It was nothing more than a stop along the Mormon trail where you had a good chance of being killed by Indians. Yet this dumb shit has the audacity to put the fucking rebel flag, which most people now consider to be nothing more than a symbol of hatred and bigotry, in the rear window of his truck!

As he climbs out of the cab I can see that he's a tall skinny guy in a ripped t-shirt and sporting a mullet. I would imagine that in this city of long shots you couldn't have gotten better than even money that the guy driving the truck with the rebel flag would wear his hair in a mullet.

"Excuse me." I say as he walks toward the hotel.

"Excuse me." I say again.

This time I get his attention.

"Are you talking to me?" He asks.

"Yes, I just wanted to point out that you splashed me." I say to him.

"I didn't splash you." He responds.

"Well then how do you suppose that my pants got so wet?" I ask him.

"How the fuck should I know." He says.

"They're wet because you had to go speeding through this fuck-ing puddle and splash me!" I tell him.

At this moment what I'm guessing is his girlfriend emerges from the passenger side. She's a short stocky girl wearing a shirt that doesn't do the justice of covering up her protruding gut. I guess she wants to show off that ugly tattoo on her back.

"Who's this goober?" She asks her boyfriend as she points to me.

"Wait, you're calling me a goober? Do you see that hairstyle that your boy is wearing? What did you two just arrive in a time machine from 1985?" I say and with that the boyfriend starts charg-ing at me.

"What did you just call me?" He asks and the truth is I didn't call him anything.

I was just pointing out the fact that his fashion style is off by at least a couple of decades. As he gets close enough to notice the fact that I outweigh his puny ass by at least fifty pounds he stops charging.

"I don't know what you're problem is buddy!" He says as bravely as he can from twenty feet away.

Behind him I see that the dreadlocked red head has emerged from hotel and is looking my way.

"If you don't get out of here I'm gonna be hafin to call the police!" He says to me.

Now the thing is, I didn't do anything wrong here but this kid has it in for me and I really don't need the police back in my life right now. Not with the trial hanging over my head.

"God, you really do need anger management counseling don't you?"

I hadn't even noticed Carl drive up but there he is sitting in his Honda Civic.

"What do you think I should do?" I ask him.

"Get in." He says and I throw my bags in the back seat climb into the passenger side and we drive away.

"How long were you sitting there?" I ask.

"Long enough to see the whole ugly incident." Carl replies.

"The asshole splashed me! Look at my pants, they're soaked!" I say.

"I don't think that he did it on purpose." Carl says.

"How do you know that? I mean there's only one fucking puddle in all of Las Vegas and this idiot has to drive right through it." I say.

"You should have been aware of where you were standing." Carl says.

"What are you saying? Are you saying that this was my fault?" I ask.

"I'm not saying that it was anybody's fault. It was just an unfortunate accident." Carl replies.

"So you're saying that I should have just let it go." I say.

"I just feel that you should think things through before you go off like that. You never know what you're dealing with." Carl says.

"Oh come on, that moron couldn't have weighed more than one hundred and twenty pounds." I say.

"Yeah but like I said you never know what you're dealing with. He could have been a black belt or worse yet he could have had a gun in the truck. He certainly looked like the type." Carl tells me.

"So you're saying that I should have just let it go." I say again.

"I'm just saying that you should think things through." Carl says.

Now I'm pissed. You would think that at least your friends would be on your side. We drive along quietly for a few minutes and I can feel the tension in the car. Carl finally breaks the ice.

"Good to see you." He tells me and I realize that he is doing me a huge favor here.

I also realize he is right about the fact that I should think before I act. It's just really hard for me to admit when I'm wrong.

"Yeah, it's good to see you too, although I wasn't really planning on spending the week here." I say.

"There are worse places that you could be stuck." He tells me.

"Well, I guess if you want to look at it that way I guess it's better than being arrested in Iowa." I say.

"Now that would suck." He says.

There you go, I've only been away from the hotel for a few minutes and Carl has already put a positive spin on my situation. At least I'm not in Iowa.

Carl has a one-bedroom place in town and it's pretty barren. It's just a bed in the one room, a sofa, television, and table with his computer on it in the other room. He also has a balcony over looking the swimming pool.

Standing out there looking down Carl tells me, "That's where the strippers that live in the building sun themselves during the day."

"You have the world by the balls don't you?" I ask.

"Oh yeah." He replies with a shit-eating grin on his face.

"Have you had dinner yet?" Carl asks.

The truth is I can't remember the last time that I've had any-thing to eat. I have too much else on my mind and haven't really even thought about food, but his asking me about it makes me real-ize I'm starving.

"No, I haven't. What about you?" I ask.

"I haven't eaten since lunch he tells me.

"Then maybe we should get something." I say.

"Chinese, OK?" Carl asks. "Whatever you want, I'm starving." I say. "Well then let's go." Carl replies and we are on our way.

We walk over to the P.F. Chang's directly across the street from Carl's building. I wolf down my food like it's my last meal.

"You really were starving." Carl says.

"Yeah, you know I just realized that I haven't eaten anything all day. I don't remember if I ate anything yesterday either." I say.

"You don't remember! How could you not remember if you had anything to eat?" He asks.

"I guess my mind has been in a whole different place these past few days." I say.

"Still, you have to eat." He says.

"I just did." I say as I swallow my last bite.

The check arrives at the table and Carl makes a grab for it.

"Don't even think about it." I say.

"Let me get it." He insists and even though I'm in kind of a bind financially over all of this I can't allow him to treat me.

"Look, you're saving me a lot of money on a hotel this week by putting me up. Not only that but you weren't expecting the company and I appreciate what you're doing for me. So I feel the least I can do is buy you dinner." I say.

Carl let go of the check and I hand it to the waiter with a credit card and add yet more to my increasing debt.

On the way back we decide to pick up some beer at a convenience store. I know that Carl is a big fan of Guinness so I grab a couple of six packs from the cooler and ask, "Is this OK?"

"I think that will work." Carl replies with a big grin.

As we exit the convenience store I notice that there is a cigar store a few doors down in the same shopping plaza.

"Are you in the mood for a cigar?" I ask.

"I'm always in the mood for a cigar. Hell we might as well go back and get in the hot tub." Carl replies.

Inside the cigar store I tell Carl to grab whatever he wants, my treat again. At this time I realize between the dinner, beer, and cigars I've spent about the same as I would have for a night at the hotel. I guess I can be thankful to have company to take my mind off things. It's just so hard for me to be thankful of anything.

So we have beer and cigars and are on the way back to Carl's. When we arrive we change into swimming trunks and go down to the hot tub. Under normal circumstances this would make for a great evening. Here we are under the stars of Las Vegas, smoking good cigars, drinking Guinness, the air outside is a bit chilly but it's un-noticeable in the heat of the hot tub and I'm miserable. That's because these aren't normal circumstances, not by a long shot. I shouldn't be here right now and that's all that keeps going through my mind.

"What a great night." Carl says and I can tell by the way that he's looking at me that he knows that I'm not enjoying it.

"Yeah," I respond quietly.

"You know some day this is all going to be funny and make a great story. You should get a decent bit out of this." He says.

"Yeah, I know. I just wish I could jump ahead to that day." I say.

"You don't want to do that. Then you would miss all of the days in between. Life's too short to wish part of it away. Look at what we're doing right now, smoking cigars in a hot tub in Las Vegas. Who wouldn't want to trade places with us right now?" Carl asks.

The thing is he's right. I know that you're suppose to enjoy every moment as you pass through life and this is one of those that you should cherish, but I can't. It's just too hard for me to get over the guilt of what has put me in this place at this time and I can be nothing but depressed. I give him a little nod in agreement.

Carl takes a long puff on his cigar and says, "Relax."

The way that Carl keeps looking at me is making me uncomfortable.

"Is there a problem?" I ask.

"I can feel the tension coming off of you." He tells me.

"Yeah, so…" I say.

"I just don't understand it is all. I mean, here we are sitting in a hot tub, drinking beer, smoking cigars, tomorrow is Thanksgiving, neither of us has anywhere we have to be and you're miserable. Why is that?" He asks.

"Because I can't be here in this moment, I can only think about what might happen on Monday." I say.

"You know, this moment right here is the only one that really exists. Monday only exists in your mind. A lot of things can happen between now and then. You could get hit by a truck, more realistically you could have a heart attack from all of the stress that you put onto yourself or a comet could hit the earth tomorrow and the world will end. Now if any of those happened wouldn't you feel foolish for wasting your last night on earth worrying about something that never even happened?" He asks.

"It's just with my luck if any of those things were going to happen it would be on Tuesday." I say.

Carl just shakes his head and takes a long puff on his cigar.

"You go ahead and wallow in your misery. I'm going to take time to think about all that I have to be thankful for." He says.

I know that Carl is right. I shouldn't be spending all of my time worrying about this hearing. It could all work out in my favor anyway. I should just relax and enjoy this evening. Monday is still a long way off. I should just take time to be thankful that I'm not in jail right now. I take a puff on my cigar and for the first time this evening I actually take the time to enjoy it instead of just letting my mind dwell on negative things. I lean back and take a look up at the stars. It's a beautiful night and I can feel the pressure leaving my body.

"That's it, just let it all go." Carl tells me.

I'm actually feeling really good right now.

"Riiiing…riiiing…"

My cell phone broke the mood. I look to see that it's my wife calling, probably to remind how bad I screwed things up. I should have never tried to relax!

FOUR

Thursday morning, Thanksgiving, I woke up around seven AM with one of the worst headaches I think I've ever had. I forgot to drink water last night. At the time I wasn't really thinking about it. It's just that between the alcohol and the hot tub and the fact that we're in the middle of this god-forsaken desert, all of the fluid has drained from my body. My brain probably looks like a shriveled prune right now and is letting me know it needs liquid by blessing me with this throbbing headache. Not only that, but also this sofa I had to sleep on has to be the most uncomfortable piece of furniture that I've ever encountered. I'm guessing it was manufactured right here in Las Vegas and is stuffed with cactus. So now I have a throbbing head, a stiff back, and a hearing coming up on Monday. Whoop dee fucking doo, Happy Thanksgiving!

About eight-thirty AM Carl is awake and comes in from his bedroom. I took a couple of aspirins about an hour ago. I've been sitting here drinking water and orange juice while watching the Macy's Thanksgiving Day parade with the sound off.

"Why are you watching without sound? You could have turned it on. It wouldn't have bothered me." He says.

"What do I need sound for? To hear the announcer tell me the Snoopy Balloon is coming down the street? I can see the Snoopy Balloon is coming, I'm not a fucking idiot." I say.

Right at that moment the Radio City Rockettes come on doing one of their high kicking routines.

"Look at this. Do you really need sound right now?" I ask.

He stares at the television for a moment and says, "You know, you're right. I think that I actually like it better like this."

Carl sits down at the other end of the sofa and we watch the rest of the parade with the sound turned off.

By the time Santa comes waving into the scene signaling the end of the parade, my head begins to feel almost back to normal. Normal as in the pain is gone, but now I find my thoughts are filled with even more dread as Santa's arrival also signals the beginning of the holiday season. I mean it's not like the stores don't put the Christmas displays out the day after Labor Day to give them even more time to ram this now overly commercialized season down our throats. It's just that now I realize it's only a month away and that song, "I'll be Home for Christmas" keeps going through my head. I just don't know if the song holds any truth for me this year. I don't know what awaits me on Monday. Am I going to jail? Am I going to be tried as a terrorist and sent to Guatanamo? If I can go home, how am I going to get there? I just wish I knew the answers.

It's only nine thirty in the morning here and the first NFL game of the day is kicking off. Everything is out of whack in this western time zone. Night games come on in the middle of the afternoon and are over by the time that they should be coming on, if that makes any sense. I know that if you are born here and grow up this way you accept it but I could never get used to it.

"What do you want to do about dinner?" Carl asks.

"I don't know. I really wasn't thinking about dinner. It's not even lunch time." I say.

"Yeah, but its Thanksgiving, we've got to do something special." He says.

"I take it you don't have a turkey ready to throw in the oven." I say.

Carl laughs as he says, "I don't even know if the oven works. I've never used it."

"Well, I suppose we could just get some more beer and order a pizza." I say what I think is jokingly.

"That sounds like a plan!" Carl responds and I think why the hell not.

Beer and pizza will do on a Thanksgiving that really makes no sense anyway.

Staying with Carl turns out to be a good move. Having company really helps the time to pass and I appreciate that. Of course after a few days we started to get on each other's nerves. Well, I know that he started to get under my skin. It could have just been me, but his anal retentive behavior became a bit much. It was constantly, 'Can you use a coaster please." Or, "Please don't put your feet up on the table."When I think about it, maybe it was just me, but that's the way that I am. I'm always looking to find fault with something in order to ruin the situation. If I wasn't that way I wouldn't be stuck in Las Vegas right now.

Sunday morning it feels like the time has passed too quickly as the realization of what awaits me the next day enters my thoughts. It's a day that I've been looking forward to with both anticipation and dread and now it's almost here.

Monday morning, I don't think I slept for more than an hour or two last night. Between the uncomfortable couch and the fact that I have this hearing today to worry about, it's not exactly the kind of night when you sleep soundly with visions of sugar plums dancing through your head. Despite my track record, I'm trying to think positive, well positive for me anyway. I'm thinking that no matter what happens at least it will all be over with. I guess that's kind of a positive way to look at it. The judge seemed like a good guy last week when I went before him and Dr. Keller said he would recommend anger management. It's just that I can't help but think about what could happen to mess things up. Like what if the judge had a horrible weekend, maybe found out his wife was screwing around on him with one of his friends or something. Or even worse she told him that she was a lesbian. A thing like that could sure change his attitude, probably send him off the deep end looking for somebody to punish. Then again I don't even know if the guy is married, but I like to prepare myself for the worst.

I'm supposed to show up by eight-thirty although they can't give me a definite time of when I might actually appear before the judge. Carl has offered to give me a ride over to the courthouse. I told him that he wouldn't have to stay and he said that he wasn't planning on it. Maybe if I was accused of murder or something interesting he said it would be worth hanging around. I was up at six and have been dressed since seven. It's about ten to eight now and I can hear Carl moving about in his bedroom. I should probably call my wife.

"Hello," she says.

"Yeah, hi it's me." I say.

"Are you ready?" She asks.

"I guess. I just wish the damn thing was over with." I say.

"It will be soon enough." She says.

"I know, it's just"…

She interrupts me. "I just want to wish you good luck and I want you to know that I love you and I want you to be able to come home."

"I love you and I want to come home. I'm really sorry about all of this." I say.

"You should be." She says.

"Yeah, I know." I reply.

"Good luck; I love you and call me as soon as you know something." She says.

"Well, I guess they'll let me have one phone call." I say.

"Quit being negative," She tells me.

"I try, but it's just the way I am. I love you too." I say.

"Bye."

"Bye."

Carl emerges from the bedroom fully dressed and asks, "Are you ready to walk the green mile?"

"As ready as I'm going to be. Let's get this over with." I reply.

With that we walk down to his car and I'm finally on my way. It's been a long six days waiting for this and at least tonight I will know my fate. That's something anyway.

Inside the courthouse I register my name and am told to take a seat. They'll call me when it's time for me to go in. There are at least ten other people sitting here and I'm hoping they don't take us in the order we showed up like taking a number at the deli counter. It doesn't seem to matter what number I get when I go to the deli anyway. I either pull thirty-eight and they're serving number two or there's only one person ahead of me who is throwing a party and buying a couple of pounds of everything, sliced specifically to their liking. Man I hate people like that!

I take a seat and begin to immediately feel out of place. Everybody else looks like a murderer, a gang member, or drug addict. Maybe all three rolled into one. What the hell am I doing here? One guy has tattoos covering his entire body. He even has one on the side of his face. I mean is that really necessary? Wouldn't it be easier and less painful to just jump up and down all day screaming "Hey everybody, fucking look at me!"

A woman comes out and announces, "Garcia, Alex Garcia."

With that a guy in a tattered leather jacket, with long hair in a ponytail and a knife scar on the side of his face stands and follows the woman. I'm guessing he's not here for a parking ticket. A short, heavyset woman comes walking down the long corridor across from where we are sitting.

"Is there a John Knight here?" She asks.

"Yes, that's me." I respond.

"Judge Ackerman will see you in his chambers, follow me." She says.

The way the other thugs are looking at me I feel like that special kid in school they realized was in the remedial class by mistake.

Judge Ackerman is seated behind his desk and I notice a short thin officer is also in the room.

"Mr. Knight, have a seat." The judge instructs me.

I take a seat in front of the desk. The judge is looking over some papers he has on his desk, then he removes his glasses and leans toward me with his arms folded on the desk.

"Mr. Knight, you have to know that in these times when somebody acts the way that you did on that airplane, they are going to be treated as being a possible terrorist. Now there were other people on the flight that were probably just as frustrated as you, yet none of them behaved the way you did, now did they?" He asks.

"No your honor," I respond.

"No, they did not. Now due to the fact that there is nothing to link you to any terrorist organization and you have no prior record and that up to this point in your life you have been an upstanding citizen I don't think you are a terrorist. However I do have to regard you as a flight risk and I am going to have to suspend your flying privileges for now. Now, looking over the report from Dr. Keller it states that you are willing to undergo counseling for anger management. Is that correct?" He asks.

"Yes your honor." I respond.

"I'm going to tell you right now that if you ever want to fly again that you will attend this counseling. When and only when a qualified therapist can give me a report stating that they feel you have conquered this problem and they feel you will no longer be a threat to yourself or others, then at that time when the report is sent to me you will have your flying privileges reinstated. Now you're probably wondering how you are going to be able to get home." He says.

"Yes, the thought crossed my mind." I say.

"I'm going to give you an option. You could walk of course or you could rent a car and drive across the country or the choice I'm going to give you is to have Lieutenant Maxwell here fly along with you as your escort, at your cost. You will be responsible for his round trip airfare and also for a night stay in the Pittsburgh area. Are you willing to agree with these terms?" He asks.

What can I do? He's really got me by the balls here. I'm not going to walk, it's at least three days drive, and I have a booking next weekend. It looks like it's going to be the Lieutenant and me.

"Yes your honor." I respond.

"OK, I'll have Margie work out the details with you." He says.

And with that it was all over, well not completely. There's still the matter of being escorted by a police officer across the country, not to mention the fact that this is going to cost me a bundle. Then of course is the fact that I can't fly anymore. I can't worry about any of that right now. At least I can go home.

On the way to the airport I am both excited to be going home and more than a little apprehensive about what lies ahead for me.

"Man I can't thank you enough for all that you did for me." I tell Carl as we drive.

"Oh come on, you would have done the same thing for me if you had to." He says. Now I really don't know that I would have but if he wants to believe that I'm not going to argue. We pull up alongside the curb outside the airport and Carl pops the trunk of his car. We both get out and I pull my bag out and give Carl a big hug.

"I owe you big time." I tell him.

"Stop it, you don't owe me anything." He says.

I look at Carl as he walks back to get in the car.

"I guess I don't know when I'll see you again. I don't know how I'm going to be able to get back this way." I say.

"I guess we'll have to hook up in Pittsburgh." He says.

"I guess that works." I say as Carl gets in the car and drives off.

It's about quarter after three in the afternoon right now. I'm supposed to meet Lieutenant Maxwell between three-thirty and four o'clock, which gives him a fairly big window. Meanwhile I have to just stand around like an idiot waiting for his arrival. I know they're just messing with me to see if they can't get me to go off again. Then they will be able to put me away for good, but I'm not going to give them the satisfaction. Carl gave me a Valium just in case I start to stress out. I don't know where Carl got them. I know he doesn't have a prescription, but it's pretty easy to get prescription narcotics these days. I've only taken Valium one other time. My mother gave it to me. She has a medicine cabinet full of shit that doesn't help her relax. The one I took, which was also during a long flight, certainly took the edge off and that's what I need tonight.

Five after four and still no sign of that son of a bitch Maxwell!

What the hell does he care? If he misses this flight we can just go ahead and reschedule it again for tomorrow at my expense and he can collect another day of over time pay. It would be different if he said he would be here around four and then I could have shown up around that time. This between three-thirty and four o'clock bullshit is, well its bullshit! What an inconsiderate bastard!

It's now about ten after four when I finally see a short balding man with wire rimmed glasses walking over toward me. It's Lieutenant Kenneth Maxwell. It's so nice of him to finally show up. I can't believe this guy is a cop. He can't be taller than five-five, five six tops and probably doesn't weigh one-thirty soaking wet. This guy is supposed to protect me? Oh, that's right; he's here to provide a safe haven for others from me. There you have the irony. I'm sure that the airline feels safe knowing that Barney Fife is going to keep me from causing a commotion.

He's friendly enough anyway as he takes the time to shake my hand and then announces, "I guess we should get to the gate."

I'd like to say something about how we wouldn't be rushed if he had gotten here when he was supposed to but I am the criminal here.

There's a somewhat long line waiting to go through security and a thought occurs to me, "You could just flash your badge and we could go ahead of all of these people couldn't you?" I ask Maxwell.

"Yes, of course I could but there's really no reason to do that. We have plenty of time." He says and then we just stand here not moving or barely moving.

I'll tell you one thing, if I had a badge I'd never wait in a stupid line again. "I have a badge so why don't you people that don't have badges just move the fuck out of my way!" I can't believe we're standing in this line when we don't have to. I mean it's not moving at all. What the hell! I don't want to miss my flight and we are just standing here and the thing is it's unnecessary!

"Why don't you just flash your badge and let's get through this line?" I ask.

He just gives me an odd smile, like don't ask me again. I guess we're just waiting.

We get to the end of this line, which only begins the next. It's here that we have to show our ID to the crack security agent. If he or she thinks that we look enough like the person on our ID we are approved and we can go stand in the next line waiting to pass through the metal detector. It's a lot of lines and waiting when you fly these days. It's a pain in the ass really and I would probably consider losing my flying privileges to be a blessing if I didn't have to do it to make a living.

I hand my driver's license to the elderly gentleman working security. As he's examining it to make sure that I'm me, Lieutenant Maxwell pulls out his ID and badge and says "I'm Lieutenant Kenneth Maxwell, LVPD. I'll be escorting Mr. Knight here back to Pittsburgh." He says.

Now the security guy gives me the once over as he hands my ID back to me. He's probably wondering what kind of dangerous felon I am and why I'm not handcuffed. Not only that but I notice the passengers around us are now looking at me with concern. Now the son of a bitch pulls out his badge! Not before when I asked him, but now when he can make me look bad. I don't know if he did it on purpose or if he's just a stupid jackass. I'm going with stupid jackass!

When I purchased the tickets I tried to get two aisle seats across from each other. That wasn't available so I had to settle for one aisle and one middle seat. I figure he can sit in the middle. As small as he is it won't bother him. As we board the plane, Officer Maxwell informs me that he would be taking the aisle seat.

"You go ahead and take the middle," he says.

Oh thank you, like you're doing me some big favor. The little shit! I don't think his feet even touch the floor, just dangling over the edge of the seat like a small child. What I should have done, to save money, was to just book one seat with a lap child. It would have been uncomfortable holding the Lieutenant for the whole flight but it would have saved me a couple of bucks. Then again, once they turned off the seat belt sign I could have just let him run up and down the aisles and bother the other passengers like most inconsiderate parents let their children do. I should have thought of this earlier. As it turns out, even though I'm the one that paid for the tickets, here I am wedged in the middle of Maxwell and some older woman that smells like she took a bath in cheap perfume. I mean I've smelled some offensive perfume in my day but this one is actually making my eyes water.

As we roll down the runway and I feel the plane lift off I lean my head back and close my eyes. I can't remember the last time I've felt this relaxed. I'm going home. It's been a hell of a week and there was a time when I didn't know if this day would ever come. I was seriously concerned that I would be doing some jail time. I guess things worked out really well for me considering what could have happened. So I have to go to therapy, I can fake my way through that. At this moment life is good, well not good maybe, but I'll settle for tolerable.

We're not even at ten thousand feet and I can sense that there might be a major problem with the Lieutenant. It turns out that Officer Maxwell has been informed that I'm a comedian and as luck would have it, he considers himself to be somewhat of an aspiring comic. The problem is that all he really has is an arsenal of bad old jokes I've heard a million times. Normally when somebody starts to tell me a long joke that I've heard before, I politely give them the punch line so they stop. Of course those people don't hold my freedom in their hands and are probably not armed. All I need is for him to go back to the judge and say I was hostile during the flight. It will be buses and trains for me for the rest of my life and I can't do that. I traveled by bus a couple of times back when I was starting out in the business. It wasn't a pleasant experience and I told myself that I would never do it again. The last time I did travel by bus I had to sit next to a guy that was not only talking to himself, he was also hard of hearing. The crazy bastard had trouble comprehending what he had just told himself. It was quite a scene. I'm not going back to that freak show. I'll just bear it for these next four hours. I decide that I have to graciously listen to each horrible joke as if I had never heard it before and then give out a big fake laugh. I feel just like a prostitute having one fake orgasm after another, telling the guy how good he is just to make a buck. The problem is that I'm not getting paid.

Here's one that I know you're gonna use." He says and I just have to say, "Yeah, maybe."

Humor the son of a bitch, that's all that I can do right now.

"So a grasshopper walks into a bar. The bartender looks at him and says, "Hey we've got a drink named after you!" and the grasshopper says, "You've got a drink named Irving?"

Then I laugh like a whore. The perfume woman is now listening in and getting a big kick out the Lieutenants bad jokes. I know this will only egg him on and things are going to get worse but there's nothing I can do about it.

I believe we're over Arizona now and Maxwell has been non-stop since we left Las Vegas. He just told the one about Cinderella sitting on Pinocchio's face and asking him to lie to her. Now I don't think that is one that you should tell in mixed company, especially since I have this woman pegged to be somewhere between sixty-five and a million but she has tears running down her face right now and I couldn't be more miserable.

"You're so funny. You should be a comedian." The woman tells the Lieutenant.

He points at me, "He's the comedian." He tells her.

She takes one look at the dour expression on my face.

"Oh, yes I'm sure." She says sarcastically.

It doesn't bother me. I'm used to it. I don't know what people expect a comedian to look like. Off stage most of us are miserable bastards and no fun to be around. Especially when we're forced to listen to bad old jokes that we've heard a million times before. The fact that this woman keeps laughing at him is only going to make the Lieutenant continue. I'm afraid that he might keep this up all the way across the country. I wonder what they would do to me if I headed for the door while we're still in the air.

"Did you hear the one about?" He starts and I just can't take it anymore!

I'm trying to block him out but he has to nudge my arm before he asks, "did you hear the one about," before he starts each joke. This woman's perfume seems to be gaining strength and I'm getting a headache from it. Between her cheap perfume and his humor I don't think that I can last much longer. I look down to see if Maxwell might be packing some heat. I could probably get the gun away from him before he even knew it was gone and just blow my brains all over the perfume woman. An event like that would surely put an end to the Lieutenant's comedy career and I'll bet this woman could never wear that scent again. Nobody would ever remember me for the hero that I was, but that's OK. A true hero isn't looking to be remembered anyway.

Something just occurred to me. I've got a Valium in my pocket. I hadn't even thought about it when I went through security earlier. Of course I had nothing to worry about since it's a legal prescription drug. It doesn't matter that it's not my prescription or even Carl's for that matter. It's perfectly legal because a government approved pharmaceutical corporation has manufactured it. Nobody is going to give me a second look for having this pill in my pocket. Now if you have a bag of pot you grew in your own back yard using organic soil and fertilizers, well that's against the law! The reason it's illegal is because you can grow it yourself and corporations can't figure out how to make money off of it and the government can't tax it, so nobody is going to make a dime. So of course you can't have that, not something you can grow yourself for heavens sake, that's illegal. But in the case of anti-depressants and anti-stress and any of the other bullshit medications that are manufactured by pharmaceutical corporations it's fine. Of course pot growers don't lobby the government and stuff money into the pockets of politicians. They also don't send their sales reps out to pay off doctors to make sure that they can get their patients hooked on the latest moneymaker.

Now what I'm thinking is that instead of taking the Valium myself, I could somehow distract the Lieutenant long enough to slip it into his drink. The image of knocking this guy out by spiking his drink makes me laugh out loud and I time it perfectly to coincide with the end of his latest torturous joke so he doesn't have a clue. OK, I'm not going to do that, leaving only one option.

"Excuse me; I need to use the restroom." I say.

Maxwell was mid-joke, but I just don't care anymore. He lets me up and I head down the aisle toward the lavatory. Once I get inside the bathroom all that I can think of is the serenity that awaits me. If I can just get the stupid thing out of my pocket… I dropped it on the floor, shit! Where the hell is it? Could the lighting in these lavatories be any dimmer? I hope I remembered to lock the door when I came in here. That's all I need right now is to have one of my fellow passengers walk in on the guy being escorted across the country by an officer of the law and here he is crawling around the bathroom floor looking for something! They would probably freak out and start screaming, sure that I'm trying to plant a bomb under the commode to blow the next idiot that sits down halfway to the moon. I don't need that commotion right now. There it is the little yellow pill. I found it. I don't even care if they cleaned in here recently. I just dust it off and pop it in my mouth.

Back in my seat and I'm not feeling anything except contempt for Maxwell. I don't know how long it takes for these things to kick in, but it had better be soon!

"What do you call a woman with one leg? Eileen." He tells it, the perfumed woman laughs and for some reason I feel myself actually chuckle.

What the hell's the matter with me? I've heard that joke at least a thousand times before and I never thought it was funny. My head feels kind of fuzzy. I must be getting delirious from this woman's perfume. I don't know what else it could…

The receptionist from Dr. Keller's office is walking toward me wearing a black lace teddy that leaves very little to the imagination. She's beginning to slide one of the straps down over her shoulder as she stares at me seductively. She's walking toward me and the teddy begins to slide from her shoulder and her breasts are about to flop out. I'm a married man and I shouldn't be here right now, but all I can think of is why am I shaking like this? It feels like somebody has grabbed my arm and is shaking me. When I open my eyes I'm looking into the face of Lieutenant Maxwell. Man, that's like a bucket of ice water in the face. Where the hell am I right now?

"You had quite a nap there." He says.

"Yeah, I guess I had a long week." I say groggily.

As I slowly regain consciousness I realize that I'm on a plane and then I feel the plane is now taxiing, we're no longer in the air. I'm home! I made it!

At this point all I wanted to do was get out of my seat and off the damned plane. Maxwell was in no hurry; he was just sitting there still telling stupid jokes as if he was unaware that we had even landed. I wonder if he even noticed that I was out for most of the flight. From the numb look on the perfumed ladies face I can tell that he must have been relentless. It started out well enough for her. She had laughed at the first few jokes he told and that was her mistake right there. He had an audience now. It didn't matter to him that I was out cold. He was going to beat this poor woman into submission. She was trapped there in the window seat, stuck by a sleeping, drooling criminal and his joke telling escort.

On the walk from the plane to the luggage carousel the Lieutenant is strangely quiet. The woman next to us told him that she enjoyed his jokes and then excused herself into the woman's room. She's probably hiding in there long enough to know that he's moved along. I'm really out of it right now. I guess the combination of the Valium and the stress of the previous week just really knocked me out. I never slept like that on a flight before but this was certainly the one to do it.

It's late and we must be the last arriving flight of the evening because the airport is deserted as we pass through.

"Have you ever been to Pittsburgh before?" I ask him hoping that it won't remind him of a joke.

"No, actually this is my first time. Of course I won't get to see much of it since I'm flying back first thing tomorrow." He says.

"That's too bad, it's a great city. You'll have to get back this way some day. Come in the summer when you don't have to deal with the weather." I tell him.

"Yeah I'll have to do that." He says as we board the train that will take us to baggage claim and ground transportation.

As we exit the train, Maxwell follows me down the escalator and out into the cold November air.

"This is where you catch your shuttle for the hotel." I tell him.

"Ok thanks." He says.

I can see the shuttle for the parking lot where my wife left a car for me approaching.

"This is me." I tell him as the shuttle stops in front. I shake the Lieutenants hand, "Thank you Lieutenant." I say.

"Best of luck to you." He tells me as we part ways.

I board the shuttle and take a seat.

"Yes, best of luck to me." I think to myself.

FIVE

I open my eyes and look around at the surroundings. They look strangely familiar to me. Holy shit, I'm in my own bed! Could it all have just been a bad dream? I look at the clock and its one-thirty in the afternoon. I never sleep this late, but man what a dream. When I finally drag my sorry ass into the kitchen to make some coffee I see a welcome home note from my wife. "I'm glad you're home, you need help!" It wasn't a dream, I knew that it wasn't but in my grogginess it just didn't seem real. I'm in a world of shit right now and I just don't see a way out of it at this time. I hate the thought of having to go through therapy but there's just no other way. I have to call and make an appointment with this doctor. This is something that I never expected to have to do in my life. I open the blinds in the kitchen that look out to our deck and back yard I see that it's a cold, gray November day and it's never looked better to me.

"Good afternoon, Dr. Jonas office." A woman's voice says to me on the other line.

I find myself at a loss for words right now. How am I supposed to explain that it's been determined I need counseling even though personally I really don't feel that it's necessary?

"Yes, my name is John Knight..."

"We've been expecting your call Mr. Knight. Dr. Keller's office called from Las Vegas." She interrupts me and at least I don't have to tell the story again.

"From our understanding you have anger management issues." She says.

"Yes, that's what they tell me." I say.

"First and foremost Mr. Knight let me just say that you have to be willing to put in the time and the work in order to achieve good mental health. Are you willing to do this sir?" She asks.

"Yes, of course." I reply.

What else could I say? These people have me by the balls right now. My first appointment will be a week from Thursday at eleven AM, which is good because it gives me time to prepare.

Around five-thirty I hear the garage door opening downstairs which means my wife is home from work. She was asleep when I crawled into bed last night. She did roll over and mumble something about welcome home, but fell right back to sleep so this is really our first encounter since I got here. The door from the garage opens and closes downstairs and I hear her walking up the stairs. As she turns the corner to walk up the flight that leads to the main part of the house she can see me standing in the living room. I can see she is trying desperately not to smile but she can't help herself.

As she reaches the top step I say, "I'm really sorry for all of this and I'm especially sorry for missing Thanksgiving."

I figure I'll take the initiative and start apologizing before she gives me any reason to. She just shakes her head and let's herself smile as she gives me a hug.

"What am I going to do with you?" She asks.

"Isn't it already enough what the authorities did to me?" I ask. With that she pulls loose from the embrace.

"For what you did they really let you off easy. You do realize that, don't you?" She asks.

"What are you talking about? I can't fly, I had to pay for a plane ticket for my escort across the country, I have no way to make a living and on top of it all I have to go to bullshit therapy!" I respond.

"They let you off easy." She says again as the smile slips from her face and she walks down the hall to the bedroom to change clothes.

I guess if I really wanted to think about it I would realize that things could have gone a lot worse it's just that I prefer not to look at it that way.

Here it is the first Thursday in December, another of those gray days that seem to go on forever back in these parts. I know that when I first came home I said the cold and gray never looked better to me, but that was over a week ago. I'm sick of it already. After living in California for twelve years, one of the hardest adjustments to make was getting used to not seeing the sunshine for weeks at a time. I swear that from the beginning of November until sometime in April you might only see the sunshine about five times if you're lucky back here in Pittsburgh. Day after day the gray and the gloom just envelope you and penetrate your soul. It can be a very trying time of year when even the smallest problem can become greatly exaggerated and lead to despair. At least it is for me. This is also one of those days when the temperature was hovering right around freezing, so there's a mixture of rain and snow coming down. Oh, and this is the day of my first therapy session. Can this day get any better?

For whatever reason, any bit of precipitation tends to turn normally bad drivers into horrendous drivers. Not that this is an easy drive to begin with either. Old Dr. Keller back there in Las Vegas thought that he was hooking me up with somebody that was close by. It's about twenty-five miles to Dr. Jonas office and that wouldn't be a problem if it were in any other direction. The problem is the route I have to travel to get there. I live northwest of the city, near the airport. To get to Dr. Jonas office I have to travel east of the city. This means I'm going to have to travel through one tunnel and get stuck in the traffic from another.

If you've never experienced driving around Pittsburgh I have to explain to you that for some reason people slow down to about thirty or thirty-five miles an hour when they go through a tunnel. These tunnels are on major highways and the speed limit remains fifty-five. They have even posted signs outside of the tunnels telling drivers to maintain their speed. That doesn't help. There are still the same idiots that slow down in the tunnel every day, causing major congestion. I've suggested positioning snipers at a strategic point along the inbound and outbound sides of the tunnels. If somebody starts to slow down the sniper opens fire on them. Now I'm not suggesting that you kill anybody. Maybe just a couple of calculated bullet holes in the hood or trunk, these would be marksman after all. You have to imagine that if you were going to come under fire, you're desire to slow down would greatly decline. Of course nobody ever listens to my suggestions so you just have to plan you're trip around the back up.

Anyway, between the tunnel traffic and the weather it looks like I'm going to be late. I gave myself extra time, having left an hour before my scheduled appointment when it should only take me thirty-five or forty minutes. Of course if he's like most doctors, I could arrive an hour late and he still won't be ready to see me. They'll just leave me out in the waiting room to read old magazines like I don't have anything better to do with my time.

The other problem is that I've never been here before and it could be a bitch finding the place. I did a computer search but they don't always help. I don't think that the people who designed map quest took into account how badly this part of the city was designed. One-way streets, dead ends, traffic circles, just one big cluster fuck. Around this part of the city my GPS unit will probably tell me "You're on your own."

Believe me, this is not the way I want to be spending my Thursday. I've never really believed in therapy. It's just some place where a bunch of whiny assholes go to grumble about their lives. Today I will become one of those people.

I'm thinking that I probably should have done some research on this Doctor Jonas. Since somebody recommended him across the country I really don't know what I'm getting myself into. What if he's just in it for the money? Maybe while I'm talking he'll just be sitting there trying to decide if he should buy the Lexus or go for the Mercedes. He could milk me for months and never give me back my right to fly. Here it is right before the holidays, my little incident cost me a small fortune and now I have to pay for therapy with money that I don't really have. For all I know the only thing this guy is concerned about is what kind of car he's going to buy! What kind of selfish son of a bitch are they sending me to?

As I approach my exit I realize that I'm going to be cutting it very close time wise. I hate to be late the first day especially under the circumstances. I mean he's going to wonder why I had such a problem with the airline for being late flying from one city to the next when I can't even make it to an appointment across town. I really don't want anybody thinking that I'm some kind of a hypocrite. I've got to get here on time.

I take the exit and bear to the left, just like my GPS tells me to do and I make sure that it coincides with my map quest. I glance down at the clock in my car and see that I still have ten minutes. There seems to be some traffic, which you wouldn't expect at ten till eleven in the morning on a Thursday. I'm supposed to make a right at the second traffic light. As I approach the first light it turns yellow and the idiot in front of me stops. "What did you need a rest?" I hate when people stop as soon as it turns yellow. Yellow doesn't mean stop. It means proceed with caution, or in this case, speed up so the guy behind you can beat the light!

We sit at the traffic signal for what seems like an eternity and when it finally turns green, dimwit doesn't move. Maybe he likes this spot. Maybe he's decided that this will be the perfect place to spend the holidays. Or maybe the asshole is on the phone and doesn't even realize that the light has changed. I give the horn a light tap to let him know that there are other people involved here and maybe some of us have some place to be. Of course he gives me the finger like it's my fault that he's a moron. What's that about anyway? I didn't lay on the horn I just gave it a pat to let him know that the light had changed. There was no ill will intended yet he feels the need to throw me the bird. Maybe he wasn't done sitting there. Perhaps he enjoys watching the shiny lights turn all the different colors from red to green to yellow and then back to red again and now I've gone and ruined this poor jackass's entertainment! So now he has to give me the finger. "Why don't you take that finger and shove it sideways up your..." We're moving and I approach the second light. The one where I'm supposed to make the right but I can't because the street is blocked by another Pittsburgh tradition, construction!

Son of a bitch! Who would schedule construction on a day like this? Living in these parts you get used to construction delays during the warmer months. It's pure hell trying to get around during the summer with road closings and lanes being blocked. It's everywhere you go, like they didn't do the roads correctly the first time so they're in constant need of repair. It seems like a big racket to me. Let's build roads that will need to be fixed every year. That way we're never out of work. There's also the fact that all road repairs are done by the same state run agency with no bid contracts so why in the hell would you give a shit about what kind of work that you do? If you screw it up, you're the one that gets to fix it! Did I mention that it seems like a racket? It gets to be really annoying and I think they should let visitors know what they will be dealing with when they get here. Maybe put up a big sign announcing to people entering the city, "Welcome to Pittsburgh, we're not quite done yet."

Today is different though. It's the middle of December, it's raining and snowing and definitely not the best day to be working on the roads. Oh and look, nobody's working anyway. There's just a bunch of guys standing around smoking cigarettes and earning a fat paycheck. I don't think I've ever passed a construction site and actually seen any work being done. If that ever happens I'll probably be struck with the fear that somehow I passed through some kind of vortex and had entered a strange dimension where things actually made sense.

"Make right turn." My GPS unit instructs.

"Yes, I wish I could but unfortunately that is impossible." I tell it, like it can hear me.

"Make right turn," it instructs yet again proving that it does not indeed have the ability to comprehend what I just said. "Make right turn," It tells me yet again.

"Fuck you! I wish I could make the fucking right turn, it's just that I can't because these idiots have decided to block off the street for what looks like a long coffee break!" I scream, this time more out of frustration than anything.

"Make right turn"…I turn the stupid thing off and for a brief moment consider tossing it out of the window.

Luckily I catch myself before I make another bone headed move. My wife bought the stupid thing and I'm not exactly on her good side right now. I toss it back into the glove compartment and try to figure this out on my own.

There's no way I can get all the way around and enter the street from the other side. That would take me at least another fifteen minutes the way things are moving right now. I'm going to have to try to park here and make a run for it. I see a car ahead of me pulling away from a parking meter. I can pull in there and if the building is where it's supposed to be, I shouldn't be too late. Now if this idiot can just remember how to drive long enough to get out of the space. "What's the hold up? Yes, I'm waiting to get in there. There you go, it's the pedal on the right, yes that's the one that makes it go, come on you can do it, oh look, you remembered. Thank you. Moron!"

I pull into the space, get out of the car and notice that there's still twenty minutes left on the meter. I reach into my pocket, pull out a quarter and put it into the meter. It gives me fifteen minutes. Fifteen minutes for a quarter? I guess that's not too bad. It's only a dollar for the whole hour. It's just that I wasn't planning to be parking at a meter. I only have one more quarter and I don't see anyplace around where I can get change. I look at my watch and it's already five after eleven. I'm late for my session already. I have fifty minutes on the meter so if I can get out of there by twelve and this gives me an excuse to do just that, the meter will only be expired for about five minutes. I might be OK. I just don't know what kind of pricks the meter police are around here.

Now I'm running down the street in a big hurry to get to my therapy session. Three weeks ago if you had told me that I'd be doing this someday I'd have laughed right in your face. Isn't it funny how fast things can change? Actually funny isn't the right expression. This isn't amusing at all, in fact this really bites! I'm getting hit in the face with ice, rain and snow and this building seems to be a hell of a lot farther than map quest said it would be. Now I'm starting to worry that maybe I'm on the wrong street. There it is, 812. I take the steps two at a time and enter the lobby. I look up at the listings and see Dr. Amile Jonas-suite 303. He's on the third floor. I press the button for the elevator and wait. It's not coming. Maybe I should take the stairs. I'll hit the button again. I wonder if this thing still works. It's an old building and chances are the thing is out of commission. Of course it is a medical building and there are probably people that are not healthy enough to use the stairs but then again, where the hell is the elevator? I hit the button again. Yeah, I know that hitting the elevator button over and over doesn't make it come any faster and that people that do this are usually classified as Type A personalities and "Hello!" Have you been paying attention so far? Wait, I think I hear it. It takes forever for the doors to open and I can't get in anyway because there's a woman that looks to be about one hundred and twenty years old helping another woman that looks like she might be her mother. The only way they could walk any slower would be to go backward. Fuck it, I'll take the stairs after all!

I'm dripping wet as I enter the office. I walk up to the receptionist window and notice that she's an attractive woman with dark eyes and dark hair but is kind of chunky. She has quite an impressive chest, which is probably just a result of the rest of her being kind of big. It may have something to do with the pile of chocolate on her desk.

She looks up at me and asks, "Are you Mister Knight?"

Yes," I reply.

She then says, "You're late. We didn't think you were coming."

"I know," I answer. "There's construction at the end of the street." I say,

"Yes, we didn't realize that would be going on until we arrived this morning." She tells me.

"I guess they don't feel the need to let us know that we're going to be inconvenienced in advance." I respond and she just looks at me and doesn't say anything.

I ask, "Is there a restroom where I could dry off?"

She points to a door across the room and says, "It's your time. The doctor has another appointment scheduled for noon, just to let you know."

I say, "Thank you, I'll be quick."

Then I think to myself, "What a bitch! I mean, what am I suppose to do? Should I just go in and sit there dripping wet and freezing?"

As I enter the office Dr. Jonas stands from the chair he was seated in and holds out his hand. He's a short, balding, pudgy man with wire-rimmed glasses. He immediately reminds me of the George Costanza character on Seinfeld.

"Hello you must be John, I'm Dr. Jonas, Amile, please feel free to call me Amile." He says as we shake hands. He then adds, "I didn't think you were going to make it."

"Yeah, your receptionist said the same thing. I'm sorry that I'm late. It's just that between the weather and then the construction." I respond.

"Perfectly understandable since this is your first time here. You know how it is driving in this city. Hurry up and wait." Dr. Jonas shoots back.

"Yes it is," I reply.

"Well next time you'll know to leave earlier." Dr. Jonas says.

"Yes," I answer as I think to myself, "Next time? He's already counting on a next time.

I guess that deep down I was hoping maybe he would just give me some kind of relaxation exercise to use when I'm flying and that would be the end of it. It looks like I'm not going to be that lucky.

"Please take off your jacket and have a seat," Dr. Jonas says as he points to a big leather chair.

I always thought you had to lie on a couch when you came to one of these places, but what the hell. I hang my coat and sink into what is probably the most comfortable chair that I have ever been in.

"Wow, what a great chair," I say. "Let me know if you're ever looking to get rid of it. I have nice spot for it in my game room."

Dr. Jonas smiles as he takes a seat in the smaller chair across from me.

"I like my patients to be at ease," He responds.

Dr. Jonas leans back in his chair. He seems to be looking me over. He's holding a note pad and pen but he's not writing anything yet. Thank God for that, I haven't even said anything so I hope he wouldn't be making a judgment already.

"Is this your first time in therapy?" He asks.

"Not exactly," I answer.

"So you have had other sessions?" He says.

"Well, just the one in Las Vegas." I respond.

"Ah, yes of course." He says as he writes something down.

"You have to write that down? You don't think you can remember that?" I ask.

"Just don't pay attention to what I'm writing." He tells me as if he thinks that is going to make a difference.

"Are you taking any medications for stress or depression?" He asks.

"Why is that the first thing that you guys ask?" I say.

"I take it that Dr. Keller asked you." He says.

"Yes." I respond

"And what did you tell him?" He asks.

"No." I reply.

"Do you think that they might be helpful?" He asks.

"I really don't want to have to take anything." I say.

"By the way that you are responding so sternly to these questions I have to assume you have a prejudice against these types of medications." He says.

"I just don't want to have to take anything." I respond.

"A lot of my patients find that they are quite beneficial." He says.

"I don't want to take anything." I say again.

"OK, that's fine." He says but I get the feeling that he'd really like to get me hooked on something so he can get his little kick back from the pharmaceutical companies. We're not off to a good start here.

"I'm sensing a lot of stress coming from you." He says.

"Yeah, I know. I just didn't want to be late the first day and between the weather and the construction…"

"You're here now, are you not?" He interrupts.

"Yeah." I respond to the obvious.

"So now that you're here there is no reason to be stressed." He says.

"I guess that I can't just let it go that easily." I say.

"That's what we've got to work on." Jonas says and then he just leans back and stares.

I don't know what it is about these guys, the way that they are always just staring at you. It's kind of creepy. Look at him, just sitting there staring at me. It was one thing for Dr. Keller to do this back in Las Vegas but I'm paying this guy!

"Aren't you going to ask me some questions?" I say.

"This isn't necessarily about me asking questions and you responding. It's your time to talk, to tell me what's troubling you." He says and stares some more.

"Hey, now that I'm over being late I feel fine." I say and I get the impression that he can see that I'm going to be difficult.

"Well let's get to know a little bit about you then. Let's talk about your family life. What it was like growing up." He says.

"Are we going back to my childhood?" I ask mockingly.

"I'm just trying to see what we're dealing with here. That's certainly not going to come about from the two of us sitting here looking at each other. So if you don't want to talk I will take the initiative and find out what your parents were like. Are they still alive?" He asks.

"My mother is." I respond.

"Were they still married when your father passed?" He asks.
"Yes." I answer.

"Ok, so there was no divorce. Did they argue?" He asks.

"They stayed married for forty–six years. Of course they argued." I reply.

I just don't know why any of this matters, probably just a way of milking me for more sessions. Now he's writing something down. I haven't really even said anything what could he be writing? Maybe he's doing the math on how many times I'll have to come in to pay for that boat he's had his eye on. The fact that we're starting on my childhood should give me some indication of what this guy is all about. Hell if he wants to he can drag this on for as long as he likes. It could be the middle of summer before we get to my teens and I could be as old as the ladies getting off the elevator before we ever get around to talking about why I'm here in the first place!

"I don't know why my childhood is relevant to what happened

on the plane in Vegas." I say, trying to move things along.

"Oh, every part of your life is pertinent to what kind of individual that you are now. Now you may not think this matters, but believe me it does in fact. You see, we've never met before, this is our first session. What I'm trying to do right now is get an overall picture of John as a person, trying to establish a guideline to what may be causing your fits of anger. Now I'd like to ask you if you would consider your father to be a stable person." He asks.

I think about it for a moment and answer, "Yes, yes he was."

"What about your mother?" He asks.

"What about her?" I ask.

"Would you consider her to be a stable person?" He asks.

For some reason that old Kenny Rogers's song, "The Gambler" is going through my head. The part about "knowing when to fold them, know when to walk away", I just know that if I don't bluff right now we're going to spend the next three months talking about my mother.

"Maybe not as stable as my father," I tell him and in a way that's not really lying.

"Did either of your parents ever take medication to deal with stress or depression?" He asks.

The truth is that my mother has been taking shit for as long as I can remember but never enough of a dose to do her any good. The woman won't even take vitamin C for fear that her body might have some kind of reaction to it. Usually she cuts what she calls her nerve pills in half. I don't know if she's afraid to take the whole thing or if it's just the fact that if she actually felt better she wouldn't have anything to complain about. I really don't want to tell him but I guess we need to be honest here.

"My mother," I tell him.

"Was there ever a time you can remember when either of your parents acted out in a way that would be considered out of control?" He asks.

The truth is I'm the only one in my family that ever caused a scene like I did on the plane. I'm unique that way.

"No." I tell him.

"I don't see how any of this has anything to do with what happened on the plane." I say.

"It all has a connection to what happened. Now the only reason I was asking these questions was to try to get things started. You didn't seem to want to open up to me but if you'd like to talk about what happened on the plane then we can do that." He says.

"That is why I'm here isn't it?" I say

"What you are here for is to get your anger under control." He tells me.

"Yes, but because of what happened on the plane." I say.

"That was the event that is responsible for your being here today, yes. But this is an ongoing problem that needs to be corrected." He says.

"Yeah, but if I hadn't acted that way on the plane I wouldn't have to be here now." I say.

"Yes, I suppose that if it didn't happen you wouldn't be here now but it did happen and you are here so why don't we talk about it." He says and I get the feeling that he's starting to loose his patience.

Now he's sitting there staring at me again.

"Well aren't we going to talk about this?" He asks.

"What do you want to know?" I respond.

I can see that he's really starting to lose it by the way that he's grimacing and rubbing the side of his temple.

Dr. Jonas leans back in his chair and takes a long deep breath.

"Ok, what I would like to know is what exactly you were feeling at that moment." He asks.

"Frustration," I respond.

"Frustration," he says. "Frustration is what caused you to act in this manner?"

"Yes," I reply.

Dr. Jonas says, "You do realize that your behavior on that airplane was totally irrational don't you?"

"I do now," I answer.

"Have you had other incidents where you would consider your actions to be unreasonable?"

I know that there have been many occasions where I may have gone off the deep end but I always felt justified by my actions. If something's not right I feel that it should be brought to somebody's attention. Of course I realize that most people consider that kind of conduct to be a little crazy. Most people will just allow big heaping piles of shit to be dumped on them without ever saying a word. I give Jonas what I believe to be the right answer.

"Unreasonable? No, I don't think that I've ever acted in an unreasonable manner."

"So you don't feel that your actions on that airplane were irrational?" He asks.

"OK, maybe I got a little out of hand there." I say.

"A little out of hand! You tried to open the door of a moving airplane!" He says.

"We weren't moving." I respond.

"Maybe not at that moment but the plane was not yet at the gate. You're going for the door is not a sensible reaction. You don't feel that it was normal, do you," He asks.

"I guess not." I respond even though I think it was pretty well established that this was not normal behavior the moment I was arrested.

"What we've got to find out here is why you acted the way that you did. We've got to get to the root of your anger. Find out what causes these fits of rage. In this way we will be able to control it before you harm someone including yourself." He says,

"Hey, I've never hurt anybody or even threatened anyone for your information." I respond.

"Well that's good. But, let me ask you this. Has the thought ever crossed your mind that you would like to cause physical harm to somebody?" He asks.

"Yeah, when they piss me off the thought has crossed my mind. I've never acted on it though. Sometimes just the thought of it helps." I respond.

"Ok, I appreciate your honesty. How far have your thoughts of physical violence gone?" He asks.

"I'm not sure what you're asking here. Do you mean like did I ever think that I wish I had a gun at that moment?" I ask.

"Have you wished that you had a gun at a particular time? Like when you feel that somebody has crossed you?" He asks.

"Sure, hasn't everybody?" I respond.

"That's an interesting answer. So you believe that everybody thinks about shooting somebody?" He asks.

"Yes, I would imagine that at one time or another in a certain situation that thought crosses everybody's mind," I say.

"Under what kind of circumstances do you find that the thought has entered your mind?" He asks.

"Oh, I don't know. I guess like when somebody cuts you off on the highway. When somebody is in front of you in the ten items or less line and they have about eighteen items. Just because they're all yogurts doesn't mean that they count as one. If you have to do more than ten scans then its more than ten items! Times like these." I respond.

"So you would shoot somebody because they have too many items?" He asks.

"I didn't say that I would shoot them. I just said that at that moment the thought has probably crossed my mind that a little gunfire might set them straight. I'm not talking about killing anyone. Maybe just a flesh wound to let them know that what they're doing is unacceptable. The thing is I've only thought about it. I don't even own a gun." I tell him.

"That's probably a wise decision." He says.

That sounds like a crack. This bastard is taking cheap shots at me!

"What did you mean by that?" I ask.

He seems to be fumbling around searching for the right answer.

"Oh, I'm sorry that didn't come out right. It's just that, I should let you know that I'm an advocate of gun control. I mean, I can see the point if you're a hunter and I do respect their rights. It's just that in general guns cause so much damage. Everyday in the news you see another senseless shooting. Children shooting each other, adults, it's such a violent society we live in anymore. I don't know how people can even get up the nerve to go outside the house. Then again, how safe are you in your own home? " He responds.

This guy sounds like maybe he's the one that needs some help.

"You're afraid to go outside?" I ask.

"Oh no, it was just a general statement." He says.

"Well that's all that I was doing. Making a statement that in certain times of annoyance the thought that you'd like to shoot somebody might cross your mind. The fact that the majority of people never act on these thoughts is what separates us from the people that are truly dangerous." I say.

"That's a very good point. There is a barrier between most people and how did you phrase it, the truly dangerous. It's just that by the way that you acted on the airplane you crossed that barrier. Do you see what I'm saying here? At the moment that you tried to open the door of the plane your actions would be considered to be erratic." He says.

I look down at my watch. It's already eleven-thirty. I've got to start thinking about an exit plan if I want to beat the meter expiring. The thing is I was already late getting here so I don't want to seem like I'm trying to rush.

"So what do you think that I can do? You know to keep myself from acting...you know irrational?" I ask.

"Hold on, hold on. Look you're not some teenager that stole the car keys and is waiting to see how long he's going to be grounded. What we've got to do here is find out what caused you to behave that way so we can prevent it from happening in the future. There's no quick fix for this. It's not something that we're going to be able to solve in five minutes. This is going to take some time. Now you may feel that you have things under control and on the surface they may be. It's the inside that I'm concerned about. Inside you're a ticking time bomb and we don't know when you'll go off. What we are going to do here is try to fix the inner you."

Fix the inner me? Did he really just say that? Who is this guy, Mister Rogers? The next thing you know he'll be telling me that he likes me just the way I am and singing to me. I'll bet he's got a couple of sweaters hanging in that closet over there. If he pulls a puppet out of the drawer I'll be out of here so fast that I'll leave a cloud of smoke behind me!

"Do you find yourself feeling pressed for time?" He asks.

"How do you mean?" I respond.

"What I'm trying to get across is that everything doesn't always go according to plan. Sometimes we just have to accept the fact that certain circumstances may occur and change the outcome. For example, the fact that you had to make that connecting flight, you were unable to accept the reality that you may miss that one and perhaps go out on the next one." He says.

"There was no next one. That was the last flight of the day going into Pittsburgh!" I respond.

"Is it possible that there may have been another way to get home? Perhaps they could have routed you through another city or even put you on another airline." He says.

"I guess I wasn't thinking about that at the time." I say.

"Were you thinking that the airline was just going to leave you stranded?" He asks.

The fact is I really wasn't thinking.

"Looking back on it I suppose that they would have gotten me home eventually. It's just that I wanted to get home on time." I say.

"In fact you would have been home much sooner if you had just relaxed and dealt with the situation, would you not?" He asks.

"Yes, but I didn't know that at the time." I say.

"Let me ask you this, have you ever heard the quotation, never run for a bus, there's always another one coming along. Do you see how that applies here?" He asks.

"I wasn't trying to catch a bus." I say.

"I know that, but do you see how the quotation applies here?" He asks.

"I guess." I answer.

This probably isn't a good time to mention the parking meter but it's now eleven-thirty five.

I can see that I wasn't as discreet as I thought when I was looking at my watch because the doctor seems to be aware of it.

"Why are you looking at your watch? Are you anxious to get out of here?" He asks.

"No, I guess it's just a habit." I answer.

"Somebody that is constantly looking at their watch and thinking about what they have ahead of them misses the moment at hand and then at the end of their life they're left wondering where all that time went." He says.

Yeah but they wont have to wonder why the hell they got that parking ticket I think to myself!

"Now let's get back to that moment on the plane when you lost control. Were you aware of the fact that you weren't acting rationally?" He asks.

"At first no, I guess if I was I wouldn't have done it. But once I was there and I could see the way the other passengers were looking at me and the fact that the flight attendants were trying to restrain me, then yeah at that time I was aware of the fact that my behavior may have been a bit irrational." I answer.

"But you didn't stop?" He asks.

"No." I reply.

"Why?" He asks.

"I guess I was really caught up in the moment. At that time I had made the commitment to get my point across and I wanted to make sure they understood." I answer.

"So you were trying to get your point across. What exactly was this point?" He asks.

"I guess my point was that their service was totally unacceptable." I answer.

"Did you maybe consider an alternative way to communicate your displeasure?" He asks.

"Not at that moment when I was stuck on an airplane that didn't have a gate to go to." I reply.

Dr. Jonas leans back in his chair and folds his hands over the note pad that is now resting on his lap. He's looking me up and down like he doesn't know what to make of me.

"Here's a word I'd like you to remember, timeout. Do you think that you can remember that?" He asks.

"Yes, I think I can remember timeout. I'm not an idiot." I reply.

"I don't mean just remember it. I mean to store it, to have it on constant reserve in the back of your thoughts and when you feel yourself getting ready to lose control, when you are about to have a moment of anger I want you to call timeout. Take time to tell yourself that there is a way to get through this without losing your temper. Take time to calm down and analyze the situation and think of ways to resolve the issue in a lucid manner. Take time to see if there is even reason to be angry to begin with. Do you think that you can do this?" He asks.

"Yes." I answer.

"This is starting today. When you leave here the word timeout goes with you, do you think that you can do that?" He asks again.

"Yes, I already told you that I could." I reply.

"Is this conversation making you angry? Do you feel like I'm treating you like a child?" He asks.

The truth is that he really is pissing me off because I feel like he's treating me like a total fucking moron but I'm not going to tell him that.

"No." I answer.

I look at my watch and it's now almost a quarter until noon. My meter is going to be expired in ten minutes. I've got to get out of here.

"There you go looking at your watch again. This is why I just emphasized the timeout over and over to you. I don't know if you are even paying any attention to me." He says.

I have been paying attention, its just that I really don't give a shit about what he's telling me because I have the more pressing matter of a meter that's about to expire.

"OK, here's what it is, I was running late this morning as it is and they pick this day of all days to do construction. Well I didn't actually see any construction being done but the end of the street was blocked so I had to park at a meter and I didn't have enough change so now my meter is going to expire in ten minutes. That's why I keep looking at my watch." I say.

"Do you see what you just told me? You're sitting here concerned with your parking meter expiring and that is taking priority of your thoughts right now. So instead of you getting all that you should out of this session you're too busy giving yourself something to be upset about." He says.

"Yeah, but I don't want to get a ticket." I say.

"Timeout, remember? Take timeout and get the meter out of your thoughts. This will be good practice. For the rest of our time here I don't want you to look at your watch, OK?" He says.

"OK," I respond.

"Now when you take the time outs there are some other things that you can try, like deep breathing. Take a couple of deep breaths and collect your thoughts. Why don't you go ahead and do some deep breathing right now." He instructs.

I take a deep breath and exhale.

"Slowly, hold the breath for a moment before you exhale. Really fill up your lungs." He says.

I take another deep breath, hold it longer and then exhale. I take another breath.

"That's it, good. Let all of that stress and anger go. Let it all out." He says.

I take another deep breath and pretend to stretch my arms out in front of me. Out of the corner of my eye I try to look at my watch without him seeing me do this. Dr. Jonas tosses his note pad on the floor and is shaking his head as he stares at me.

"You're really not trying at all! The whole point is to just let it go. Get it out of your mind. It's very simple."

"Oh sure, it's easy for you," I begin. "You're not the one that's going to get a ticket!"

"How much time do you have?" Jonas asks.

I look at my watch.

"About nine or ten minutes," I respond.

"You'll be fine," Dr. Jonas says "I'm sure that they're not just sitting there waiting for your meter to expire. I don't think anything will happen if you're a few minutes late."

"But, you don't know that for sure," I say.

"Let it go, come on you can do it," Dr. Jonas says.

"Ok." I say.

"Now really, I hope that you are listening because I want to talk to you about an exercise that I would like you to try this week, until our next session. Now what I would like you to do is to keep a journal or a diary for the next week. Anytime that you find yourself becoming frustrated, instead of going off the deep end, take time out and just keep the thing that was upsetting you in mind, then write it down. Do this for the whole week. I think that by doing this you'll be more conscious of what is upsetting you and it will help to control your feelings."

Oh great, now I'm getting homework. The first day of school too! I always hated those teachers that gave homework the first day of school, as if to show you what a hard ass they were going to be. In case you thought we were just going to ease into this, I'm sorry, you were sadly mistaken. Here's some work for you and it's only going to get worse from here.

Dr. Jonas goes on, "I think that by taking your actions into context and giving them some thought you will find how easily they can be avoided. Instead of going into an all out rage, what you will be doing is analyzing the situation and looking for ways to enter them into your journal instead. Then when you come in next week we can discuss them."

"What if I don't have any moments that cause me to get aggravated?" I ask.

Jonas looks at me like this is the dumbest thing that he has ever heard in his life.

"Do you really think that you can go through a whole week without something upsetting you?"

"Probably not," I answer.

"OK, when you come in next week, bring the journal along with you and we will discuss it. Then you let me know if you think it helps."

Now Dr. Jonas is just sitting there staring at me, he's not saying anything. What the fuck is this about? I think he's just messing with me now. My meter's about to expire in two minutes and this asshole is just sitting here staring at me! Is he going to dismiss me? Do I have to wait for the bell to ring? I've never done this before. Is it up to me? Should I just take the initiative and say goodbye?

Finally Dr. Jonas starts to speak, "You're still thinking about the meter aren't you?"

"Of course not," I answer.

Jonas smiles at me knowingly as he continues, "Well I can see that we've certainly got our work cut out for us here, but I believe that over the course of time, if you are willing to do the work, you'll be able to handle things in a controlled manor. You won't let little things like parking meters get to you."

"Are we through?" I ask.

He just sits there smiling at me.

"I've forgotten all about it." I tell him.

"That's good," he says and then he just sits back and stares at me and smiles some more.

Now this is getting really annoying. I mean, are we done? Why am I just sitting here? Does he want me to get a ticket? Why is he just sitting there staring at me like that? I can't take it anymore and I leap from my chair.

"OK, I'm thinking about the meter. Actually what I'm thinking about is the ticket that I'm going to get if I'm not down there in about ten seconds!" I say.

Dr. Jonas lets out a long breath and shakes his head.

"You're not going to get a ticket." He says.

"How do you know?" I ask.

He's silent for a moment and then says, "Fine, I guess we're done for today. I can see that we've got a long road ahead of us."

What's he saying? We've got a long road ahead of us! I knew it. This son of a bitch is going to try and bleed me for every last dime!

"Is there anything else that you would like to discuss before you leave? We still have time." He tells me.

"No nothing," I say.

I leap to my feet and put on my jacket. I shake Dr. Jonas hand and thank him, although for what I have no idea. He looks very disappointed with me as I leave the office. I rush past the receptionist who is stuffing her face with candy.

"Would you like the same time next week?" She asks.

At least that's what I thought she said. It was hard to tell with her mouth full of chocolate.

"Yes, that's fine." I say as I rush out the door.

I decide not to wait for the elevator and race down the stairs. I look at my watch; it's eleven fifty-eight. I know the meter is expired but I figure I still have time. Dr. Jonas is probably right, it's not like they're just sitting there waiting for the time to run out.

I step outside and find it's colder than it was when I went in. There is no longer rain mixing in with what is now just a light snow. I race down the street, turn the corner, and head toward my car. As I get close, I can see it, there perched on the wind shield is a parking ticket! I think to myself, "Jonas, you son of a bitch!"

SIX

Monday

MY WIFE WAKES ME THIS MORNING BEFORE SHE
LEAVES FOR WORK TO INFORM ME THAT ONE OF THE
CARS WON'T START AND OH, BY THE WAY THERE WAS A
LOT OF SNOW LAST NIGHT.

As I was lying in bed before I got up, I remember thinking to
myself that I was really going to try to make the best of the day
and not let anything upset me. That's the last time I'm ever going to
tell myself that SHIT! The snow is one thing. We live in a part of the
country where it snows in the winter and its winter now. You learn
to deal with it. I hate dealing with it but there's nothing you can do
about it except move to a warmer climate. I've suggested moving
but my wife likes it here. Of course she's never the one that has to
shovel.

Like I said the snow is one thing but now I also have a car that
won't start. I know that my wife told me it won't start and I know
that she's been driving for a long time. She should know how to
start a car, but I still have to see for myself. Even though I don't
know anything about cars I still think to myself that maybe she did
something wrong. At least I hold out some hope anyway. I have to
see for myself so even before I make my coffee I head down to the
garage and give it a shot. I turn the key in the ignition and nothing
happens, it doesn't even seem to try. So now it's confirmed, the car
won't start.

Son of a bitch! As I look outside at the cold gray and the snow coming down I wonder why the hell I even bothered to get out of bed this morning. Of course the answer is so I can be irritated.

Hopefully it's just the battery. I could probably get one of my neighbors to help jump start the stupid thing but what the hell have I been paying those AAA dues for all these years? I call AAA and they say they will be right over. I make myself some coffee and oatmeal. I shovel the entire driveway and sidewalk. All of this took me a good hour, maybe an hour and a half and there is still no sign of AAA. I'm beginning to wonder if they know what "we'll be right over" means.

AAA finally shows up half an hour later which means that "be right over" is actually around two hours in case you ever need to know. The guy gets out of the truck and he looks like a stoner. This probably explains why it took him so long to get here. He can't be more than twenty years old and doesn't look like he would know how to turn on a light switch let alone get a car started.

"Dude, I'm sorry it took me so long to get here. We're getting like a ton of calls today." He tells me as we head to the garage. "Dude, you wouldn't believe it. It's like nobody's car will start today. I don't know what the problem is."

I look around and say, "It could have something to do with the weather."

"Dude, you're probably right. I wasn't even thinking."

The fact that he "wasn't even thinking" doesn't surprise me at all and I guess we've established the fact that I am dude. Now as far as this guy getting the fucking car started... I'm not going to be holding out a lot of hope.

"When was the last time that you tried to start it?" He asks me.

"About two hours ago." I tell him.

"Why don't you try again?" He asks.

"Yeah, maybe it just needed a rest." I say sarcastically and I can see immediately that the irony is lost on him.

I know that this is futile but I guess I have to show this idiot that the car won't start. I get in the car, turn the key and nothing. I get back out of the car.

"Yeah dude, that's not gonna start." He says.

It's that money I keep sending to AAA that gets me this kind of quality service. The kid goes to his truck and grabs a battery charging device.

"Pop the hood." He instructs.

I do this and he hooks up the device to the battery. Now, I'll be the first to admit that I'm not the most optimistic person in the world but I'm thinking that there's a better chance of this moron blowing up the entire house than getting the car started. I walk about halfway down the driveway, just in case. Bingo! The car starts right up. Son of a bitch, I never would have thought he could do it.

"All right dude, you're good." He tells me as he climbs into his truck and drives away.

Probably off to freshen up his buzz somewhere. The good news is it's only the battery, shouldn't run more than sixty bucks.

When I pull into the station where I usually go when my car needs some kind of service, I see what appears to be everybody else that lives in town is already here. It seems that anybody that thought they should probably get new tires or some other repair done before winter waited too long and now that they see we are actually going to have winter decided to come in today. The guy behind the counter explains to me that it will be a while. He then tells me that he would imagine every other garage in the area is probably just as busy and that at least he has more mechanics on hand. I don't have much choice. If I turn off the engine the car will never start again. I suppose I could just have the stoner follow me around with his battery charging device wherever I go but I found him to be rather annoying. I decide to wait it out.

Ninety minutes later, and don't think that it didn't seem a hell of a lot longer; they finally get to my car. Five minutes after that, Jim the manager, calls me up to the desk to inform me that this particular car requires a special battery that will run me one hundred and fifty dollars!

I say, "It's a Toyota for God's sake. It'll run on flashlight batteries!"

As it turns out it won't, it will only run on one hundred and fifty dollar batteries.

So let's add it all up. Between the parking ticket yesterday and the battery today I'm out around two hundred bucks that I don't have. Oh and Christmas is only a few weeks away. This just keeps getting better and better!

Wednesday
I'M HAVING COMPUTER PROBLEMS SO I CALL THE HELP LINE WHICH IN TURN IS IN A FOREIGN COUNTRY AND IT TURNS INTO THE CONVERSATION FROM HELL!

Normally I do everything I can to avoid dealing with customer service these days. Under most circumstances you can do whatever needs to be done on the internet now. It's easier and less aggravating that way. It's just that the particular problem I am having is an issue with my computer. It's a new lap top and I'm trying to use the DVD burner but it just keeps rejecting my blank disc when I try to make copies. It uploads the original OK and then it tells me to insert a blank DVD. After I do this it spits it back out and tells me to insert a blank DVD. This is when I scream at the stupid thing, "I just fucking did that!" When these computers are finally outfitted with a device that allows them to have a conversation we are really going to have it out. Until then I just scream at them and they just sit there like they haven't heard a word I said. It's really annoying. So for now all I can do is insert another blank disc. It spits that out, tells me to insert a blank disc, I scream at it and we start the whole process over again. I've tried two different types of discs, Sony and Memorex, so that can't be the problem. That's why I've come to the conclusion that it can only be that my new computer is a piece of shit and should be destroyed! Of course I should pay it off first.

That's why I am calling the customer service line, which they should rename "You're Journey into Hell!" You know if you have called any of these lines in the last few years that it has become a joke. Press one for English, ha! Why not Press one for broken English that you will need a translator for. I call the first time; the person on the other line is speaking what I can only make out as some form of gibberish, so I hang up and dial again. This time it is even worse and I realize that there is no way I will be able to com- municate with this person. I hang up once more. I have at times asked to speak to somebody in the United States. All that will get you is the person in India that they have decided speaks the most comprehensible English, so no sense in even trying that.

The third time I call is the worst. All I can make out is allo and what sounds like something about trying to win a toaster. Did I call the wrong number? Was the computer company giving away toast- ers? Or was it just that this person spoke English so poorly they should not be doing a job that involves having a discussion? Anyway the important thing was that corporate was saving money by not having to hire employees they had to pay a fair wage to, not to mention benefits and providing better service for the customer. It's all about the bottom line now folks and you don't matter at all.

The fourth time is the best of all, "Allo wulcum fu Dahl cosomer hulp lion, deece is Dwayne, how may I hulp yew?"

Dwayne? The son of a bitch said his name was Dwayne! What are the odds? What are the chances that of the over one billion people living in India, I was speaking to the only Dwayne? I couldn't pass up my chance to speak to what was probably the only Dwayne in India.

"OK Dwayne," I start and try to say that with a straight face, "I'm having a problem with my DVD burner."

"Wha modal you huv?" He asks and I assume he wants to know what type of computer.

"It's a Dell lap top," I explain and I give him the model number.

"Wha ees problem?" He asks.

I explain the problem to him.

"What tep of deesk you use?" He asks.

"Could you repeat that?" I say.

"What tep of deesk you use?" He asks again.

"I haven't been using my desk. Actually I have it on the kitchen table right now. Is that a problem?" I ask.

"No, no. no, not tep of deesk, tep of deesk." He snaps back and it sounds like he's saying the same damn thing.

I really don't know what the hell he's talking about.

"Tep of deesk…tep of deesk…" He utters again.

I see what he's trying to say now. He wants to know what type of disc I have been using.

"Sony plus." I reply.

"OK, dah shuw work." He tells me.

"Yeah, but it doesn't." I tell him.

"OK, whut will do is, I wheel take ovah you computah." He says.

What's he telling me? He's going to take over my computer? Well you can take over the payments too my friend.

"Puwl up internet." He says.

"I don't understand what you are trying to do here." I tell Dwayne.

"Whut we will do is I will take over you computah. Den we will see what ees problem. Now puwl up internet." He tells me.

I do as instructed this time.

"All right, Dwayne, we're all set." I let him know.

"OK, now put in d ass in daove…"

Now I don't know if he his saying d as in Dave or as in Dove but it doesn't matter because they both begin with D.

"Then N ass in nuncy, C ass in cundy…"

His giving me these words for help is really just making it more difficult to decipher and I'm beginning to lose my patience. After a long series of letters, numbers, slashes and dots, Dwayne asks me to read it back to him.

I do as I'm instructed and Dwayne says, "OK, now hit enteer."

What do you know? I got it right! I hit enter.

"Ok, I now have control of yaw computah." He tells me.

"Now, try to make copy of deesk." He tells me.

"I told you it doesn't work." I say.

"Lesse." He says.

It sounds like Dwayne doesn't believe me which has been happening a lot lately. Between Jonas and the parking ticket and the stoner guy that didn't believe that the car wouldn't start, I'm beginning to have a complex here. I'll just have to show him. I put in the disc that I was trying to copy and start the whole process over.

It takes time to copy the file to the computer and Dwayne hangs in there with me. I hear him breathing on the other end of the line and I'm thinking that we should probably be having a conversation while we're waiting but what the hell am I going to talk to this guy about? "How's the weather in your country?" I really don't care. We can just listen to each other breathe. After about five minutes the machine spits out the original and instructs me to put in a blank disc.

"Go head, put in deesk." Dwayne tells me.

Once again the machine spits out the blank and tells me to put in a blank.

"Thees is nah working." Dwayne observes.

"That's what I was telling you!" I say.

"Vedy good then," He replies. "We must get uwe new burner."

I watch as my computer goes about pulling up a search engine and I'm hoping that Dwayne isn't going to some strange porn site on my computer, not when I have him on the phone anyway. I am helpless as I watch the cursor pull up and begin to download a large program.

"We get uwe new burner now." He tells me.

It's a huge file and I can see from the progress report that we are going to be here for sometime. I wasn't planning on this taking so long. There's a hockey game that I was hoping to watch that's coming on in five minutes.

"Dwayne, this is going to take a while, should I call you back once this is finished downloading?" I ask.

"No, I will wait, tank you vedy much."

I take the phone with me from the kitchen table where my lap top is and into the living room where my wife has the hockey game on.

With the game in the background I walk back and forth checking on the progression of the download. Over the phone I can hear Dwayne speaking to somebody in his native tongue. It seems that somebody has brought him some food because I can hear him crunching in the background. Dwayne is chomping away, saying something to somebody that I don't understand and laughing away. Here on this side of the globe I'm starting to get pissed.

After about twenty or twenty-five minutes the program is finally fully downloaded.

"It looks like we have it Dwayne." I say.

No response.

"Ah, Dwayne are you there?"

"Yessir." He responds.

"Are we done here?" I ask.

"No sir, less try. Put in deesk and try to burn please." He instructs.

I put in the original disk that I've been trying to burn and Dwayne pulls up the program he just downloaded.

"Dwayne, this isn't going to work. It looks like you gave me an MP3 player." I tell him.

"Oh, dees is no good." He says.

"No, no it's not." I add.

"No, dees is not good…OK, then." He says and before I can stop him, he's scrolling through a list of programs, finds one and begins another long and torturous download.

Entering the living room I ask my wife, "What's the score?"

"It's two to nothing, Penguins are winning." She informs me and I can see that it is between periods.

I missed the whole first period dealing with this idiot. I can hear Dwayne is back in conversation with somebody in India while here in the United States I regret ever making this call to begin with.

Over the next two hours I miss the rest of the hockey game including overtime and a shootout. During this time Dwayne has managed to download for me, a program for photos, and a program for faxing and at one point I think my computer was able to brew a pot of coffee. It could do everything except what I wanted it to do, make copies of DVD's. "Dwayne, I think we should just call it a night." I say. "No, no…we get it dis time." He says. I can't tolerate this anymore. "No, Dwayne, thank you but I'm going to have to call back tomorrow." I say. "Vedy well, have you been satisfied with our service?" He asks. "No, actually Dwayne you've been absolutely no help at all. The only thing that you managed to do was waste my entire evening." I say. "Vedy good, tank you for calling. Have a good night." He says and with that he's gone. Did he understand what I was telling him? Did he even give a shit or was he just reading a script? We have phones now that allow you to watch television, listen to music, get information from the internet, do your taxes, get directions and GPS tracking, we have phones that do pretty much everything except wipe your ass for you and I'm sure that is coming. We have phones that do all of these things but we don't have a phone that you can reach through and wring the neck of the fucker on the other line!

The next day I drive over to my brother in law's house, who is an expert with computers and we find out that the problem is that I need to use minus disks instead of plus. This takes all of about three minutes to determine. Unfortunately I can never get back the three and a half hours of my life that Dwayne wasted but at least he's saving the corporation money.

SEVEN

Another Thursday and another session with Jonas, this time I give myself extra time to get to the office. I leave an hour and a half before my scheduled eleven AM appointment. I probably didn't have to leave at nine-thirty but after what happened last week I didn't want to take any chances. I think I should ask Jonas if he could maybe recommend somebody closer to where I live. With the commute both ways I'm wasting three or four hours just for an hour of his bullshit.

The weather is fine today. There is no traffic or construction and I am able to get into the parking lot adjacent to the building. The only problem is that I'm here forty-five minutes early! This really sucks. What the hell am I supposed to do now? I'm anxious to get to my session today since I brought along my parking ticket to shove in the doctor's face. I still have three days to pay the stupid thing. I hope that he will at least have the courtesy to deduct it from the bill since it was his fault in the first place.

I decide that rather than sitting around the waiting room I will walk around the neighborhood for a while. Of course there's a Starbuck's on the corner and I'm sure if I walk a block or two there will be at least one more. I believe if I live long enough there will eventually be a Starbuck's right inside each of our homes. It will come with the house when you buy it. "In the kitchen you will see that there are marble counter tops, an island, all the latest appliances and of course a Starbucks. No home would be complete without a Starbucks, this way you can get a five dollar cup of coffee without having to get into your car."

There is a store next to Starbucks that sells used CD's, so I opt instead to rummage through other people's discarded items. I can't believe that this store is even able to stay open. Almost every music store that sells new music has gone out of business and this place stays open selling used shit. Nobody buys CD's anymore, they just download it to the IPhone and there is no need for a disc. Then everyone walks around with their ear buds in and nobody communicates. No, people just live in their own little worlds, only receiving the information that they want to hear. That's why there are so many morons. At least that's what I think.

Hey look, in the back of the store they have a rack of albums. If hardly anybody is buying CD's, I have to believe that not a single person is buying albums. Here it is the week before Christmas and I'm the only one in the store. Sure it's only ten-thirty in the morning on a Thursday, but I don't think that I'm ahead of the big rush of people looking to buy used crap to give as gifts, not even in this economy. This place has to be a front for something, just look at the guy behind the counter. He looks to be around forty, long hair in a pony tail, AC/DC t-shirt covering his massive gut, he must be selling drugs in the back room. Look at the way he's eyeing me up, probably thinks I'm some kind of a nark or something. Calm down pony boy, I'm just browsing through these old albums killing time waiting to go into my therapy session. What irony here, I have to go to therapy and this idiot is looking at me like I might be up to something.

"Is there something that I can help you with?" Pony boy asks.

"No, I'm just looking around. If I need something I'll let you know." I reply as I think to myself. Yeah, why don't you grow the fuck up! You're not in High School anymore.

Of course he probably hears that on a daily basis from his mother that he probably still lives with. Walking into his bedroom is like taking a walk back in time. I can see it now, with the old Van-Halen and Mettalica posters hanging on the wall. The same as it was when he was eighteen, back when there was some hope that someday he might have a girl friend or even a chance at casual sex. Those dreams are gone now along with the hope that someday he may actually amount to something. It's amazing how much you can tell about a person by being judgmental.

Here's an album I used to have, "The Beatles-Rock and Roll Music." Holy shit! Sixty-five dollars! I wish I still had this album I could use sixty-five bucks. Here's what bothers me about this. If I were to buy this album, which is no longer in print and give it to a person that really likes the Beatles and if they still had a turntable, I would be like a big hero. On the other hand, if I still had the album and I wrapped it up and gave it to the same person, I would now be considered a cheap asshole for just giving away shit that I don't want anymore rather than paying sixty-five dollars for something that somebody else didn't want. It just makes no sense.

I glance down at my watch and see it's now ten-forty five. I've accomplished what I set out to do in here, kill time. I should probably walk over to the office. I feel kind of bad leaving without making a purchase, especially the way this guy is eyeballing me. I think he's really counting on me for a sale, but I didn't come in here to buy anything. Besides I don't think shelling out six bucks for a used Poison CD is going to help this idiot make the rent next month. It's a good thing he has that drug thing going. I walk past the terminal teenager out into the cold December air and down the street to the office building. I enter and take the two flights of stairs rather than wait for the ancient elevator to come down. That's all I need is to get stuck inside the elevator and arrive late again, especially since I've been here for half an hour already.

"Oh, Mr. Knight, you're early. Dr. Jonas is running a little behind schedule this morning. If you could just take a seat he will be with you shortly." The receptionist tells me.

That's my luck, I'm early and he's running behind schedule, we just can't seem to get this time thing to jive.

"All right then," I say and I take a seat and shuffle through the pile of old magazines.

Now you know that people in the medical profession charge a fortune and they make good money, so why is it that they can't spend a few bucks on decent magazines. "Hunting and Fishing" and it's the March issue for God's sake! I don't hunt and I don't fish so why would I want to read about them? Not only that, but there may be new innovations in hunting and fishing since March. But that's my only choice, either that or "Lady's Home Journal." I guess that's the doctor's opinion about his patients. If they're a man they're an outdoorsman and all the women are housewives. Anyone that would read "Newsweek" is certainly too intelligent to come here. I begin to glance through an article about the best bait to use when trout fishing in Michigan and wait for Dr. Jonas.

The door to the office opens and a frazzled looking middle age woman walks out. Her messed red hair is graying and she looks as if she'd been crying. Now I don't know what her story is and I really don't want to. I'm sure that it's long and sad but I really don't have that compassionate side that would allow me to listen and actually give a dam. Of course she may just be somebody that wants attention. Either way she looks like she really needed to be here. Well it's my turn now and I may never find out if I would be better off using minnows or a lure, but what the hell, that's not why I'm here. Let's get this torture over with.

Lisa, the receptionist tells me, "OK, Mr. Knight, you can go in now."

I enter the office and Dr. Jonas shakes my hand and says, "Take a seat, sorry I'm running a little late."

He then grabs a tissue from the box on his desk and blows out what sounds like about a gallon of snot.

"One of the kids brought home this damn flu and I can't seem to shake it."

"You're sick?" I ask. "Why did you shake my hand?"

Jonas gives me a look like I was being silly and says, "You're not a germaphobe are you?"

"No," I shoot back, "I just don't want to be sick at Christmas. Do you have any kind of disinfectant that I can rub on my hands?"

"Oh, you'll be fine," He says.

This is the same thing that he said about the parking ticket last week and we know how that turned out!

Now I'm afraid to touch anything in the office. Who knows what this guy has been touching and breathing on? I take a seat and hold my hands out in front of me, I surmise that if I can keep my hands from touching my mouth or nose until I can give them a good scrubbing I'll be all right.

"Are you going to sit like that for the whole session?" He asks.

"Yes, until I can wash your germs away," I answer.

"If it's going to make you feel more comfortable, why don't you go out to the restroom and wash your hands then" He says.

I stand up and head toward the door.

"Could you open it?" I ask.

Jonas shakes his head as if I'm being ridiculous and opens the door.

"And leave it open," I shout as I head toward the restroom.

Here it is a week before Christmas and the last thing I want is to spend the holidays walking around like some kind of mucous factory. You would think a man in the medical profession would know better. You don't shake a person's hand when you're full of bacteria. I give my hands a thorough cleansing and find myself faced with another dilemma. What if Jonas has been in here and touched the door knob? I grab a handful of paper towels to open the door and head back to the office.

I enter and kick the door closed with my foot. Jonas is mid-sneeze as I enter and fills up another tissue. I don't know how in the hell I'm going to be able to sit through this for an hour. The poor bastard sounds like he could drop dead at any minute and every breath he takes is filling the surrounding atmosphere with his contaminated particles.

As I take my seat in the comfortable chair across from the Doctor I can sense something trying to invade my system in this virus riddled office.

"So, did you keep a journal like I suggested?" He asks.

"Yes, I did," I reply.

"OK, let's start with the first day." He says.

"Thursday..." I begin and "Ahhhhhhh....chooo!!!" Jonas lets out a loud, disgusting, Kleenex filling sneeze.

"Jesus." Is all that I say.

"I'm so sorry about that. Go on then." He instructs and again I begin.

"All right, I leave my therapy session and find a parking ticket on my windshield."

"Really, you did get a ticket?" He asks.

I pull the ticket out of my pocket and hold it up to show him. He reaches for it and I pull it away.

"Don't touch it with your germs," I say. "I think that you can see what it is."

"I'll be damned. I wouldn't think that they would jump on you that fast, must be because of the holidays." He says.

"What are you going to do about this?" I ask. "It's going to cost me thirty five dollars!"

"What am I going to do about it, why should I do anything about it?" He says.

"Because I feel that you're responsible, that's why." I answer.

"How am I responsible? I'm not the one that parked the car in front of that meter and didn't put in enough money." He shoots back.

"Because you're the one that said I wouldn't get a ticket, I had nothing to worry about!" I say.

"I don't remember saying that." He says.

"Well you might not have said it exactly like that, but it was implied." I respond.

"Look, if you want to we can waste the whole hour arguing over twenty-five dollars…"

"Thirty-five," I interrupt.

"Ok, thirty five. We can use the whole hour discussing the ticket or we can spend this time trying to help you. It's up to you." He says.

Now if it was really up to me I would spend the hour arguing over the ticket and I'm pretty damn sure that he would end up paying it but that would only cost me another session in the long run.

"All right, drop it," I say.

"Good, that's a good move on your part," he says. "Now let's talk about that journal."

I can't believe the nerve of this guy. He just wants to change the subject. The least he could do is offer to pay half. It was his fault after all. He knows that he has the upper hand here. If we spend the hour arguing and I convince him that he should pay the thirty five dollars, he makes four times that by having me come in for another session.

"I just really think that it's your fault that I got the ticket in the first place. I mean, I told you I was concerned about getting back to my car in time and yet you went on and on about how I should just get it out of my head. That it was a good way to get control of my emotions and then I get the stupid ticket anyway." I say.

"I thought that we were past this." He says.

"We are. It's just that I don't think that you are really feeling the responsibility for this that you should." I tell him.

"Do you see what you are doing here? You are transferring blame to somebody else. Although you were the one that was running late. Because you didn't take the time to plan your day and take the proper precautions you were presented with the predicament of being parked at a meter that was not going to give you enough time. Had you not taken our session for granted, as I feel that you did, you would have had enough time to make it into the lot outside of the building. If in fact the construction did hinder you from doing so, you would have had enough time to acquire change and make sure that you deposited the proper amount in the meter. See, it was you that made the decision to not give yourself enough time to get here. I'm guessing because you feel you are being forced to come here and if that is the case we are not going to get anything out of these sessions. Do you see that?" he asks.

"Yes." I reply.

"Good. What I'm trying to get across is that what transpired last week was a result of your own actions, but you want the fact that you received a parking ticket to be my fault. Now let's move on." He says.

"I still think that if you would have let me out of here five minutes sooner this could all have been avoided." I say.

The doctor leans his head down and places it in his hands. He's shaking his head back and forth, as if he's disgusted with me. Why should he be upset with me? I'm the one that has to pay the ticket after all. He sits back up and leans way back in his chair. He pauses for a long moment.

"I'm all right." He says and then just stares at me for a long time.

"Hopefully we are beyond this now. Did you find that by writing things down, that it helped to control your emotions?" He asks.

"I guess, in some cases, maybe," I answer.

"You don't seem so sure," he replies.

"Well I wrote them down," I say.

"Ok, besides getting the ticket which I think we've spent more than enough time on, what else happened?" He asks.

I tell him the events of Monday, with the snow and the car problems.

"These are the kind of things that happen to everyone. By beginning to realize that and the fact that they are minor occurrences, will help you to keep your emotions in check. What was the problem with the car?" He asks.

"Battery," I reply.

"And it's fixed now?"

"Yes," I answer.

"There you see it was a minor problem that's easily corrected was it not?" He asks.

"Yes," I answer.

Then Jonas lets out a sneeze that sounds like it came from the deepest region inside his body.

"Wow!" I say. "I know that you're going to get me sick!"

"Oh, you'll be fine," He insists.

Yeah, I'll be fine, just like I wasn't going to get a ticket last week and a hundred and fifty dollars for a battery is a minor problem. This guy knows all of the answers. They're all minor problems, sure because they happened to me!

"These may seem minor to you but I'm really on a tight budget right now. Between the cost of my incident and now therapy, not to mention that I don't know when I'm going to be able to fly again, I'm really stressing about money." I tell him.

As I glance at him I get the impression that he's not even hearing me. He's looking kind of gray and fuzzy. Then he closes his eyes, leans his head back and I'm sure that he's about to black out. He shakes his head as if he's trying to clear the cob webs and rubs his eyes.

"You really look terrible," I say. "If you don't feel that you're well enough to continue I will totally understand." I say.

I'm trying to give myself an out here, I really can't stand to look at him anymore and I sure as hell don't want to be trapped in here with this disease riddled son of a bitch any longer.

"No, no I'm fine," he says. "Now what else happened?"

At this point I can see he didn't hear a word of what I just said. That's when his head snaps straight back and he almost falls backward in his chair. My first instinct is to grab him and keep him from falling, but I realize that I don't want to touch him. He recovers on his own and leaps from the chair.

"I'm sorry, I'm terribly sorry," He says. "Just give me a moment here to pull myself together."

I'm ready to just run out of the room but I'm going to need him to open the doorknob for me.

"You know what," I say, "You're not feeling well and should probably go home and get some rest, why don't we just call it a day."

Dr. Jonas is now pacing back and forth across the room.

"No, I'm fine. Just give me a moment here."

I look down at my watch and it's only eleven-fifteen. "You're looking at your watch again."

He says. "Did you park at the meter again?"

"No, I just wanted to see how much longer that I have to sit in this germ infested room." I reply.

"Once again you're focusing on something other than why you're here." He says to me as if I should just ignore the fact that he's a walking snot factory!

Dr. Jonas is now rubbing his temples as he sits down.

"Ok, I can get through this," he says. "I have an idea. Why don't you take the one incident that you found the most frustrating and we can discuss that?"

The one incident that I found the most frustrating, that's easy.

I begin, "I believe the thing that upset me the most last week was dealing with the computer help line, in India. I couldn't understand the guy I was talking to half of the time and I never accomplished anything. All it did was waste three hours of my life." I tell him.

"Go on," he says.

I look at him carefully before I start, to make sure that he hasn't blacked out. There's nothing worse than talking to somebody and realizing they're asleep. It happens with my wife all the time and she never understands why I find it so aggravating.

"I just don't understand why in the hell I can't talk to somebody in this country!" I tell him.

Jonas grabs yet another tissue and hacks up a phlegm ball.

He says, "This is just the way that things are now. You can't let it get to you."

"Doesn't it bother you?" I ask.

"Well, I suppose that when I have to deal with it, I can find it to be a bit annoying," He answers.

"If it's not somebody in India, you're dealing with an automated system. Those are even worse. You can spend hours pressing one for this and four for that and in the end you have no satisfaction. Eventually there will be no place that you will be able to deal with a human being. Not even one that you can't understand, and do you know what happens then?"

"What," Jonas asks.

"When you really need answers, when you really need somebody to speak with and there's no one there. When there's no longer a human voice to communicate with, that's when civilizations break down!" I say.

Dr. Jonas is staring back at me blankly. I don't know if it's the flu or if he's trying to dissect how calling customer service will lead to the collapse of civilization. He's staring without blinking for quite some time now. I'm beginning to think that he may have died during my last outburst and I know that somehow I'm going to get blamed for this. I can see the headlines now, "Crazed Flyer Kills Doctor during Anger Management Session." I should have never agreed to this therapy crap in the first place! His lips begin to move as if he's trying to speak, which means he's still with us.

"Wow," he says. "That's quite a summation. So you think that our civilization is going to break down?" He asks.

"I think it's almost gone right now." I reply.

"Interesting," He says as he scribbles something on his legal pad. "Ahhhh....ahhh...Chooo!"

Jonas covers his nose and mouth with his bare hand as he lets out this massive sneeze. Now I can see that his hands are decorated with the slime that is oozing out of his face.

"Excuse me." He says as he grabs a handful of tissues and attempts to clean the mess from his hands. "I'm sorry I'll be right back." He mumbles as he leaves the room.

I really don't know how much more of this I can take. He's obviously really sick or I might think that he was testing me to see how far he could go before I snap.

When he comes back into the office he is drying his hands with a paper towel.

"Sorry again about that. Now where were we? Oh yes our civilization is collapsing."

As he says this I can detect the sarcasm in his voice.

"I can see that you think that I'm going too far with this." I say.

"I didn't say anything. We're just getting to know each other and I find that your answers are giving me an insight into your persona." He tells me.

Insight into my persona my ass! I can see the way that this guy is looking at me and I know he's thinking to himself that I'm totally out of my mind. There's no way in hell this guy is ever going to let me fly again.

"Would you consider yourself to be a negative person?" He asks as he grabs a tissue to blow even more disgusting goo from his nose.

"Oh man, I know I'm going to get sick." I say.

"You didn't really answer my question but you did." He says.

"What are you talking about?" I ask

"I asked you if you consider yourself to be a negative person. You in turn said that you know that you are going to get sick. You're already defeated. You know that you will get sick. Where as a positive attitude would be to think that you are not going to get sick or better yet to not even have any thought on the matter at all as if the germs in this room didn't even exist." He says.

"That's kind of hard to do with you hacking out phlegm like there's no tomorrow over there." I say.

"You still haven't answered the question. Do you consider yourself to be a negative person?" He asks.

"Obviously you do." I reply.

"Avoidance, do you realize that you are doing everything in your power to avoid answering this question?" He asks.

"I do now." I say.

"Now try to answer this question. Do you consider yourself to be a negative person?" He asks yet again.

He's right; I really don't want to answer the question. Maybe by admitting it I will be admitting something to myself that I really don't want to know. On the other hand if I don't I'm probably never going to get out of this virus workshop.

"Yes, I guess that I'm a negative person." I finally answer.

He writes something down on his pad and leans back in his chair smiling.

"It took a lot for you to admit that, didn't it?" He asks.

"Yes it did." I answer.

"Now by admitting this to yourself we can begin to rectify the situation. The fact that you are already accepting defeat before seeing what the actual outcome is going to be is a major contributing factor in your anger. Can you see how that would affect your attitude in general?" He asks.

"Yes, I guess." I answer.

"You see by understanding that you are looking at the situation in the negative, if you understand this, by knowing this in advance you can change your outlook. If you realize that everything does not always have to turn out bad or against you then you will be able to eliminate a great deal of your anger. This will take a great deal of effort on your part, but if you are able to accept that positive things can happen to you and will happen to you if you allow them, then your mental attitude will change. Most of your anger will dissipate. Do you see what I'm saying?" He asks.

I knew that he had been talking way too long and I could hear that he was filling up with mucous as he droned on and on. It doesn't surprise me when Jonas reaches for a tissue and fills it then reaches for another and fills that one up too. Nobody should have to sit through this disgusting display.

"You still didn't answer my question," he says as he wipes the last bit of slime from his nose.

"Yes, I understand." I reply.

"Now this is something that we have to work on. I want you, for the next week, actually it will be two weeks before I see you again with the Holiday break, but what I want you to do is take time to analyze each thought that you have. Take time to see if what you are thinking can be construed as pessimistic. Now if you come to the conclusion that you have already admitted defeat then I want you to take the time to consider that by changing your outlook, to realize that everything does not have to come out for the worst, there can be some positives in every circumstance. Try to find some good in what you are thinking. Do you think that you can do this?" Jonas asks.

"I guess I can try. But what if things don't work out? What if I would have been right all along?" I say.

"Of course things will not always work out. Life's not perfect after all. It's just that I think that you always expect the worst and are probably only happy when you prove yourself right. When things don't work out you can tell yourself, see I knew this was go-ing to happen. Am I right?" He asks.

I think about it for a few moments and realize that he is probably correct.

"Yeah, maybe," I reply.

"So we're going to work on fixing this, OK?" He says.

"Yes, OK. But it's going to be tough. I've been this way for a long time." I say

"I know that it's going to be tough. Anything that's worth while is tough." He says.

There's a long silence between us. Jonas is just staring at me again and I don't know if he's waiting for me to respond to what he's just said or if he's gone into a coma from this nasty flu that's infiltrated his body and is probably working its ungodly way into my system right now. Finally Jonas reaches for the tissue box and empties his cavity yet again.

"It's Christmas after all, you should be enjoying this time. There's no reason to be unhappy. Are you going to spend the holidays with your family?" He asks.

"Yes." I answer.

"Well you see right there you have something to be appreciative of. Isn't that a positive thing?" He asks.

"You don't know my family. Why do you think I'm this way to begin with?" I answer.

Jonas lets out a phlegm-filled laugh and stands.

"I want you to really work on this these next few weeks. Make this part of your journal. Write down any negative thoughts that you may have." He says as we walk toward the door.

"I will." I say.

"And enjoy the time with your family."

Now I don't know if he meant that in a good way or a bad way. All I know was that at this point all that really mattered to me was being able to escape this germ-infested office.

"Are we done?" I ask.

"Yes, I think that's enough for today. I think this was a good session, considering that I wasn't myself." Dr. Jonas extends his hand. "I won't see you until after the holiday, so have a Merry Christmas," He says.

I look down at his hand and say, "Are you kidding me? Just open the door." Dr. Jonas opens the door and I say, "You have a Merry Christmas too and feel better."

Jonas has a big smile across his ghastly pale face and gives me a wave as I head out.

Before I exit the building I head into the restroom and scrub myself like I'm about to perform surgery. I wash my hands, lather up my face, the inside of my nostrils, my lips; I roll up my sleeves and even scour my arms. I've got to kill these germs. Down the steps and out to the parking lot I walk to my car. I know I'm going to get sick.

Saturday

AGAINST MY ADVICE WE MAKE AN ATTEMPT TO GO TO THE MALL ON WHAT IS THE NEXT TO LAST SATURDAY BEFORE CHRISTMAS.

I can't really blame this on my wife, although in the end I probably will. I hate to take responsibility for a plan that goes wrong and this was one of the dumbest ones that I ever came up with. As I've mentioned the money has been mostly going out these days and not coming in to replace it. Usually around this time of year I pick up some jobs entertaining at Christmas parties, but with the economy in the toilet everybody is afraid to spend. Add to that my continuing expense of my little tirade in Las Vegas, car problems, and whatever other bills there are and you see why I have not been in the jolliest of moods this holiday season. My plan was to explain to people that we were really tapped out this year and ask if we could just not exchange gifts. My wife wasn't in agreement with that arrangement.

She says "We only get so many Christmases in our lifetime and there is no reason to not enjoy this one just because we may not have as much money as we'd like."

So we've decided to do what most people do at this time of year, put everything on the credit cards and hope for the best in the New Year. Because of the fact that I've been debating the issue for weeks now and my wife has finally convinced me that we should go for broke with very little time left, we find ourselves at the mall on the worst possible day of the year.

There's something about the holidays that makes people insane. What reasonable person would do this? When you're driving around acres and acres of parking and not one space is open what would make you continue to search, knowing that at least one person from each of these vehicles is crowded inside of this concrete hell. Hot, jammed together, looking like zombies or people waiting for sweet death. What makes us do this? I can count on one hand the number of times that the look on the person's face when I gave them the gift was worth the hassle that I went through.

"Let's just go home! There's no place to park!" I say to my wife.

"If we do that when are we going to get this done?" She asks.

"Why don't we just order everything on line?" I suggest.

"It's too late. It would never get here on time." She replies. "There's a car leaving!" She tells me.

I pull toward a woman and what looks like her teenage daughter loading packages into the back of an SUV. I wait patiently as they slowly slide each package into the back and then stand there and arrange them.

"What are they going to do, stand here and gift wrap?" I shout.

"Just be patient." My wife says to me.

"They see us waiting here, what the fuck are they doing?" I shout.

"I see that therapy is doing you a lot of good." My wife says sarcastically.

"I've only been there twice." I tell her.

They finally get the last of the packages into the back of the SUV, close the door, and then… turn and head back to the mall!

"Son of a bitch, they weren't even leaving!" I shout.

"Just calm down," my wife tells me.

"Calm down? I should run them over!" I say.

"Let's just go find another space." She says calmly.

With my teeth grinding and the anger seething inside of me I drive to the farthest region of the parking lot.

We finally find a space so far away that the mall looks like a small blip in the distance.

"It's not that far." My wife insists as we face the cold wind and walk for what seems like miles to get to what should be nothing short of insanity.

"We could have just walked from the house. We're really not that much closer." I say.

"Can you ever do anything without complaining?" My wife asks.

We walk in silence the rest of the way.

As we enter the Mall through Macy's I can see it's worse than I could have ever imagined. The store is so jammed pack that you can't breathe. No sense in even trying to find anything in here. I grab my wife by the hand and lead her through the mass of people.

We snake our way slowly through Macy's and out of the store into the corridor. It's swarming with people here too and I'm beginning to feel claustrophobic. If I don't get out of here soon I'm going to lose it.

We try to walk but we're getting nowhere fast. I have the feeling of being trapped in quick sand. Each step I take I plunge a little deeper. We walk past what looks like one thousand children waiting to see Santa Claus. Santa's got the fake smile painted on or maybe its drug induced. You really couldn't blame old Santa if he showed up for work everyday stoned on his ass. That would make it so much easier. Some over indulged brat that reeks of urine and spoiled milk breath rattling on with their long list of toys and gadgets that they feel they deserve and you don't even hear it. You can just sit watching the twinkling lights and not listening to a word. I think that's the only way to get through that job.

I can't remember that time in my life, but it must be a wonderful feeling to be so innocent. Imagine believing a man in a red suit that flies around the world and brings you anything you want just because you're good. Sorry kids but it doesn't work that way. Being a good person in this world will get you absolutely nowhere. It's the slimy, evil, cutthroat bastards that make all of the money, but you'll find that out soon enough.

We head past Santa and my wife drags me into the candle store. She wants to get something for the girls at work. Again, you can't move. Why are there this many people in a stupid candle store? To me it seems like the most thoughtless gift you can give.

When you hand somebody a candle you're saying, "I didn't put any thought into this at all because I really don't give a shit about you, but at least I gave you something."

My wife can get what she needs in here and then meet me in

JC Penney. It's a time saving plan. That is if we don't get hopelessly lost in the crowd and we can't find each other until February. I'm figuring that by the time she gets out of here I will have purchased the items we were planning to get from Penney's and then we can go home and hang ourselves. As I enter the store I'm overwhelmed with the feeling that I've never seen this many people in one place in my life! It seems that Penney's is running a once in a lifetime sale with up to twenty-five percent off. That means by Monday it will all probably be forty percent off, but hey we can't pass up a bargain.

I fight through the crowd and grab the items that we had decided on and then I'm going to pick up a few gift cards for people that we have no idea what to get at the check out counter. As I approach the line I realize it is so long that I may not get out of here until I'm eligible for social security. The weekend is now shot and I think about saying to hell with it, but I'm here now and this has become a quest!

As I position myself at the end of the line I realize it's so long that I can't see the counter from here. I figure I must be in the right line because there can't be this many stupid people that would stand in the wrong line. Of course I know the answer to that and if you want to try an experiment sometime; just start your own line. Start standing around somewhere like you're waiting for something and watch how many people line up behind you. The results will frighten you.

Behind me a woman with a screaming child in a stroller enters and I think to myself, "At least I'm not the last person in line anymore. I'm ahead of somebody." Let me tell you something. If you think a child cannot scream at the top of their lungs for forty-five minutes without their mother doing anything about it, well you would be wrong. Not only is this woman allowing the child to continue with the annoying screaming, but also each time we move, she bangs me in the back of the leg with the stroller. At first I'm concerned that maybe she's blind and is using my leg as a guide. When I glance back at her I realize she has sight, which means instead she's just an ignorant fucking bitch!

By the time I finally reach the front of the line, if somebody were to ask me if I would rather be waited on or shot in the head, it would be a tough choice. I see my wife looking for me and I wave to her as the woman behind me bangs me one last time. There seems to be a problem with one of the customers that is trying to check out. He's a sad looking little guy and the only thing he is purchasing is a package of underwear. You must really need underwear to stand in a line this long. It seems there's a problem with the package. It won't scan in the computer system. They try it four or five times and then decide he must have picked up a bad one. The woman cashier is explaining to him that all he has to do is go upstairs, grab another package and get back in line. This would waste another hour of his life. The man doesn't say anything. He looks numb and desperate. If it was me I would probably demand that somebody go and get them for me while I wait here, but not this guy. I mean the poor son of a bitch is just tying to get himself some new drawers. It shouldn't be this difficult.

I can't believe that he's just standing there and putting up with this bullshit. He's just standing there with no expression at all on his face. What kind of a guy are you? The cahier is done explaining what he will need to do and dismisses him. That's when the guy walks right out of the store with the underwear in tow.

"Good for you buddy! Good for you!"

I couldn't believe what I had just witnessed, a person that was willing to stand up and solve the problem on his own. I wonder at what point he had come to the conclusion that he would just walk right out of there. He didn't say a word, just stood there taking it, but thinking to himself, "Yeah right, I'm going to go grab another package of underwear, stand in the stupid line for another hour, and take the chance those ones will scan. How about instead I walk out of the store with these and you can kiss my ass!"

Despite the crowds and the fact that the store is so hot it feels like it's on fire, I have to admit that at that moment I got a rush of holiday spirit I hadn't felt since I was a child. I felt like the Grinch on top of the mountain when the Who's came out to sing even though he had stolen all of their shit. My heart grew three sizes that day my friend. But alas, it was short lived.

A female cashier, not even the one that had been waiting on the underwear guy says next and I approach.

As I arrive at the counter she makes the realization what had happened and says to no one in particular, "That man just walked out of the store without paying for those."

I say what I think is loud enough for her to hear, "Yeah, I guess he didn't feel like standing in this line again."

She pays no attention to me. Instead she walks away, picks up the phone, and asks for security. In the meantime, the cashier that had actually been waiting on the man announces next. Old bumper stroller and her screaming little monster walk up and received immediate service!

My cashier is on the phone, trying to get through to security and you know that by now the guy is probably half way to Arizona. He's probably one of those serial underwear thieves you read about in the paper but pray you never cross paths with. It's when the male cashier across the way calls over the next person in line that I lose it.

"Excuse me! Can I get some service over here? I'm not invisible am I? I've stood in this line for an hour and now I'm at the cashier. Nobody is paying attention to me! Just like the man with the underwear I'd like to pay for my items, but if nobody wants to help me I'm walking out of here too!"

I feel that sometimes you have to take matters into your own hands or they'll just shit all over you. I may have mentioned this once or twice before. The woman puts down the phone, realizing now that I should be her first priority. I make my purchase and calmly walk out of the store with my wife.

When we get back out into the corridor my wife says, "You know, you really embarrassed me in there."

I ask, "And why is that, because I stood up for myself? That woman was just ignoring me. She called me over and then ignored me!"

My wife says, "You didn't have to yell like that, everybody was looking at you."

"That's because they become confused when they see somebody actually standing up for their rights! Most people forget that they actually have rights anymore." I reply.

My wife says, "Still."

And I ask, "Why didn't you just pretend that you didn't know me?"

She doesn't say anything and I can tell by her demeanor that I'm going to have to do some serious ass kissing if I want to have sex later but that's nothing new to me.

I guess I could have tried one of my time outs or taken a series of long deep breaths until I calmed down enough to not cause a scene, but I have to admit that the thought never even crossed my mind. This anger management thing is still kind of new to me. At least I wasn't arrested this time.

Meanwhile, he's still out there as his legend grows. I'm sure that will frighten many and they won't step into a mall until he's caught, but not me. No, I hope they never catch him. Remember I've seen him up close and lived to tell about it. My advice is to not try and be a hero if a man with a package of under shorts walks past you and heads for the door. Just let him be and he won't bother you, I know what I'm talking about. I've been there after all.

Well, it's Christmas Eve and I'm sick as a dog. It started about three days ago with chills and fever, followed by horrible congestion. I spent the first day in bed but there's just too much to do around here to get ready for the holidays. I'm doing all I can to keep myself upright today. If it was up to me I would just cancel Christmas this year and stay in bed until the New Year, but that would ruin it for everybody else. My plan is to get everything done and then numb myself with alcohol.

The worst part of having the type of flu that lasts for a week or more is that you forget what it's like to feel normal. Everyday I wake up hoping to feel better but it's not to be. There is only one thing that keeps me going through all of this. The one thought that is totally consuming me right now, "Jonas, you bastard you're going to pay for this!" I know that I shouldn't be having thoughts like this especially around the holidays but hey I'm really sick and my head is clogged and I'm not thinking straight.

EIGHT

It's the first Thursday of the New Year and after a two week break for the holidays, it's time for another session with Dr. Jonas. It was nice not having to deal with this for awhile. Of course I spent a large amount of that time trying to get over the dreaded flu that Jonas had infected my system with. I have a booking in Baltimore this weekend and have to go in a day early to do morning radio, which usually sucks, but its all part of the job.

Since I will be traveling east for Baltimore I decide to pack up the car and head out from here. This way I will avoid going through the stupid tunnel traffic twice in the same day. Baltimore is only about a three and a half to four hour drive from Pittsburgh and the weather is cooperating. The only problem with leaving after my session around noon is I will probably end up hitting nasty rush hour traffic once I get into the Baltimore area, but I won't have to deal with the tunnels twice. I'm screwed either way and the best scenario would have been to fly but hey, the courts have decided that I need my therapy.

I time it perfectly and arrive five minutes before my scheduled eleven o'clock appointment.

I enter the office and Lisa says, "Oh, hello Mr. Knight, Dr. Jonas will be right with you."

I no sooner hang my coat and sit down than the office door swings open and the frazzled woman steps out. It's obvious she's been crying again which means Dr. Jonas isn't doing her a hell of a lot of good, not if she leaves here crying every week. Then again maybe she just saw her bill. There's a part of me that would like to know how long she's been coming here and if Jonas has been any help at all or if we are just wasting our time getting parking tickets and a horrible virus. It's just that at this stage of my life I know better than to strike up a conversation with a crying woman.

Dr. Jonas pokes his head out of the office and says, "C'mon in John."

I follow him in and he shuts the door behind us. He extends his hand to shake mine and I give him a long exploratory look. There's no way that this guy is giving me another bug. He seems to be OK, so I shake his hand.

"Take a seat," he says.

I sit down in the big comfortable chair and he sits down across from me.

"So, how was your holiday?" He asks.

"Not too good," I reply. "I was very sick."

"Oh, that's a shame," he says, "There was a lot of that going around."

"Yeah, especially in this office!" I say.

"Oh, come on. You're not blaming me because you had the flu." He says.

"Of course I'm blaming you! The last time I was in here you were sneezing and hacking up phlegm like nobody's business. I wasn't around anyone else that was sick, so where else would I have gotten it?" I ask.

"Something like that, you just never know where you pick it up. I'm sure you were going to different stores and probably malls, weren't you?" He asks.

"Well, sure," I answer, "but..."

Jonas interrupts. "Well there you go. You never know what you'll pick up in those places. Somebody's sick, they touch a door and then you touch it and the next thing you know, you have the flu."

So there you have it. This man of medicine, this man who attended medical school, a man of science is unwilling to admit that possibly the fact that I was in his presence when he was coughing and hacking flu germs into this enclosed area is the reason that I got sick. No, it happened from touching a door at the mall. It must be nice to be able to pawn off your responsibilities on people that you've never met. I think I may be in the company of a future politician.

Dr. Jonas shuffles through his notes from what I'm guessing was our last session.

"So, how did we do with the positive thinking?" He asks.

"I've got to tell you, it was hard to think about anything except for the fact of how bad I felt." I reply.

Jonas has a look of disappointment on his face as he starts, "Don't you see that by dwelling on that, you were looking at the negative side. It probably kept you from enjoying the holidays."

"Yes, it did." I answer.

"That's too bad." He says.

"How were your holidays?" I ask hoping to hear the worst.

"Oh wonderful, yes just wonderful everything was great. I was sorry to see them end." He replies.

"Son of a bitch!" I think to myself.

"Ok, I'm going to ask you some questions and I want you to answer them honestly. Are you willing to do this?" He asks.

"Yeah, sure," I reply.

"What this is, I'm going to try to get a read on you emotionally and remember to be honest in your answers or you won't be doing yourself any good, OK?" He asks.

Now he's really starting to annoy me. I already told him that I was going to be honest.

"Yes, I told you." I say.

"What I want to know is if you've had any of these feelings in the past week. Were you at any time angry?"

"Yes."

"Bitter?"

"Yes."

"Rebellious?"

"Let me think about that one...No, I wasn't rebellious. Wait a second would that include wanting to get back at somebody for what they did to you?"

"Of course it would."

"Ok, then I was feeling rebellious."

"Annoyed?"

"Very."

"Furious?"

"No, I honestly think that I was too sick to be furious."

"Resentful?"

"Yes."

"Were you at any time looking to get into a fight?"

"Again, too sick."

"Frustrated?"

"Yes."

"Disappointed?"

"A lot of these are pretty much the same thing aren't they?" I ask him.

"No, not really. They are all different forms of emotion." He says.

"OK then. Yes I was disappointed."

He leans back in his chair and begins to write furiously. Wow he's really writing down quite a bit. I'm thinking that I may be the subject of a novel or some medical journal he's hoping to get published. He finally finishes and takes a long hard look at me.

"Do you realize that every answer that you gave me is a perfect example of a person that has anger management issues?" He asks.

"That's why I'm here isn't it?" I respond.

Dr. Jonas seems to be agitated by my answer.

"Yes, that is why you're here but it seems to me that you don't want to do anything to help yourself." He says.

I have no immediate response to this because he may be right. I wasted the holiday season dwelling on how sick I was instead of trying to enjoy the moment at hand. Then again, I was really sick.

"You know, I think that I really could have worked on the positive thinking and I really wanted to until I got the stupid flu and then everything went out the window." I say.

"Do you see that would have been the perfect opportunity to take a positive attitude? It may have even helped you to get over the flu sooner. You may have even been able to avoid getting it in the first place. Do you realize that stress is a predisposition to infection? Negative thinking can influence your health you know. Instead of dwelling on the fact that you don't feel well look at the fact that what you have will eventually go away. You didn't have anything life threatening. What you have to realize is that life isn't perfect. Things are going to happen that you can't control. The way you deal with these things is going to determine what kind of person you are. Are you able to accept that sometimes things happen and just deal with them in a rational manner or are you going to fly off the handle whenever things don't go the way you want them to?" He asks.

I have nothing to say to this.

"Are you happy with the way you are?" He asks.

The truth is that I'm not. I don't like getting upset all of the time. It's just the way I am and have been for as long as I remember. I'd like to be able to change.

"No." I answer.

"That's a start, admitting you are unhappy with the way things are. Now it's going to be up to you to do something about it. You're in control here, do you understand that?" He asks.

"Yes." I respond.

"Then why aren't you doing anything about it?" He asks.

"I don't know, like I said I was sick last week. Now I'm feeling better so I can start now." I respond.

"You can't keep making excuses. I was sick or my day didn't go as I planned. Do you see what I'm saying?" He asks.

Now Jonas is really starting to get repetitive and it's occurring to me that maybe I should just start lying to him. Tell him what he wants to hear.

"Yes, I see what you're saying." I reply.

"OK, let's start fresh. Last week is behind us. Let's look at what you have going on now." He says and then he just sits there.

I guess he's not going to ask me another question.

"I'm going straight from here down to Baltimore." I tell him.

"That's a pretty good drive isn't it?" He asks.

"It's not so bad. Besides what choice do I have? I'm not allowed to fly." I say.

"That's true." He responds.

Now he knows he's the one that holds the key to that problem for me. I decide to work on his sympathy.

"Of course the way the price of gas keeps going up it's actually less expensive to fly right now. Not to mention the convenience." I say.

"You didn't actually find it to be convenient the last time you were on an airplane, now did you?"

Ah, yes there's that. Hey I gave it a shot anyway.

"Well the weather won't be a problem. We're not supposed to get any snow this weekend. And a nice drive can be good for you. It'll give you time to clear your head." He says.

"Yeah I guess, that's if it is a nice drive." I say.

Now he's looking at me curiously.

"Why do you say that?" He asks.

I keep forgetting who I'm talking to. I guess I can't go back on my statement now.

"It's just that I rarely drive somewhere that everything goes smoothly. I either get held up with construction or stuck in traffic. It's always something." I tell him.

"So you don't like traffic?" He asks.

"Who likes traffic?" I respond.

He catches what he just said and laughs.

"Yes, you're right. I didn't word that correctly. What I meant to say was do you find yourself losing control when you're in traffic?" He asks.

"Yes, sometimes." I reply.

He writes something down.

"You realize there is nothing you can do about it?" He asks.

"Yes I realize there's nothing I can do about it. That's what makes it so frustrating. I have no control over the way the other idiots on the road are driving." I say.

"That's interesting. So you feel that you are a better driver than these other people?" He asks.

"I'll tell you this much, I've never been the reason for a major jam. I've never looked in my rear view mirror and seen a line of cars that are backed up because of the way I'm driving." I say.

"So you don't feel it has anything to do with the fact that there are maybe too many people all trying to go in the same direction at one time?" He asks.

"Yes, that's a contributing factor. We wouldn't have this problem if people would take their head out of their ass. I mean how hard is it to maintain a speed and take your turn merging instead of changing back and forth between lanes? These drivers assume that one of the lanes is going to be magically faster. It's the idiots that think that they can some how beat the traffic that only make things worse!" I say.

He just smiles and says, "You realize there is nothing you can do about it?"

"Yes, that's what makes it so damn annoying!" I answer.

"What you have to do is just deal with it. Realize that eventually the traffic will end and you will begin moving." He says.

"I don't know, I've been in some pretty bad traffic. There were times that I've given up all hope that it would ever end." I say.

"But it did end, didn't it? Or else you wouldn't be here right now. You'd still be stuck there."

He's got me there.

"When you find yourself getting agitated why not try something like oh, counting to ten until you calm down." He says.

"Because by the time I get to ten I probably wouldn't have moved even an inch. I could probably count to a billion if I wanted to." I respond.

"You could try listening to some soothing music." Jonas suggests.

"What like mood music?" I ask.

"No, it doesn't have to be mood music. Whatever music you like can be calming if you concentrate on it." He tells me.

"Yeah, maybe, it's just that when I'm in traffic it all blends to- gether for me. It's all just white noise at that point." I say.

I can see now that Jonas is starting to become a bit upset with my answers. I mean it's not like I wouldn't like a solution to keep me from losing it in traffic, it's just that he's really coming up with some half-assed suggestions.

"Have you ever tried a mantra?" He asks.

"A mantra?"

"You know like a phrase or song that you repeat to yourself until you are calm. Have you ever tried that?" He asks.

"No." I tell him.

"I have to tell you that all of these things I am telling you have been proven to provide stress relief, yet you seem to just dismiss them as nonsense. I think maybe the problem with you is you might feel you are above all of this." He says.

"I don't feel that way. It's just that it sounds like a bunch of bullshit to me." I say.

Jonas has his arms folded over his chest and is looking at me like what I just said is the most ridiculous thing he's ever heard.

"So you don't even want to try?" He asks.

I really don't but I'm afraid that if I tell him that it will hurt his feelings.

"Yes, I can give it a shot, go ahead and give me a mantra." I say.

"Once again I'm getting the feeling that you are not cooperat- ing because you want to but because you feel you have to." He says to me.

"What's the difference?" I ask.

"The difference is that if you do something because you have to you're probably not going to give it the same effort as you would if you were doing something you wanted to do." He responds.

"I told you I would try it, now give me a mantra!" I respond.

Jonas looks at me as if he's not fully convinced by my response but then realizes that this is probably all he's going to get out of me.

"Now I can give you something but I think it might be better if you came up with one yourself." He says.

"Give me an example." I say.

Jonas seems to be searching through that brain of his for the mantra greatest hits. I would have thought he would have had an example handy.

"Oh I don't know, it can be something simple like "Everything is fine" or "I'm at peace." It's really up to you to come up with one that will work. Like I said it could be anything." He tells me.

"What like "uh-oh Spaghetti-o's?" I ask.

"Uh-oh Spaghetti-o's? What's uh-oh Spaghetti-o's?" He asks.

"It just popped into my head. Don't you remember that commercial, uh-oh Spaghetti-o's?" I respond.

"I think I remember. Did you like Spaghetti-o's when you were a child." He asks.

"Please! My mother's Italian. We didn't eat spaghetti out of a can. It just popped into my head." I say.

"Well if it works for you go for it. If not that try to come up with something else. The time that you spend trying to come up with a mantra will be time that you won't be getting agitated by the situation." He tells me.

"Now another thing you may want to try is to take yourself to a relaxing place in your head, a place that you can find peace. Can you think of a place where you find yourself relaxed?" He asks.

"I don't know." I respond.

"Concentrate!" Jonas commands.

I really have to think about this one. I really don't know if there is ever a time in my life when I am relaxed. I really don't know if I can come up with anything…and then it hits me.

"On the beach, at night when it's quiet, with the moon shining down on the water and the sound of the waves and the breeze blowing over you. Walking along the beach at night is very relaxing to me." I say.

"Very good, very good, I can see that you really put some thought into that. Now you have something you can use when you are feeling stressed. Just take yourself to the beach in your mind. Picture yourself walking along the beach at night. Maybe holding hands with your wife, is that OK?" He asks.

"Yeah, she can be there." I respond.

"Good, now you have a mental image, a place that you can go to when you find yourself overcome with anxiety. Do you think you can do that?" He asks.

"Yes," I reply.

I can see by the way that he's looking at me that he's really not buying it.

"You don't look like you believe me." I say.

"Well the thing is with you, I'm really not getting the impression that you want to do this." He says.

"Yes I do!" I demand.

"OK, maybe you do initially but when the time comes to apply what I am telling you here, you just forget about it and continue in your old ways. The only way to overcome your anger is to put these things into practice. It comes from in here."

He points to his chest which of course means the heart.

"And in here."

Now he's pointing to his head in case the first part wasn't cliched enough. The theme of our session today seems to be that I don't want to help myself and I guess deep down he may be right. I can be a real stubborn son of a bitch at times. The thing is that in reality I would like to get over this problem. It's not enjoyable to allow yourself to get pissed off at the dumbest things. OK, that's wrong, when something dumb happens I'm going to get pissed off and I feel that I have every reason to be. There's just no excuse for stupidity. I guess what I mean to say is that I shouldn't allow myself to get annoyed over things I have no control over.

"I really want to do this." I proclaim to Jonas.

He gives me a smile and says, "OK, then."

We spend the rest of the session going over and over the same thing to the point where he is becoming a real pain in the ass.

"These are all proven stress relief methods."

He keeps telling me as if I don't believe him. I do believe him. The problem is going to be to put them into practice. He even goes so far as to tell me of a technique where you hold a polished stone in your hand to relieve stress.

"Do you really think that I should be arming myself like that?" I ask.

After giving it some thought he just shrugs and says, "It would probably be wise for you to try some of these other methods first."

As I leave the office and get into my car I see that it's only ten after twelve. This is a great time to leave. I'm already through the Pittsburgh city limits so I don't have to worry about any problems there. I'm thinking that I will be able to make the trip in less than four hours, even with a quick stop for gas. I should be able to avoid the worst part of rush hour traffic and get to the hotel by four, maybe four thirty at the latest. That will give me plenty of time to get a shower, grab something to eat and have time to relax before going to bed.

NINE

It's only quarter after three and I'm just thirty miles outside of Baltimore. It didn't look like I was going to have any problems and I was honestly starting to believe that until I hit complete gridlock. Interstate 270 looks like a parking lot. I don't think I've even moved one car length in the last ten minutes and I'm beginning to become agitated! This is when I normally would call my wife on the cell phone and start screaming, but this time I don't.

I decide to give Jonas' strategy a try. Let's see if I can't come up with a mantra and get myself calmed down here. Nothing is coming…I look around for inspiration. There it is in the rear view mirror. No, not the asshole behind me, "Objects in mirror may be closer than they appear." Objects in mirror may be closer than they appear, objects in mirror may be closer than they appear, and objects in mirror may be…This one's not going to work. All I keep thinking is that if the idiot behind me was any closer he would be in my back seat right now!

I've got to come up with something else. OK, I've got it, how much wood could a wood chuck chuck, if a wood chuck could chuck wood. How much wood could a wood chuck chuck, and who really gives a fuck! That one's no good either. All right, here's one, "no pain, no gain. No pain, no gain." What the hell am I thinking? This is a pain, sitting here not moving. Screw that one. Let me think, what about "does this look infected to you?" "Does this look infected"…no, that one's wrong for so many reasons.

Maybe a song, one of those stupid songs that you can't get out of your head no matter how hard you try. Let me think. I know, I'm feeling hot hot hot…I'm feeling hot hot hot… and how the hell does the rest of it go? I'm feeling hot hot hot…I'm really not not not…that guy should be shot shot shot…look at that fat bastard, he must eat a lot lot lot. To hell with this, let's give that ocean thing a try. I've been to the beach before I know what it feels like, maybe if I really concentrate.

Here I am at the beach. I can feel the breeze and hear the waves. I can see the moon reflecting off of the water. Come on concentrate, I can really do this. Feel the breeze, listen to the waves. Nothing better than a walk along the beach at night, feel the breeze, look at the moon shining. Just let it into my head, block out what's pissing me off, feel the breeze, listen to the waves…Hey, this is starting to work! I'm really feeling it. This is really working. Ah, I feel so calm right now, so calm…BOOM!

I just hit the guy in front of me! Shit! I probably should have been paying attention to the road instead of trying Jonas' silly nonsense! There can't be any damage, we're hardly even moving. Not only that but there's no way to get over to the side of the road anyway, what's the guy going to do? Are you kidding me? The idiot is getting out of his car in the middle of this mess and he's signaling for me to do the same. Son of a bitch!

He's examining his back bumper as I approach. He's a heavy set guy in a gray shirt with pit-stains under the arms. Obviously he sweats too much from all of that fat and gray probably wasn't the wise color choice for a shirt. He's also wearing a neck tie with what looks like a mustard spot. No surprise there. He's got a mess of hair, what's left of it anyway that he seems to be attempting to do some kind of bizarre comb over with. I'd like to tell him he's not fooling anybody but we can just let that go since I'm the one that hit him. Now I can see that he's got one of those blu-tooth's growing out of his ear. People like to wear those to show the rest of us just how important they are. What a jerk! Oh, and of course he's driving a Mercedes.

"What are you in a big hurry?" He asks.

"Even if I was it wouldn't matter, we're not moving." I say. Then I ask, "Is there any damage?"

"I'm not seeing any right now, but I might have to have my mechanic check it over tomorrow." He says.

"Are you kidding me? I was going like one! You're going to have your mechanic check it out?"

At this point I'm about to grab him by the tie and jerk him up against the car and maybe talk some sense into him but uh-oh-Spaghetti-oh's, uh-oh Spaghetti-oh's!...

Then he says, "Maybe you should give me your driver's license and insurance, you know just in case."

"Do you really think all of that is necessary?" I ask.

"Well what am I supposed to do if I need to get a hold of you?" He asks. "I'll give you my phone number." I say.

"How do I know that you're not giving me a fake number?" He asks.

"I'll pull up my home number on my cell phone and you can copy it down from there." I answer.

"How do I know that's your real number?" He asks.

"What do you think I did? As soon as I saw you get out of the car, I erased my old number and put in a fake one?"

That's when it occurs to me that would have been a really good idea.

He's writing down my phone number and now the cars behind us are blowing their horns, even though traffic couldn't have moved more than five feet in the time we've been standing here.

"Where do you think you're going?" I scream to no one in particular. "We're not even moving!"

Nobody cares and they just beep their horns more.

"You know I really think I should get your insurance information." The guy says and I imagine there will be a whiplash case in his future.

The hell with it, let my insurance company deal with this fat bastard if he wants to commit fraud. He'll tell them he has a nagging pain in his back which he probably already had. Not from me rear ending him at one mile an hour either. No, his back probably hurts because it has to carry around his front. As I walk toward my car to get the insurance card out of the glove compartment the horn blowing intensifies.

"Yeah, I know you'll all feel much better when you get five yards further up the road. Life is so much better there. It's just that you're going to have to wait a few more minutes but just think, it will be so much better when you finally get there." I say, once again to nobody specific.

I hand him the insurance card and he begins to write down the information. He finally has it all written down and since there's no sense in us continuing to exchange pleasantries here in the middle of the road, I walk back to my car. He gets back into his and begins to move forward, I follow carefully and there we are, ten feet farther up the road. I hope all the idiots that were honking at me are satisfied.

What an asshole! I'll tell you that I have met my share of assholes in my day, but this guy was the king. If they ever held an election for the biggest asshole on the planet this guy would win by a landslide. Now you may consider yourself to be an asshole, you may even take pride in it. I know people like that. They get a charge out of being a total asshole. I don't care. If you met this guy you would be in complete awe.

The nerve of the guy! He went over his car as closely as he could without using a magnifying glass. There wasn't a mark in sight, but that's not good enough! No, he has to take it to his mechanic and make sure that it didn't suffer any internal damage. Maybe you shouldn't pay that much money for a car if they can't handle the impact generated at one mile per hour!

The other thing was the damn blu-tooth. As soon as you see one of those you know you're going to be dealing with some pretentious piece of human slime. There was a time when people were embarrassed to wear hearing aids because they were a big ugly thing that you had to attach to your ear. Now people wear a big ugly thing hanging out of their ear like it's a badge of honor. Oh, look at me everybody, I'm so fucking important! I'm so important that I could get a phone call at any moment and I'm so damn busy I don't have the time to bring the phone up to my ear. No, instead I have this piece of shit that hangs out of the side of my head so I can continue on with my busy life while I talk on the phone. The fact that I'm so busy means I'm so much better than you mere mortals that have the time to answer the phone like a normal person! The most annoying part of those things is when you hear somebody say "hello" and then as you are about to answer them you realize they're not even looking at you. It used to be that if somebody was walking down the street talking to themselves, you knew they were out of their mind, but no more. No, we can't tell who the crazies are anymore. Then again, maybe we can.

Traffic has been rolling along at a pretty good pace for a while now and I was so entrenched in thought of the different ways I would like to see the son of a bitch in the Mercedes die, that I didn't even notice when we started moving again. At least I found a way to take my mind off the traffic. Mantra, my ass!

We're moving along really well in this direction but going the other way looks like a nightmare. There's an accident in the middle of the highway and the police are directing three lanes of traffic into one. Oh, look at all of those poor bastards on the other side of the highway. I'm glad I'm not going that way because that would really suck and I think I just drove past my exit! Son of a bitch! I should have been paying attention to what was happening over here. Now I have to drive up to the next exit and come back the other way, in the massive traffic jam! Nothing ever goes easy does it?

The next exit is two miles up the road. I turn around and get right into the jam that I was so happy to be avoiding just a few minutes ago. It just goes to show you that life can take a turn for the worse in just a brief moment. It takes about forty-five minutes to trudge those two miles that I should never have had to travel. When I finally arrive at the hotel it's almost seven o'clock and what should have been an easy three and a half to four hour trip has turned into seven hours of hell!

When I get to the room I call my wife to let her know that I have arrived and of course share the details of my ordeal. Then I take a quick shower and grab a sandwich to go at the place next door. I eat, give my wife another call and check my e-mail. Then I relax and watch some TV, and finally get to bed around one AM. I have to get up to do stupid morning radio after all.

Let me just say that nine times out of ten doing morning radio sucks! There was a time back in the eighties when you might be on with just one guy or one woman and at least you had a chance. Most of the time they asked for notes they could use to lead you into material and then actually let you finish what you were saying

∽ 144 ∽

before asking the next question. Of course you would run into the occasional jerk that felt like he had to help you and would step on and shit all over what you were talking about, sucking all of the humor out of it. You never knew what you were going to run into but at least it was usually a unique experience each time.

Then came the time when corporations began to take over the stations and make them all into the same annoying garbage. There's no longer one person doing the morning show, now we have the morning zoo or the wacky morning team and it's all the same, sad, low brow shit no matter what city that you're in. Until reality television came along, morning radio was the lowest form of entertainment on the planet.

It's easy for these people to be funny on the radio. They're not in front of an audience. They only have to make each other laugh and since they all share the same juvenile sense of humor, that's easy to do. Then there are the names. You rarely do a show with people that have normal names. "Hi, you're on the air with Dave and Ted." No, that wouldn't be wacky enough, now you have to do shows with people that have the nerve to call themselves things like "Big Earl and the Butt Man" or "Mookie and Stinky" or sometimes one of them will have a normal name like "Freddy and the Tuscaloosa Kid." Of course he won't actually be from Tuscaloosa. It doesn't matter. It's all just very maddening.

As far as doing material, forget about it, now it's just a matter of survival. They might ask for some notes and they might even lead you into a bit, but they never let you finish. It's almost guaranteed that one of them is going to jump in and destroy what you were about to say. I don't know if it's a sense of insecurity or if their ego's are really too big for them to realize that they have absolutely no talent. Then there are the times when instead of setting you up, they tell you to just feel free to join in with whatever it is that they are doing. Oh, that's great, I'll just dive head first into this festival of shit that you're presenting!

Now I don't want to say that it's always like this. Like I said before it's usually nine times out of ten but there is that ten percent out there. I have had some very enjoyable experiences on the radio with intelligent people that truly get it and are very aware of how to entertain the audience. It's just that these are few and far between.

I'm supposed to be picked up at the hotel at seven-thirty in the morning, so I set the alarm for seven-fifteen. That gives me time to comb my hair, brush my teeth, and throw something on. No need to look my best, its radio after all.

At about seven twenty five the phone in my room rings and there's a woman's frantic voice on the line. She informs me that she is the club owners' wife and that she will be picking me up. Then she tells me that she's running a little late and that she probably won't make it until about quarter of. We were not off to a good start.

Now I'm standing outside of the hotel in the cold, waiting. It's about ten to eight now and no sign of anybody yet. I feel like just going up to my room and climbing back into bed but then I would be the asshole. The fact that I was ready at seven-thirty like they asked me to be and that I could have slept another twenty minutes or half an hour if they had told me last night that they were going to be this late doesn't matter to these club owners. Like everybody else, the only thing that matters to them is the bottom line, how much did we take in? It never factors in that you are the one doing them a favor by arriving a day early and getting up to do the radio show in the first place.

A silver SUV pulls up in front of the hotel and the woman driving is looking at me like she wants me to get in. This is probably my ride and not just some random woman staring at me but I'm not going to just climb in, just in case. That's all I need at eight in the morning is to be arrested for being a suspected killer or rapist or some other thing just because I got into the wrong vehicle. No, I think I'll just wait for her to signal me.

When I finally get my signal and climb in the woman acts as if she's annoyed with me. I'm sorry did I interrupt your busy schedule by doing promotion for your business? I just can't believe the attitudes of some people. She moves some children's toys from the seat so that I can sit down. There are empty fast food bags and candy wrappers on the floor of the vehicle and I work my feet around them. For those of you out there that think show business is nothing but glamour and limousines, I hate to inform you that it's usually like this, sorry to burst your balloon.

The woman is dressed in a sweat suit and has a frenzied pace about her as we leave the parking lot.

"I'm on my way to a meeting and I'm running really late." She tells me.

I'd like to mention the fact that if she had picked me up on time she wouldn't be rushing around like this but it's early and I'm not really in the mood for confrontation yet.

"I'm just going to drop you off at the station and my husband will pick you up later, after he gets the kids off to school." She informs me.

Wow isn't it nice of these busy people to take time out of their schedule to allow me to advertise for them so that they can make more money! I'm getting a real sense that things will only be getting worse as the morning goes on.

As we drive along she tells me that I will be doing the top rated station in the city and that it really helped to generate business at the club.

She then asks, "Would you like to listen to the station that you will be doing?"

She has the radio playing and I was under the impression that we were already listening to it.

"This isn't it?" I ask.

"No, I can't listen to those guys," she answers.

Again, not a good sign.

She puts on the station that I will be doing. The one that we had been listening to was playing jazz and there was a news update about to come on. What was I thinking? Of course this isn't the station that I would be going to. There's no way in hell that a jazz station is the number one rated in any city. Not in this day and age anyway. If you ever listen to jazz radio you know that the DJ's are usually refined and intelligent and know what the hell they are talking about, not like this mess that I am now hearing which I can only describe as sheer hell. What's going on is, the DJ's or the morning zoo or the wacky guys or whatever the fuck they want to be known as are taking calls from their listeners to discuss different nicknames that they have given to their penis's. At this point I would like to ask her to just turn around and take me back to the hotel or at the very least, let me just get out and jump in front of the car while she speeds over me, but she's running late already and either of these suggestions will probably send her over the edge.

We arrive at one of those generic office parks where all of the buildings look the same. This is usually where you find radio stations these days, probably three or four stations tucked inside the same building and all controlled by the same corporation. She tells me that she can't really remember which building the station is in because her husband usually brings the people to the station and stays with them. I think to myself, "Oh, rather than strand them out here like you're about to do to me," but I don't say it out loud.

"Maybe the building with the black van with the call letters of the station that I'm about to be on parked in front of it could be the one." I say and I'm pretty sure that she doesn't sense the sarcasm and disdain in my voice.

"Yeah, I think that's it. I just don't know which door it is that you should go in." She tells me and this day just keeps getting better and better.

"What about the big glass double doors that lead to the reception area." I say.

"Yeah, I think that might be right." She says as she pulls in front of the building.

I'm feeling that her only chance at getting to her meeting is for me to stick around and guide her, but I've got radio to do. She'll have to make it on her own. This is her town after all.

As I climb out of the SUV carefully as to not knock any of the garbage under my feet onto the ground she tells me. "You'll be on for at least an hour and probably two. My husband will be here when you are done."

I find no comfort in those words as I head toward the door. She doesn't even wait to see if I make it in and just speeds away toward her meeting. I'm no longer her problem.

I go to the reception desk and tell them who I am and why I'm here and I'm surprised to find that they were actually expecting me. The receptionist, a chunky older woman acts like helping me is the last thing that she wants to be doing right now. I feel bad. I did take her away from her book of jumbles after all. Anyway she takes the time to actually do the job they are paying her for and makes a call. She then informs me that the producer would be right with me. Now, producer sounds like an important position but when it comes to morning radio it's usually some pimple faced kid that looks like he spends all of his free time playing video games and jerking off.

The producer arrives and I'm not disappointed, he meets all of the criteria. You really hate to shake the guys hand when you think of what he spends most of his time doing with it, but that would be impolite. He leads me down the cookie cutter hallway past the dull gray cubicles and I could be doing radio anywhere in the country right now and it would look exactly the same. He leads me into the kitchen, which is where they always make you wait and asks me if I would like some coffee. I decline. He tells me that I will be going on in a few minutes and he will come and get me.

For the next hour I sit in the kitchen and watch various employees come and go, grab coffee and snacks, and I think to myself that I should have never answered the phone this morning. I also am aware of the fact that there isn't anybody here to take me back to the hotel. Even if I wanted to act like a "Prima Donna" or a "Diva" or whatever term applies here and demand that I shouldn't be treated this way! It wouldn't matter because the truth is I'm stuck here. I really don't think that it is acting like a "Prima Donna" for standing up for your rights but that's how people always get labeled. Every club owner has a story or two about the asshole that threw a fit because the people at the radio station didn't kiss their ass. Of course the club owners never mention the fact that the person is probably getting up in the middle of the night to do this radio spot. They don't take into account how far we had to travel the day before to get here. They also never bring up the fact that we were picked up from the hotel late by somebody that didn't know where they were going, or how we had to sit around a kitchen for an hour waiting to do a few minutes on a moronic morning show. No, they never mention that part.

Pimple face finally remembers that I'm here and takes me over to the studio. He introduces me to the DJ's. I don't remember their names, all I remember is that one was a black guy and the other was white and I think that the black guy was more arrogant, but it was really too close to call. They introduce me and we go over the formalities. Where are you from? Do you have a web site? How long have you been at this? Is this your first time at the club? And then they thank me and go to break. I'm done! This wasn't two hours, it wasn't even one hour, it was five fucking minutes! I just wasted my whole morning for five fucking minutes on this stupid show.

I walk out to the reception area and ask the receptionist if the club owner had shown up yet. She has no idea what I'm talking about and in fact I don't think she even remembers who I am. I guess that it's been over an hour since I was taken hostage and put into the kitchen holding cell and her short term memory probably isn't what it used to be.

Usually these club owners make a weekly appearance at the station and get to know the people involved with running things, but I was getting the impression that type of thing didn't go on here. Hell, he can't even take the time out of his busy day to be here to take me back to the hotel! I guess they just drop us at the door and then we're to fend for ourselves. I decide to take matters into my own hands. I walk back down and find the producer kid and ask if he had any contact information for the owner. As a surprise to me, he happens to have his cell number. I probably should have his cell number too, but I guess he doesn't want to be bothered by some pain in the ass that he left stranded in the middle of nowhere and might want to get back to their hotel room.

I dial the number and I don't even get voice mail. All that I get is a message telling me that this person was not taking any calls at this time. Son of a Bitch! He's probably where I would like to be right now, in bed. I can't believe the balls of some people. Have somebody do you the favor of promoting your club so that you can make money and then if they would want to get hold of you for a ride back to the hotel, well they can just go fuck themselves!

The receptionist is doing whatever she can to avoid me and I can see that she really doesn't want to be bothered, but she's my only hope. I ask her if there was any way to get a cab out here and she's nice enough to make the call for me. Either she's being nice or doing what she can to get me out of her life so she can get back to her important puzzle book. It really doesn't matter to me. I just want to get the hell away from this place. The receptionist hangs up the phone and informs me that it would probably be at least half an hour or forty five minutes before the cab would be here. Then she goes back to the jumbles. She's done with me, just like the woman that stranded me here. I am no longer her problem. I can tell by the way that she's acting that she would rather I just go away so I decide to go outside and wait.

Now I'm standing outside in the cold, ready to go with the first person that comes along. The cab, the club owner, hell at this point if a guy in a van came by and offered me some candy to go for a ride I would probably jump right in. I just want out of here. It's now about quarter of ten in the morning and I've spent the last two and a half hours doing five minutes of radio. I have no ride and it seems like nobody really gives a shit about me so I'm just standing here like a jerk in the cold waiting for my cab.

It's five of ten when the blue SUV races up in front of the building and rolls down the window.

"Are you John?" The man inside asks.

Now, I could be wrong but it doesn't seem like the kind of spot where people would spend a lot of time loitering, but from what I've experienced so far this morning, I have to assume that I'm dealing with a total moron here.

"Are you my ride?" I ask.

When I get in I'm greeted by the loud crying shrieks coming from the small child strapped into the car seat behind me. It's like an added bonus, just in case this day wasn't infuriating enough.

"I'm really sorry. I just put on the show and heard that you weren't on anymore and I raced right over." He says.

"Do you know that if you had put it on an hour ago you could have heard I wasn't on anymore and I wouldn't have had to wait around like an idiot?" I ask.

"I'm really sorry. They usually have the acts on longer. I don't know what happened. I'm really sorry."

He apologizes all the way back to the hotel and between that and his whining kid it's really a long fucking drive.

All I want to do is climb back into bed and get a nap. I realize that the rest of the world gets up at seven AM or earlier everyday, but they don't keep the same hours that I do. When they're crawling into bed around eleven at night, I still have a show to do and am expected to be at my best. I need to get some sleep. It takes a while, but I finally doze off and am in a deep sleep.

BANG! BANG! I'm suddenly awakened by a series of bangs on my door. I'm not sure if it was a dream or, BANG! No, that's not a dream and it's not somebody knocking. BANG! I don't know what the hell is going on. I throw on a pair of pants and open the door to find a group of five kids are playing hockey in the hallway of the hotel and they have set up the net right in front of my door.

"Do you think that you guys could do that someplace else? Why don't you go down and play in front of your own room?"

One of the little snot nosed punks' answers me. "We can't play in front of our room our parents are trying to sleep."

"Hey guess what, I was trying to sleep in here too. That's what people do in hotels! Do you think that you could find another spot away from here?" I ask politely. "OK," the punk assures me and I crawl back into bed.

BANG!

"Bastard kids!"

The problem with hotel room doors is that they open in. If I only had a door that opened out right now, one quick swing of that door would take out the net and at least two of the kids at the same time. That would put the fear of God into them. Yes, that's all it would take, one quick jolt from this door and game over. Who designs these stupid hotels anyway?

It turns out the five minutes on the radio is actually the high-light of the weekend. During the Friday night late show a fist fight between a group of drunken adults in their forties and fifties breaks out in the hallway while I'm on stage. The owner knew they were probably going to be a problem. He told me as much before the show.

"There is a group in here that are really loud and they could be difficult. They already had to throw them out of the restaurant upstairs. I'd probably ask them to leave but they are running up a pretty good tab." He told me.

There you see it, the bottom line. How much is this guy putting in his pocket by selling alcohol to already intoxicated idiots? The show doesn't matter. If it did he wouldn't allow these fuckwads to shit all over it. After the show he's already patting himself on the back for the way he ushered them into the hallway when the fight started and then finally asked them to leave. The fact that the hallway was about ten feet from the stage and the rest of the people in the audience couldn't help but pay attention to what was going on there doesn't even enter his thoughts.

Saturday, the second show is filled with more drunks with short attention spans that need constant attention. It sucks but I get a paycheck and this is what you have to do when you're not famous. Sometimes it's just about getting the money and getting the hell out of town. That's what I'm doing now. The weather is fine and I leave after the second show and head for home. I'm on the road by midnight and if you can do it, it's the best time to drive. There's almost never a traffic tie up at three AM unless you live in Los Angeles.

LOS ANGELES

Twelve years, twelve long years we lived there and I can only say that I wish I would have had the same attitude about the place when we got there as I did when we left. That way we probably would have only stayed for about a week and a half. It's all part of the learning experience.

"You have to go to L.A., it's the place where everything is happening." I heard that from everybody back then and why would I think everybody was full of shit. Surely everyone can't be wrong can they? Of course the reason to go to Los Angeles is so you can be discovered and become famous. The problem being that everyone in town is there for the same reason. Oh, except for the Mexicans, the

Mexicans are just there to work but everybody else is there because they think there is something special about them. When you are surrounded by nothing but people that think they are special it can be really fucking annoying!

It really is a beautiful place that has everything. It has scenic mountains where I could see snow in the distance during January while I was enjoying seventy degree days. It has a great coast line that we used to enjoy driving along. Where else can you ski and take a dip in the ocean on the same day? I'm sure you can do it in parts of New York if you really wanted to, but the water is going to be like ice.

There really is a lot to like about the place except for the special people. Millions of them and none of them want to talk to you or have anything to do with you. Not unless you can help them in their selfish quest to be famous. If you can advance them in any small way, they will attach themselves to you like the blood sucking leeches they are. Millions of special people, all of them in their cars at the same time and I hope you're not in a hurry to get anywhere because you can't.

Some of these special people become executives making important decisions. Not because they're qualified mind you. I really don't know how most of these people got to the places of power but I have a theory. If you know deep down that you are really an idiot with no qualifications and have no business being in the position that you are in, when it comes time to hire somebody to work below you, they would have to be even dumber and less qualified than you are. Then these people get promoted and have to hire somebody less qualified than them and this has been going on for so long you now have nothing left but a group of mutants running the entire town. I've heard talk of intelligent Hollywood executives but just like Big Foot I'm going to have to actually see one in order to believe they exist.

When I refer to the special people I'm not necessarily referring to people you might recognize because they've made it. Usually those people will at least give you the time of day if you're not too big of a pain in the ass when you approach them. They should be nice. The people that approach them are the reason they are living the good life to begin with. Sure, some of them are real pricks and bitches but there are pricks and bitches that work at the bank or the supermarket. Some people just can't help themselves.

The people that really get on your nerves in L.A. are the wannabe's and phonies. These are people that try to act like they are something they are not. They are always trying to give off the illusion that they are important. I can't tell you how many times I felt like taking a cell phone and shoving it up somebody's ass because they wouldn't even take the time to acknowledge the person waiting on them. The thing is most of the time they weren't even on the phone until they get into the check out line. The phone doesn't even ring. No they make the initial call as they work their way through the line. When they get to the person helping them they just throw their groceries at the cashier or plane tickets at the gate attendants at the airport. Then not even pay attention to that person as if to say "I'm too good to have anything to do with a peon like you!" Oh, but if somebody grabs the phone out of their hand and smacks them on the side of the head while saying, "Don't ignore this person you stupid piece of shit!", then you're the bad guy. Some things just don't make sense.

Of course it wasn't all bad. You can't live in a place for twelve years without some positives coming out of it. I made some good friends that I remain close with to this day. Not only that but I had a large group of friends and acquaintances I had met over the years in the business that had also decided to make the move to the Promised

Land. Some of my friends went on to become successful in TV and films as actors and writers while others struggled and just left the business completely. Others like me just keep chugging along. I've gotten close a few times only to have the rug pulled out from underneath me.

The closest that I got was the thing that really helped to open my eyes about how dumb and meaningless it all was. I think I still have the contracts somewhere. The ones that told me how much I was going to make per week for the first three years we were on the air. It was really going to happen...and then it didn't.

It was my next to last year living out there, although I didn't know that at the time. I was invited to do the Chicago Comedy Festival. A lot of people I know were going in and some people I hadn't seen for a while were going to be there. One of the people I hadn't seen was my old friend Tony. He had a lot less hair than when I had last seen him and put on a few pounds, although he was heavy set for as long as I had known him. He had been writing for television, mostly cartoons and was in town to do the writers seminar. I knew him from Florida and it turns out he was now another of us living the dream in L.A. We exchanged numbers and decided to hook up when we got home.

At the time the internet and dot-coms were just starting to take off and we decided to try to get into that business. Just come up with some bullshit idea like everyone else was doing and then sell it for millions, if not billions and retire. It seemed simple enough.

What we decided to do was produce short shows and films that would play over the internet. I was a free lance writer for "National Lampoon Magazine" at the time and we were already online. Tony was a bit of a computer geek so it seemed like the natural way to go. The only problem was that to do this sort of thing you would need a lot of equipment and money that we didn't have. So our dream was put on hold.

That's when Bobby comes into the picture. Bobby is a soap opera actor. He is also a pretty boy type and a womanizer who likes being out on the town. Tony as I mentioned is heavy and a homebody that would rather spend his evenings watching television or writing. He's not the type to stay long at parties. In some way that I really don't understand Bobby and Tony had become best friends. Anyway, Tony called me with exciting news one day. "My friend Bobby is trying to start a web site called Buzz. He has the equipment we need and guys working for him that actually can do all of the editing. All we have to do is come up with some ideas for shows." The dream was alive again.

I have to admit that on a shoe string budget and not much to work with we came up with some pretty good shit. Tony took apart one of those annoying singing fish, re-wired it, put it against a brick wall and it became "Sal the stand-up Salmon." We had a guys doing bizarre and funny cartoons. My bit was a play on my name, "Knightline" where I would do a rant and usually something would happen to me during or at the end. This was before YouTube and I really believe that had it been around then we would have been huge.

The thing was that most of the guys involved were just hoping to make the big sale and get out. We had potential investors and buyers coming into the office everyday. I should probably describe the office, since it wasn't really an office at all. Actually it was a house just off of Wilshire that Bobby was renting but not living in at the time. In one of the rooms we painted the wall green to use as a green screen background where we would shoot and then could add in background using computers. Tony had the office upstairs in a converted bedroom since he was the Vice President. We all had titles. It didn't matter what your title was because nobody was making any money. After a couple of months Bobby either left the girl he was living with or she threw him out. He moved back in the house and had his bed next to Tony's desk. The computer room was the living room where a piece of plywood on top of a pool table made a space for all of the computers. It was kind of cozy in there with the fireplace going. In another room downstairs we set up the editing equipment. We had one cameraman and one editor. Tony and I would help out with whatever we could. Everyone pitched in. The young guys would skate board to work. It was a lot of fun. We just didn't have any money.

Tony came up with the term, "dog and pony show." That was when we would clean the place up and be on our best behavior for the presentation to these potential investors. Everyone loved us or at least they said that they did in front of us and had it been a year earlier we probably would have cashed in. Unfortunately we came around at the end of the dot-com boom and everyone was cautious. Timing is everything in this business.

One day when I came in I was introduced to Jeffrey, a British gentleman who had been around Hollywood for years. He was a producer for a couple of hit television shows in the sixties as well as films. He loved what we were doing and just wanted to get involved. He was going to hook us up with this friend of his, Bruno, a potential investor with deep pockets. At a meeting Bruno was shown what had already been done but also pitched ideas for full length shows that we had in development. Bruno was blown away and promised us a million dollars for the first year to keep us going until he was finished building our new state of the art studios in the Valley. Now we weren't just going to cash in on a buy out. We were going to become a legitimate production company. Everybody was very excited about this prospect. The future was looking bright. Just before Christmas we received a down payment, which was small, but it was enough to pay some guys, including myself that hadn't been paid in months.

The thing Bruno explained to us was the investment money was coming from these guys in Spain. Now from what Jeffrey told us, Bruno had money but people don't just go and invest their own money in things like this. During Christmas break Bruno was going to meet with these people in Spain and the check would be in the bank by the beginning of the year. When my wife and I went home for Christmas that year I was planning to come back and work full time with the company and not have to go out and do stand-up as much. I figured I would only go out for maybe a week a month to the clubs that I liked just to keep my chops up. I was about to be part of a successful production company after all.

We got back to L.A. a few days after the New Year and I gave Tony a call to hear the good news. What he had to tell me was not very good at all.

"Nobody can find Bruno. Jeffrey doesn't know where he is and we never got the money. Not only that but the guys say they're not going to work anymore without getting paid and do you want to hear the best part? Bobby hasn't paid the rent in three months. The landlord is going to throw us out. If you have anything in the office you want I suggest you come down and get it."

This was definitely not the news that I was expecting to hear.

The dream was over, Buzz was a bust and it was time to come up with the next idea. That's the thing about being one of the special people living in Los Angeles. When one thing falls through you move on to the next. Things don't pan out as an actor, well then I'll give writing a shot. They don't like my screenplay, I'll just write another. The production company isn't going to happen, well this time I didn't know what the fuck was next.

When I first moved to Los Angeles it was right after I had done a bunch of television and was known around the clubs in New York. I had some, what they call "Heat" on me. There were a lot of network people that said they had me in mind for different projects. None of these projects ever panned out and the heat went away. So now like an idiot, instead of just taking no for an answer, I spent the next nine years banging around trying to find some way to get the "Heat" back.

It looked like somehow I was finally going to do it. Even though it wasn't what I originally had in mind it was a way to make a living in the business and we were really enjoying what we were doing. The fact that we were some of the first people to present programming for the internet made us feel like pioneers.

This one really sucked the wind out of me. It was so close and it fell away in just a matter of a few weeks. I just didn't know what was next but it had to be something. Like I said, I didn't know at the time that this was going to be my last year in Los Angeles. I had put so much time and effort into this place that I felt like it owed me something and I wasn't leaving until I got it!

January in California is a hell of a lot better than it is back east but I couldn't help feeling the grayness and depression creeping over me. It was the sense of hopelessness, not knowing where to turn next that was really getting to me. I had a booking in Las Vegas and just decided to go in and make the best of it. I could still make people laugh and feel better about themselves even though I wasn't feeling very good about myself at the time.

Around the middle of the week in Vegas my cell phone rang and it was Tony on the other line.

"John, wait until I tell you what's going on. Do you remember when the guys from ICA came in last month?"

I really didn't know, like I said we had so many different people coming in and out all of the time that they just seem to blend together.

"Not really." I answered.

"Well, it doesn't matter. Do you know who ICA is?" He asked.

Again, I had no idea.

"No." I answered.

"They're a huge management and production company out here. They handle a lot of big stars and produce shows for television. Well it turns out the two young guys they sent over were so impressed with us that they brought their boss over yesterday and he loves us. He thinks we can sell this idea to one of the networks. We're going to have a big meeting with them next week and go over our presentation. It looks like Buzz isn't dead yet!"

Wow, this news was huge. When I woke up this morning I didn't know what was next and now this comes along. The fact that this thing just won't die is encouraging. It just feels like it's meant to be. This was not the path we had envisioned when we started, it's even bigger!

It was weird walking back into the old studios. We had all said our goodbyes to each other a few weeks earlier when we came in to clean out our shit and here we were back to life like some kind of monster that couldn't be killed. The meeting was on a Wednesday evening around six o'clock. We had to come in early to get the place in shape and make it look like we were still in business.

Just after six the three guys from ICA came in, two young guys and the boss, Andrew. The meeting consisted of Andrew telling us his vision for the pitch meeting. Normally when you do a pitch meeting with a network it's just a couple of people walking into an office and telling their idea to some idiot behind a desk. We already had product to show these people. Andrew came up with the idea that we would turn the office into a big club house with a party going on and bring the executives to us. We then would present them with the short shows that we were doing including Knightline. His vision was that we would be a new "Laugh In" We were all in agreement that it was a great idea. On my way home over the hill to the Valley that night I was in the clouds. I had seen the "Hollywood" sign everyday on my way home from here but tonight I could feel like I was really going to be a part of it.

You have to realize that when you get really good news it's usually followed by a long hard punch in the gut, just to bring you back down to earth. Tony called with the bad news the next day. "The presentation is going to be the first week in February which is a big problem since the landlord is threatening to throw us out at the end of the month."

Oh well, back to reality.

Now we were facing the possibility that when the network people showed up for the pitch meeting they would be greeted by a padlocked door. Chances are they wouldn't want to get involved with such irresponsible people.

"Has anyone found Bruno yet?" was one of the recurring jokes as we sweated things.

That one and one that "Sal, the stand up Salmon" did on one of our little films. It was the old joke where the guy walks into a bar and orders five drinks and then downs them really fast. The bartender asks, "Why are you drinking so fast?"

The guy replies, "You'd drink really fast too if you had what I had."
The bartender then asks, "What have you got?"

The guy answers, "No money!"

We got a lot of mileage out of that one,

"If you had what we have."

That's all we had to say to each other and then the nervous laughter.

The thing about Bobby is that he's not just a pretty boy actor but a real charmer. He was able to somehow convince the landlord that if he would just give him a few extra weeks he would not only get his back rent but a nice bonus on top of it. None of this was true of course, but the guy bit.

Two days before the big pitch we were going to have a rehearsal. I showed up at the Buzz studios and it was filled with a hundred people I had never seen before. These were the people that were going to be at the party and hopefully for most of them, they too would be discovered and get to be part of the show. The fact that we had put in all of the work and that none of them had anything to do with what we were presenting didn't matter to them. The leeches come out in droves when you can help them.

On the day of the presentation I woke up early and packed because I was flying out of Burbank airport into Florida for a gig the next day. I knew it would probably be a long day and I wouldn't feel like packing when I got home. When I arrived around noon there were already people everywhere. Most of them I didn't know since they really had nothing to do with us and I had only seen them at the rehearsal. The house-office had been transformed into a big party with balloons and dancing girls in bikini's and a naked tool man wearing nothing but a tool belt. We had monitors set up around the computer room, each one loaded with a different one of our little shows. The most important thing was the surf board-bar that was set up when you entered. We were going to be plying the visiting executives with alcohol, which we figured could only help our cause.

Starting at around three in the afternoon the various networks began showing up and were given the same tour. They would be greeted at the door where they would be served a glowing appletini and then brought into the party. At the party Bobby and Tony became the tour guides. They led the executives around from monitor to monitor as well as some live presentations including our white trash soap opera, "The Edge of Nowhere." We hadn't shot that yet but hoped to include it as a part of our show. At the end of each presentation the executives would be whisked off to a waiting ambulance where they would be joined by Bobby, Tony and Andrew to talk business. If nothing else we were giving these bastards a performance like they had never experienced in a pitch meeting before.

The first to arrive would be the people from a huge corporation that owns a host of networks. They were scheduled to show up at three in the afternoon. At about ten minutes to three a friend of Bobby's, who happened to be a famous in Hollywood for reasons other than show business wandered in. I don't know how they became friends, I can only speculate. This person had never been in the office before and really had nothing to do with us, but I figured Bobby was just trying to give the networks a little taste of celebrity, no matter who it might be. This person may have stayed all of twenty minutes but happened to be in the room when the idiots from this corporation took the tour. This is important to the rest of the story.

We would end up doing our run through for various networks and production companies until about eight o'clock that evening. I think it was six or seven times all together that we put on our little "Dog and Pony show." The most important one we ever did. When the first corporation arrived we were still working out the kinks and once or twice the monitors didn't work and had to be re-booted. During one of these lulls, Bobby took it upon himself to introduce these people to the infamous celebrity and mentioned they would be part of our show. This person looked as shocked as the rest of us to hear about this, since it was something that had never been discussed. It was no big deal, he was just killing time waiting for a computer to come back up and since they weren't seeing a sample you would think they would just forget about it. At least that's what a rational person would think.

I was very proud of the particular Knightline we were showing them. In this one I appear to be seated at a desk ranting about the lowbrow toilet humor that Hollywood was presenting as comedy. At the end of the two minute rant when I described various scenes where shit and fart and cheap laughs were used in movies I make the following statement.

"Hollywood, if this scatological humor is the best that you can come up with you should be fucking (Bleeped) ashamed of yourself!"

Then the camera panned out to reveal that I was sitting on the toilet with my pants around my ankles. It was a great use of irony and also an important part of the rest of the story.

The infamous person left before the corporate people had even finished the tour. When the infamous person left I figured it would be the last we would ever see of them. At least that's what I thought at the time.

At the end of each walk through I would hear the executives saying to each other that this was the most fun presentation for a series that any of them had ever experienced. If nothing else they would at least remember us. Something had to come from this, we were so close to dead so many times and we just kept coming back. It just seemed like it was meant to be.

It was a long day. I don't think that I got home until about eleven that night.

"So how did it go?" my wife asked as I entered our apartment.

"I think it went really good. I have a good feeling about this." I said and at the time I really did.

My flight was at eleven the next morning and even though I knew it was still early, I figured I would give it a shot and call Tony before I got on the plane to see if anyone had shown interest yet. To my surprise he informed me,

"That big corporation, the first ones in, called early this morning. They want to meet with us later in the week to make an offer. Nobody else yet but it's early. Hopefully this will turn into a bidding war!"

It was certainly exiting news and I felt like I wouldn't need an airplane to get to Florida. I could pretty much just ride the cloud I was on.

As the week in Florida went on I kept in touch with Tony to find out what was happening. It turns out not too much, nobody else was calling. Calls were finally made to the other networks and producers. They all gave the same answer,

"We really enjoy what you are doing but it's just not something that we are looking for at this time."

That's Hollywood's polite way of telling you to go fuck yourself. The people in that town never just say no. It's always that they are not looking for this or it just doesn't fit in with what they are doing. These idiots are too afraid to just say "no" or "you suck!" That way if you go on and do great things, then they weren't wrong about you, it's just that you weren't right for them at the time. It's a load of bullshit but its how people that are filled with insecurity and fear operate.

There was going to be no bidding war and we weren't going to have a choice of whoever was going to give us the best opportunity or the most creative leeway. Our deal was going to be with the first ones that called and we could be happy we had that. Buzz was back from the dead yet again. I was about to find out that there was going to be no creative freedom at all. The nightmare was about to begin.

This particular corporation had just taken over what was at the time, a country network which they were going to turn into a hip new network. They thought that we would fit in well with that kind of programming and were trying to decide whether they wanted us for just one night a week or maybe as a strip show (One that airs five nights a week). What they wanted from us first was to shoot a ten minute pilot presentation that would give a feel of how the show would look. They also said they were interested in shooting a pilot for "The Edge of Nowhere". A month ago it looked like everything was over and now I was going to be involved with at least one and maybe two shows. That's how fast it can happen...or not. Oh and there was one condition, the infamous celebrity had to be part of it or there was no deal.

That just goes to show you how stupid and name driven these executives are. They had never seen this person do anything. This person was just sitting on a sofa and did no more than nod at the executives, yet they wanted this person. They didn't know if this person could act or even speak, which it turns out this person could not. That didn't matter. They were going to have a show with this famous person as one of the stars!

It didn't matter to us at the time what the conditions were. We had a shot at getting on the air! There are millions of people in Hollywood that would jump at a chance like this so you have to take what you get. When I first came to town my goal was to keep my integrity in tack and not lower myself to do some bullshit show just to get on television. After all these years of nothing happening

I was willing to make some compromises. Besides the other things we had were pretty good and who knows, maybe this person will surprise us all and really add to the show. At this time I was totally unaware of how much I was going to have to compromise or how bad things were going to get.

One time after a show in Chicago, I went out with the opening act and his brother for drinks. His brother was in town from Los Angeles where he was trying to make it as a playwright. The brother's girlfriend was with him, she currently was teaching at the University of Wisconsin, but just a year earlier she had been an executive with a major studio. During the course of the evening she told me of her experience there and that part of her job was to give notes to writers. She also was stable enough to admit to me that she had no idea what she was doing but the higher ups insisted that she give notes and suggestions to the creative people. This woman was the only one I've ever met that admitted that it probably wasn't a good idea.

It was decided that my temper was too volatile to allow me to go into meetings with the executives that we were now working for.

"You could blow the deal for us." Tony told me.

Looking back he was probably right, but I think I would have felt better about myself in the end. As it was I had to get the notes second hand and just accept whatever it was they wanted.

We had two great animators working with us that were doing very edgy cartoons. These executives decided instead of that we would use a hack they had a deal with. They sent us over what were supposed to be his best work to look at. What they turned out to be were cartoons of jokes that were so old that the original versions were found by archaeologists in ancient cave etchings.

The idea for the Knightline that we would do for the pilot had me smoking a big cigar and complaining about the anti-smoking laws and how it was impossible to find a place to smoke these days. At the end it would be revealed that I had been on a crowded elevator and we would use smoke machines to really enhance the effect as the choking passengers followed me from the elevator. Now of course I was not allowed to attend the meetings but from what I was told, the way it went down was like this, after pitching the elevator idea, one of the female executives sternly said,

"We can't do smoking; Another comedian does a bit about smoking! He did it on a comedy special"

So in effect, even though what we were doing was completely different than what this comedian had done, in the eyes of these idiots he had cornered the market on smoking material. This was not the worst part of it. After that statement, the head executive, who could have been the dumbest man in Hollywood, stood up and laid down the boom,

"No, no, no…he's the guy on the toilet!"

That's actually what he said which meant that he just didn't get it at all. The fact that what I had done in the rant he saw was a parody of toilet humor didn't register. All he saw was the guy on the toilet, to him that would always be the punch line even if it made no fucking sense!

Finally I was going to get my big break in Hollywood. I was going to be the guy on the toilet! After all the years of sticking to my guns to be pure and not sell out this was going to be my claim to fame. Wherever I would go people would point and yell,

"Hey look, it's the guy on the toilet!"

Clubs and theatres would be able to bill me as, "Coming next week, The Guy on the Toilet." Be careful what you wish for in this business I guess is the lesson here. I can't tell you how pissed I was about the news or the fact that nobody had stood up and explained what a stupid idea this was at the meeting. The thing is when money and fame are on the line it changes everything as I was going to find out.

My initial reaction was to just quit the project and believe me I did quit many times only to be talked into coming back.

"You'll let everyone down."

They would say to me and reluctantly I would return and so would the headaches.

That was the thing, the more ridiculous the notes became, and the show would become a bigger piece of shit, the more the back of my head would throb. I had never had migraines before and at first I thought I might have a tumor or something. It took my wife to explain to me that it was stress, the stress of having to whore myself out to make this thing work was giving me the headaches.

Tony was the one that would take the daily calls from the executives and he did at times try to explain how ridiculous their notes were but to no avail. The corporate people decided that instead of the new Laugh-In, we would be a parody of a reality show.

"They're doing these things and they aren't aware they are on camera."

Was the idea that they came up with even though anybody that's ever been on a reality show is totally aware of the fact that they're on camera. It didn't matter, the idiots had a vision. They just didn't realize their vision was a big pile of garbage. They didn't want me to be looking at the camera when I did my piece. At one point Tony, in defense of me, explained,

"John does a rant. If he's just walking around talking to himself he's going to look like some kind of lunatic."

The executives came back with, "You'll figure it out."

Everyone that had become involved with Buzz from Jeffrey, who brought in the guys from ICA to the guys at ICA themselves, had told me I was the main reason they had gotten involved. They loved my Knightline episodes and thought that it stood out among everything else we were presenting. It was just that now I was more or less an after thought. Oh, I was still part of the project but nobody gave a fuck that what they were having me do was trash.

It was an amazing thing to watch as people began to argue over what their positions would be on the show. Who was going to be executive producer, the highest paid and so on. Tony, Bobby, Andrew and now Bobby's manager was involved. He had never had anything to do with us at all but now that we had a deal he decided he wanted to be part of it. Remember the leeches. Anyway, these four fought amongst themselves on a daily basis over who was most important. The thing is we didn't even have anything shot yet and what we were about to shoot was a load of shit that I knew was never going to make it on the air. How did these guys not see it? Money and fame, remember, they can really blind you. The real kicker was the day that Tony told me,

"If we do get picked up there's a good chance that the executives will want to go with a younger John Knight type to do Knightline."

Can you imagine being replaced on your own creation with a younger version of yourself? Tony told me I would just have to accept it and maybe there would be a writer's job for me. Oh good, I could write the words for the guy that was doing me. C'mon, you can't treat me this way. I'm the guy on the toilet after all!

The project was a disaster, the infamous celebrity was a nightmare, and could barely speak. If a word had more than two syllables it was almost impossible for this person to spit it out. Not only that but this person took twenty percent of the total budget given to us for everything, including camera equipment, shooting locations and editing. It was an experience I would never wish on anybody and of course in the end the executives looked at what we handed in, exactly what they asked for and decided that it was awful.

Now I don't know if those executives are still in show business. It would be nice to think that they were fired long ago and are now doing what they are actually qualified to do like pump gas or bag groceries. Could you imagine these morons bagging groceries for you? Of course the eggs would be on the bottom beneath the canned goods and when you would say,

"You broke my eggs! What am I supposed to do with broken eggs?"

They would just smugly reply, "You'll figure it out."

Hopefully all copies of what we shot were destroyed, I would hate for any of it to ever see the light of day. After the executives passed on our project, there was an attempt to shop it around to other networks and of course they all turned it down. Why would anybody want this piece of trash that even the people that envisioned it didn't like? I think it was right before my birthday; the first week in August that we found out we were out of options. Buzz was now defunct, the thing that wouldn't die finally died a long and painful death. Bobby was already in New York where he got a part on a soap opera. Tony went back to writing cartoons, the guys at ICA, well they still had their jobs despite the fact they had been involved with us. The thing is I didn't know what my next move would be. I still didn't know that it was my last year in Los Angeles so I was looking for the next way in. The whole experience had really soured my opinion of the town and deep down I had really had enough but I wouldn't admit it to myself just yet.

I was working in Las Vegas that first week in August and my wife and some friends came in to celebrate my birthday with me. We had a great time. My wife came on stage and surprised me with a cake at the end of the show and then the two of us and a group of our friends went out on the town. It was the first week of August 2001, I was a year older and had no idea what I was going to do next but it didn't matter that night.

Labor Day weekend my wife and I drove up the coast to San Simeon where Hearst Castle is located. The first time we went it was just to visit the Castle but we were impressed by the rugged coastline and the weather and the hotel where we stayed. After that we tried to get up there for a weekend every summer to get away from all of the congestion and aggravation in Los Angeles. We would get a room overlooking the Ocean and just enjoy the quiet for a couple of days. This time it was hard to relax because back in Pittsburgh my father was in the hospital. He had been having health problems for a few years but they were starting to become more severe now. It was apparent that his best days were behind him and his days ahead were numbered. It was weighing heavy on my mind.

We had been back at our apartment in L.A. for a week now. My father was home from the hospital back in Pittsburgh, but things weren't looking good. My wife wasn't even up for work yet so it couldn't have even been six AM when the phone rang. My wife answered, she didn't seem overly concerned about what she was hearing,

"Oh, really…you're kidding…OK, thanks for calling."

She hung up the phone and rolled over to get her last few minutes of sleep before the alarm went off. I had to know.

"Who was that?" I asked.

"Oh it was Bruce."

Bruce was our close friend from Pittsburgh who was now also living in Los Angeles and had come to Vegas for my birthday.

"He said a plane flew into the World Trade Center and that it's on fire." She told me.

We both envisioned some small plane had gone off course and mistakenly crashed into the building. No big deal.

Chrissie got up for work a few minutes later when the alarm went off and switched on the television.

"You have to see this." She said as she entered the room and woke me up.

What I watched that morning and the rest of the day is something that none of us who witnessed it ever imagined we would experience. It is something that we will never forget. It was a life changing experience.

I was supposed to fly back to Pittsburgh that Thursday for two weeks of shows in and around town. I was looking forward to seeing my father and being home but at this moment I couldn't imagine myself ever getting on another airplane.

The first weekend's shows were canceled as the whole country was still in shock. The airports finally started to reopen and the airlines were very flexible on rescheduling flights. I knew that it was something I would have to do eventually and decided to fly out on the red eye from Los Angeles to Pittsburgh on Sunday night. My next show wasn't until Wednesday so I gave myself time in case there were any problems. Not only that but for whatever reason I just felt like the over night flight would be safe.

On the Saturday night before I was to leave we were invited to a birthday party at some friend's house. These friends were doing well financially and were going to put on a big bash. It was the husband making the money but the wife liked to show it off. Even though most of the country was in mourning she was still going to have her event, live band and all. I tried to talk to people at the party about the tragedy the country had experienced just a few days earlier. Nobody at the party wanted to discuss any thing except themselves, just like normal in Los Angeles. "If we're not going to talk about me I don't have anything to say." The special people, remember, it was the last straw.

I finally made it back and I was sitting on my parents back porch smoking a cigar. My dad was doing OK and I was glad to be there. I was just sitting there with a calm breeze blowing and I remembered something my wife had said to me when I was working on our disaster of a show.

"If this doesn't go I don't have five more years to give to this town."

She meant that she couldn't see wasting five more years in Los Angeles while I was trying to figure out my next move and making myself more miserable. Sitting there with my cigar and the serene evening I thought to myself, "Why am I not living like this?" That's when I made the decision that it was my last year in Los Angeles. I called my wife and asked,

"Would you like to move home?"

"Can we?" was her response.

It was the second week in September then and we were out of there by the first week in December. As we drove out of the city limits I rolled down the window, stuck my hand out and gave the town the finger. Twelve years of life behind us, we were on our way to the next adventure.

TEN

Here's the plan. I got home from Baltimore last night. It's still January, which is probably the worst month of the year. I know that it's cold and gray around here in December but at least you have the holidays to look forward to. February is the same and sometimes worse than January but at least there is the hope that spring is not far away. January on the other hand has no redeeming quality at all. There's no need for it really and it would be nice if it somehow could be eliminated all together. Unfortunately that is impossible so you have to find something to get you through. That's where the football play-offs come in. The first round started yesterday and I didn't get to see much because the games started late and I had my shows to do. Today there are two games, the first at one PM and the second whenever that one ends. So the intent is to go to the grocery store and pick up enough junk food to sustain my wife and me through both games. I guess I could have sent her out to do this but for whatever reason going to the grocery store has become my job.

One of the items on my list is cheese from the deli counter. I grab a number and look to see that it is twenty-nine. As I look up I see they are now serving number six. Are you kidding me, six? How can they only be on six? That means there are still twenty three people in front of me! There are only two people working behind the counter, an older woman and a fat guy with a gimp leg. At least he's walking like there's something wrong with him. It could just be a sympathy ploy. Get us all to feel sorry for him and just walk away. That way he can go sit on his fat ass and wait for his shift to end. I look around and can see there's not much sympathy going on here. These people look like they're hungry and willing to wait this out. This of course is not good for me.

All I wanted to get was some cheese. I guess we could do without it. Cheese clogs the arteries and is bad for you anyway. Plus if I just walk away I will avoid the stress that will surely overcome me if I stand here waiting it out. Health wise this is a good move all around. This could be a new approach for me. Instead of trying one of Dr. Jonas' stupid mantras or picturing myself at the beach, neither of which work, I can just avoid any situation that will aggravate me altogether. If I keep this up I'm going to add years if not decades on to the end of my life.

Of course the thing about adding years on to the end of your life is that they do come in fact at the end of your life. You know when you're getting really old and feeble and your mind starts to go and your skin is wrinkled and loose and some of us will end up wearing diapers like a baby because we can no longer control our bladders and bowels. So here I am a wrinkled up, senile, diaper wearing troll, all because I took care of myself. It just doesn't seem worth it. I mean what do you really get out of it, wisdom? All of life's experience will be yours. You will know what truly matters and the mistakes that should have been avoided in your youth. At this point you will have the perception of all of your years on earth and you still won't be able to help shitting in your pants.

"Number seven, who has number seven?"

The old woman behind the counter is up to the next person and she changes the six to a seven on the sign.

A well-dressed redhead standing near the counter holds up her number and announces, "I have number seven."

The woman behind the counter asks, "What can I get for you?"

The red head reaches into her purse and pulls out what looks to be a lengthy list.

"Let's start with…"

That's all that I could hear. The rest of what she said went totally blank inside my brain. "Let's start with…" That means that it was going to be a long and painstaking order. I look again at my number, twenty-nine. A moment ago I was thinking about my golden years. At the time I wasn't planning to reach them as I stood in this line. I crumble up my number and toss it away. Guess what number thirty, you just moved up a slot.

I'll just grab the other items I came for and get the hell out of here. If I chop a few more things from my own list I could probably be at or under the limit for the express lane. The problem with this is the fact that most people don't necessarily pay attention to the rules of the express lane. It you've ever been behind somebody with twenty-three items in the eight items or fewer lane, you know of what I speak. Maybe it's just that they're so bad at math they think twenty-three comes before eight. Or maybe it's just that these people are so fucking special the regulations that apply to the rest of us don't pertain to them!

I remember an incident in Los Angeles when my wife and I were picking up a few items at K-Mart. We headed for the express line. The sign clearly stated four items or less, cash only. If you don't understand that, it means that if you have between one and four items and are going to be paying with cash, then you can be in this line. Well, in this case there were three women in front of us including the one that was currently checking out. She was the problem. She had nine items (I counted) and not only that, but also had the nerve to be writing out a check!

I kept my cool and very politely stated, "Isn't it a shame how many people reach adulthood and are still illiterate."

I thought that I was showing concern, I mean here was this poor woman that looked to be in her mid-thirties and yet she was unable to read a sign!

The woman checking out didn't apologize or even acknowledge what I had just said. No, she just went on with what she was doing, either she was too embarrassed or knowing the people in L.A., she really didn't give a shit what I thought because she was going to do whatever the fuck she wanted anyway! It was the woman waiting in line in front of me that really bothered me. She turned around and gave me this dirty look, like I was the rude person here. You should be applauding me and here you are looking at me like I'm the jackass! Somebody has the balls to point out that there is actually supposed to be a system in place here, so people that follow the rules don't have to wait through all of the bullshit and you're giving me a dirty look! Maybe you were planning on writing out a check and having to show two forms of ID and have the rest of us waiting here like morons while we wait for the check to be cleared and now I've ruined it for you! Good, if that is indeed the case then I've done my good deed for the day. I can only hope the woman with nine items has fleas in the socks she just purchased. Then they breed and infest her home and it has to be fumigated and even that doesn't help. In the end her skin will be constantly itching until it drives her insane and she spends the rest of her life in the asylum. Then it would all be worth it.

If I think about it there is really no reason to be in such a hurry to get home in time for the start of the first game. I really don't care about any teams playing today. It's just that I have set a goal to be out of here and in front of the television at a certain time and when I set a goal for myself like this, well I usually wind up extremely annoyed. I should have put at least small wagers on the games just to make them more interesting but none of them really jumped out at me like they were sure winners although that never seems to help me. I think out of every sure thing that I bet in my life I hit on half, maybe less. Of course if I could pick all of the winners we would be living in a big house in Las Vegas, probably next to Wayne Newton. Every Sunday I would go down and place my bets and come home in the evening with hundreds of thousands of dollars and invite the neighbors over for a big celebration barbeque that I would light with a hundred dollar bill! Maybe it's best that I'm not able to pick all of the winners, I don't know if I could take hanging out with Wayne Newton.

With everything I need in tow I head for the check-out lines which are jam packed with people. Most of them have carts overflowing with what looks to be enough groceries for the rest of the month. What happened to the sagging economy? Of course most of these people are probably just going to put their charges on a credit card they are never going to repay thus making the economy tank even further. It's an endless, vicious cycle that was brought on by greed. Nobody in this country is satisfied with what they have, everyone always wants more and they think they deserve it. Me, right now I would be satisfied if I could be checked out and on my way home within the next ten minutes. I know it's probably just a pipe dream but I'm clinging to it all the same.

I'm going to need some kind of strategy if I hope to make my dream come true. I decide that my best bet will be at the self check out. If you've ever done the self check out you know that it can be really hit or miss. Sometimes the machine can be a little squirrelly and more times than not I end up standing around like an idiot waiting for an employee (usually some high school kid) to come to my aid. Although most of the time it's the best bet because people are either too stupid or too lazy to use the self check out. I wonder who the first CEO was that realized by eliminating a few cashiers he could put an extra couple of bucks in his pocket at the end of the week.

"Let the assholes check themselves out!" He probably exclaimed as he told of his new idea.

This is only the beginning of self reliance. The more jobs that can be eliminated the more money goes into the hands of the select few. Isn't that the way it works now? Believe me if these guys can figure out a way to get us to grow our own fruits and vegetables and raise our own cattle, pigs and chickens, slaughter and butcher them and then hand over what we produced on our own so they can turn around and sell it back to us they're going to do it.

Then there is the fact that these stores have cards that have to scan to get the discounts on the overly inflated items. Of course this is just a method of tracking your buying habits. It's a way of spying on you. You may want to spend the extra twenty cents on the rat poison that you planned to bake in a cake for the neighbor that pissed you off. The latest scam is an APP for your phone that let's them follow you around the store and offer coupons for items depending on what aisle you are in. No thank you! I don't need Big Brother knowing that I'm buying toilet paper.

Self check out is definitely the way to go here if I'm going to have any chance of getting out of here without wanting to kill somebody. There are three possible choices for self check out available and I will analyze each before making my decision. The first one has an older woman that has a shoe box filled with coupons and is looking through them all to see if she has a coupon for each item before she scans it. I notice that if she can't find a coupon she just sets the item aside. Of course the intelligent and polite thing to do would have been to make this determination before she got this far. Of course that would have also made it easier for anyone waiting behind her, like me. Obviously she doesn't give a shit about anyone except herself and the rest of us can go to hell.

The next line has a woman with a small child that keeps running away and then the woman has to stop with her check out and chase the child. She scans an item, chases the child and brings him back, scans another item the kid runs off. This is not a game that I want to watch. I'm trying to get home and plop my ass in front of the television.

I settle on the third line which has a man with only about fifteen items in his shopping cart including chips and snacks. He probably wants to get home for the game too. This looks like the place to be. The first item that the man takes from the cart is a bag of grapes. He runs them over the scanner and nothing happens. He tries again, nothing. He picks up the bag and tries to adjust the bag around the bar code and gives it another shot, nothing. Now he turns the bag around so that the bar code is facing up, no chance in hell that this will work and of course it doesn't. He turns the bag back around and runs it over the scanner again, nothing, again, nothing. This goes on for another ten or twelve tries and I actually back away for the fear that he may start a friction fire. I glance at the other lines, coupon woman is carefully going through her files and I notice that she has now more discarded items than items she is going to purchase. Lady with child has only scanned about a quarter of her items and is now trying desperately to remove her kid from the candy rack. I'll stay put behind Mr. Grapes.

It looks like he's finally given up on the grapes, he puts them back into the cart and grabs for the chips. Bingo, we have a winner!

The pretzels scan easily and the dip goes through with no problem, now as long as the machine doesn't freeze up I should be up to the plate shortly. All of the items are through and son of a bitch, he's reaching for the grapes again! He's not going to try again is he? I can't believe it, what did he think that maybe they just needed a little rest in the cart and then they'd scan? What an idiot! He's going at it another ten or twelve swipes. Here's a man that refuses to take no for an answer. Wait, what's he doing now? It looks like he's finally given up. It's starting to sink in that this item isn't going to scan. Just give up on it. Grapes don't fit in with the other crap that you are purchasing. If you mix grapes in with all the chips and dips it's going to throw your whole system out of whack. Wait, he's not done yet. Now he's gone to the produce screen to search for grapes. That's not it. Not that one either. Why don't you just get somebody that works here to help you? Why's he looking under lettuce? Now it's bananas. Does this guy even have a clue? It could be that he doesn't speak English and is unfamiliar with our alphabet. Maybe I should try to help.

"Excuse me sir, why don't you look under R?" I suggest.

"Why under R?" He asks. Well he does speak English after all which means he's just an idiot.

"Because they're probably going to be fucking raisins by the time we get out of this stupid store!" I reply.

One of the store employees was helping him when I left. Coupon lady looked like she was settled in for the evening and could care less if anybody else wanted to use that line. It was the woman with the kid that finally wised up and put him in the cart while she finished scanning the rest of her items. It's good to see the occasional person that realizes it's not all about them and that there might be others behind them. Of course, she may have just wanted to get her child away from the angry man in the store yelling at the grape guy. Either way it worked out to my advantage. I'm leaving here with my sanity intact just a little bit older than I was when I walked in.

ELEVEN

On my way into my session with Dr. Jonas I only have one thing on my mind today. I have a bit of a dilemma. What it is, I have a date coming up in Laughlin, Nevada and I'm going to have to be able to fly to get there. You really can't fly directly into Laughlin so what I have to do is fly into Las Vegas and take a rental car down to Laughlin. I know it's like returning to the scene of the crime. Actually it is returning to the scene of the crime since I was arrested the last time I flew there. My problem is that I don't know if Dr. Jonas is willing to give me clearance to fly now since I've only been here a few times. From his attitude I get the impression that he doesn't feel I'm making much progress.

When I enter the office Dr. Jonas is in the reception area talking with Lisa the receptionist.

He turns as I walk in, "Hello John. Good to see you. My ten o'clock canceled so we can go in now. As a matter of fact if you'd like to move to ten they'll be open from now on. My usual ten o'clock won't um…"

There's a hesitation in his voice, like he's trying to hide something.

"She left town, yeah. So she won't be coming here anymore. That means if like you can move to ten."

"I'm good coming in at eleven." I answer.

So the ten o'clock on Thursday time slot has opened up. That's when the frazzled woman was coming in. He's telling me that she left town, but there's no way to find out if he's telling me the truth. It could mean that she decided to really leave town, check out for good if you know what I mean. She looked like the type anyway or maybe it's just that she's given up on this guy ever helping her. That would mean he's probably not going to be able to help me either. She left the office crying every week and he still couldn't do anything for her. I've never left his office in tears. I've left to find parking tickets. I've left with the flu but never in tears. Now I'm curious to find out why she left.

I hang my coat and follow Jonas into his office. He points me to the comfortable chair and takes the seat across from me. This is all becoming too familiar but not in a good way. It seems like the same thing is happening over and over and there is no end in sight. Another gray Thursday, another eleven O'clock with Dr. Jonas and on and on it goes.

"So how was your week?" He asks.

"This is the best part of it so far if that answers your question." I reply.

"No, it really doesn't answer my question. All that your sarcastic attitude does is give me the impression that you are still looking at everything in a negative way." He says.

"It just wasn't the best week." I say.

"When things look bad you have to tell yourself they will get better eventually." He says.

"And what if they don't?" I ask.

"There you go being pessimistic again. Let me ask you something. Have you been in situations when things seemed really bad and that they would never get better?" Jonas asks.

"What do you think?" I respond.

"There you go with the sarcastic tone again. Just answer the question. Have you been in situations when you felt like things would never get better?" He asks again.

"Yes, of course." I reply.

"And they did in fact get better, didn't they?" He asks.

"I'll let you know." I respond.

He gives me a long hard stare and writes something down.

"Now when you left our last session you were on your way to Baltimore. How was the trip? Did you have any problems getting there?" He asks.

"I hit some traffic." I answer.

"And how did you handle it? Did you try any of the techniques that we discussed?" He asks.

"I was imagining that I was at the beach. That worked for a while." I answer.

"Only for a while, what was the reason for that?"

"I hit into the car in front of me. It kind of ruined my day at the beach!" I respond.

"Was there any damage?" He asks.

"There should have been damage to the guy's face. Stupid piece of shit! There wasn't one mark on his precious Mercedes and he was going to take it to the mechanic! I was only going about one mile an hour when I hit him and he's going to take it to his mechanic, stupid piece of shit!"

Dr. Jonas is looking at me in a way that makes me realize that I probably shouldn't show him this side of me. Not if I hope that he will ever give me my release which I need real soon.

"A Mercedes is an expensive car. The man, it was a man wasn't it?" He asks.

"Yes, it was a man." I answer.

"I wasn't quite sure since you kept referring to him as, stupid piece of shit, was it?"

"Yes," I answer.

"That's quite a moniker to put on somebody, don't you think?" He asks.

"He deserved it." I answer.

"I'm just saying, a Mercedes is quite an expensive car. Maybe he worked and saved his whole life just to get this car and then you come along and hit it. Now how would you feel if that was you in that situation?" He asks.

"Like I really wasted my whole life saving up to get a stupid car," I answer.

"You're missing the point here. See, you hit into him, he had the right to check out his car and make sure you hadn't caused any damage. Do you understand what I'm saying here?" He asks.

"He didn't have to take it in to his mechanic, he was just being ridiculous. There wasn't the slightest mark on his precious car." I answer.

"Now if you had been the one that had been hit wouldn't you have checked out your car to make sure there was no damage?"

"Yes, but I wouldn't have been an arrogant jerk about it." I answer.

"Jerk, piece of shit, asshole, you certainly have a way of labeling people." He says.

"Hey, I never called him an asshole!" I respond.

"Are you sure?" He asks.

I think about it for a moment.

"Yes, I'm pretty sure." I say.

"I'm guessing that his car was fine and you never heard anything more about it." Dr. Jonas states.

"That's where you would be wrong." I say.

"Really, he did find some damage?" Jonas asks.

"As a matter of fact the fat son of ... (I catch myself) the guy that I hit, is trying to get a medical claim." I say.

"How fast did you say you were going?" he asks.

"About one." I reply.

"You're telling me the truth?" He asks.

"Yes, we were in gridlock traffic. There's no way that he could have been injured." I say.

"So, what do you think is going on here?" Jonas asks.

"Oh, I don't know. Maybe somebody is trying to get one over on the insurance company." I say.

"That's fraud!" Jonas says.

He's so innocent this guy, it's like he's never heard of anybody trying to get one over on an insurance company.

"Yes, I believe that is what they call it." I say and I become aware that he can once again sense the sarcasm in my voice.

"Now let's try to get a read on what is happening here. Let's discuss the gentleman that you hit. You don't mind me calling him a gentleman do you?" He asks.

"You can call him whatever you want, you didn't have to deal with the jerk!" I say.

"There you go again, jerk, stupid, asshole…"

I interrupt him. "I never said asshole!"

"Wouldn't you agree that it was implied?" He asks.

I think about it for a moment.

"Yeah, I guess." I say.

"Couldn't we say the fact that the man was driving an expensive car probably means he has a good job and that would mean he probably isn't an unintelligent person?" He asks.

"Maybe he gets all of his money by milking the insurance industry with bullshit lawsuits. And even if he does have a job that pays him an astronomical amount of money that doesn't mean he's smart. There are a lot of people out there being paid a great deal of money to do jobs that they have no clue of what to do. You know that I'm right here!" I demand.

"I'll agree with you that you may be able to get away with it for awhile but eventually you'll be found out. What I'm trying to say is that it's usually impossible to keep your job if you're totally incompetent." He says.

"What about George W. Bush?" I ask.

The way that he's looking at me right now I'm not sure if I just stumped him or that maybe he's one of the people that voted for Bush twice. Either way he has no response.

I don't know what he's thinking right now although he has to realize that it was really a half assed statement. Just because a person drives an expensive car and has a high paying job doesn't mean they deserve it. Maybe there was a time when that was true although I'm sure nepotism and fear have always played a role in deciding what person gets the job. Ineptitude has been the driving force in this country for as long as I can remember. Why try harder when you are rewarded for failure. It's just that when you fail you have to fail big time. You need a failure of such great magnitude that the federal Government will bail you out with the taxpayers' money. Then you can throw lavish parties and take expensive trips. Everybody will get their huge year end bonuses even though the corporation is in the tank because the people getting bonuses screwed up in the first place. This of course will all be done at the expense of the American people. It would be nice if this was just one of my psychotic delusions but this one really fucking happened!

"I want you to close your eyes and picture the man that you hit. Do you think that you can do that?" Jonas asks.

Man he's really going to town on this guy and I'm beginning to wonder if he might be a relative or something. I decide to humor him and I close my eyes.

"Can you remember what the man looked like?" He asks.

"Of course I can. It happened just the other day." I reply.

"That's good, now I want you to do your best to describe him to me."

I begin to think about the guy. He was a real ugly sucker I remember that.

"His hair, what's left of it is going every which way. It's that nasty matted kind of hair and I think he's growing it too long to compensate for the fact that there isn't a whole lot left." I say.

Jonas voice seems to be agitated when he says, "Look at him closely. Isn't there something positive that you can find?"

I think about it, "It's a nice shirt that he is wearing." I say.

"There that's something, so you like the shirt that he's wearing." Jonas says.

"Yeah, except for the nasty pit stains under his arms. This guy really sweats, probably because he's so fat…"

Jonas interrupts me and I open my eyes. "There you go again, he's bald and he's fat and there's nothing positive at all?"

"Not that I can see." I respond.

"You realize that male pattern baldness is hereditary and there's nothing you can do about it?" He asks and I can tell that his feelings are hurt probably due to the fact that he's sporting a nice cue ball look himself.

"Yes I realize that and I shouldn't have insulted the man because of his lack of hair. Although if you remember what I said I never mentioned the word bald, I simply stated that there wasn't a whole lot of hair left." I respond.

"Your insult was still implied." Jonas states and he's right.

"Yes, I know and again I'm sorry." I say.

"Then there is also the matter of the man being overweight. I can't tell you how many patients have come to me with weight problems over the years."

I interrupt, "Weight problem? It's not a problem, it's a choice." I say.

"It's not a choice." He shoots back sternly.

"Hey I was heavy as a child. I was heavy until I was about twenty years old and do you know why I was overweight?" I ask.

"Why?" He asks.

"Because I ate too much, that's why! There's no mystery to being overweight, if you eat too much you get fat." I say.

"Well, yes to put it in simple terms, but for many people it's not that easy. It's good that you were able to take the weight off and keep it off, most people can't do that." He says.

"I never said that it was easy. It was really tough. I lost seventy pounds and now I have to work to keep it off. No, it wasn't easy, but anything can be accomplished if you're willing to work at it." I say.

Dr. Jonas leaps from his chair as if something just stung him in the ass. He's looking at me excitedly and waving the pen and pad around.

"That's it! Did you hear what you just said? Anything can be accomplished if you work at it! That's exactly right. Now, if we can just get you to apply those same principles to controlling your anger." He says.

"I thought I've been doing that." I say.

"No, not exactly, I get the impression that you don't feel like you belong here. Like you've been forced to come here but actually you are above all of this." He says.

What is this guy, some kind of mind reader?

"If you are willing to work at this like you did with your weight you are going to be a different man. Don't you feel that you were a changed person after you lost the weight?" He asks.

"I can't really remember exactly, it's been so long but looking back I guess that I did feel better about myself." I respond.

"And you can do that again!" He exclaims.

Jonas is really on some kind of a high right now. It's almost like he's just discovered an alternative fuel. This might be as good a time as any to bring this up.

"I have this booking coming up in a few weeks that I really am going to have to fly in order to get there."

Jonas looks completely deflated. It's as if what I just said sucked all the air out of the room.

"Do you ever pay attention to anything I say?" He asks.

Of course I listen it's just that I don't always want to hear or really care about what he has to say.

"Yes of course I do." I respond.

Jonas sits back down in his chair. His brief moment of excitement with me is gone.

"What am I going to do with you John?" He asks quietly.

"What do you mean?"

"Here we were talking about how you were able to overcome your weight problem with hard work. I was explaining to you how you can overcome your anger issues if you are willing to work at it and the next thing I know you're telling me about a flight that you need to take. It's as if what we were talking about didn't even enter your conscious. You have one thing on your mind and that's all that matters to you. This is your biggest problem. It's like when you are traveling, be it driving or flying, all you can think about is getting where you're going. You never take into account the fact that certain problems may arise during this time. Then when these instances do occur you're unable to handle them and you turn to rage. Do you hear what I'm saying?" He asks.

"Yes," I reply.

"I know that you hear it, but do you actually put it into practice?"

I really don't have an answer for him.

When I am unable to respond Dr. Jonas looks like a little boy that's just had his feelings hurt. It's not that I don't want to do what he's telling me. Most of what he's saying really makes a lot of sense it's just that…I guess I really don't know the answer. If I did I wouldn't be the way I am.

"Take for example what you were telling me about the traffic situation. Here you are saying that you were totally relaxed imagining you were at the beach and then when you banged into the car in front of you it all was lost and you exploded." He says.

"I didn't explode." I argue.

"Ok, but were you able to remain calm?"

"No," I answer.

"Wouldn't you agree that if you were totally relaxed you would have been able to remain that way? What I'm trying to ask is would the situation have been any different had you remained calm?"

"No," I reply.

"In fact maybe things would have gone more smoothly had you not been filled with hostility when you confronted the man whose car you banged into, would you agree?"

"I don't know, this guy was a real horse's ass over his precious car!" I respond.

Jonas is staring at me as if he doesn't know what to make of me. He's been doing it long enough now that I am really starting to feel uncomfortable. Say something already would you!

"I just don't think I can give you the clearance to fly right now."

Ok, just don't say that, but you did say that, shit!

"I'm just not seeing any progress here. You have to understand that if I say you are OK to fly and there is another incident then it comes back to me. Do you understand?" He asks.

"Nothing is going to happen. That was a one time thing." I protest.

"But you can't guarantee that can you?" He asks me.

"I'm almost positive." I exclaim.

I can tell by the way that he is just smiling and shaking his head that wasn't good enough for him. I need to work on his sympathy.

"Look, I really put myself into a bit of a financial hole with the incident in Vegas and the fact that I had to cancel another week because of that. This is a big week for me money wise and if I can't do it I'm probably not going to be able to afford to come in here and get the help I need."

I'm trying to hit him in his wallet here too. I figure he's already lost one patient this week. He can't afford to lose two can he?

"The guilt angle won't work with me." Jonas says.

"I wasn't trying to make you feel guilty." I say.

"John..."

Is all he says and I can see he's got me here, "OK, I'm sorry. I should know better than to try to use guilt on a psychologist." I say.

Jonas lets out a laugh and just shakes his head as he stares at me.

"Where do you have to get to?" He asks.

"Laughlin, Nevada." I tell him.

"So you have to fly into Laughlin?" He asks.

"No, I fly into Las Vegas, then rent a car and drive down to Laughlin." I tell him.

Jonas begins to laugh again as he asks, "Are you kidding? You're going back into Las Vegas?"

"I see that the irony isn't lost on you." I respond.

Jonas is really getting a kick out of all of this.

He's still laughing as he says, "Let me think about this."

At least Jonas had a good laugh during our session today because I have to tell you I don't have a lot to smile about as I head out into the cold to my car. It's starting to snow a little bit and I can't remember the last time I saw the sunshine. There's something about the gray and cold at this time of year that make all of your problems seem exaggerated. Of course I've got a pretty big problem on my hands even in the best of weather. I need money, to get money I need to fly, to fly I need Jonas to say that it's OK and he's going to think about it. What's there to think about? This is a crucial situation here, throw me a bone!

I'm in a foul mood when my wife comes home from work. I give her a kiss hello and retreat back to the computer in the room we use as an office. I've been pricing flights that I won't be able to take. I don't know why I'm even bothering. I've also sent out some e-mails to some clubs in the area to let them know I may be available that week. The money won't be the same but at least it won't be a total loss. I'm sure everybody is booked that week anyway but it doesn't hurt to check. The phone rings, I let my wife answer. This is so frustrating, I can get a great price on an airline ticket if I book it now but I can't because I don't know if I'm going to be able to go.

My wife enters the room and hands the phone to me.

"It's your therapist office." She tells me as I take the phone.

"Hello…"

"Hi John, its Lisa from Dr. Jonas office, please hold for Dr. Jonas."

Now I'm holding for Dr. Jonas and wondering why he couldn't just call me himself. I hope this is good news.

"John, Dr. Jonas. How are you?"

"I'm all right."

I tell him even though I'm really not. What's going on here? Is this some kind of bonus session?

"John, I've been doing some thinking about your dilemma with the flight and I've come to a decision. Go ahead and book a flight and then call back with the flight information."

"Why do you want me to do that?" I ask.

"I've decided that what I'm going to do is fly out to Las Vegas with you. I haven't been there in years and we can use it as a prolonged session. I'm thinking that it will be good to observe you in action. Not only that but it gives me an excuse to spend a few days in Las Vegas and the best part is that I can deduct the whole thing as a business expense since you are my patient. Isn't that great news?"

I don't know whether it is or not, I mean I do get to make the trip so that part's good. But then Jonas is going to be with me so that part's not good. I'm going through a whole range of emotions here. I don't know whether to jump for joy or out of a window.

"Yeah, that's great news Dr. Jonas."

"Ok, call me with the flight information."

"I'll do it right now and then I'll call you back." I say as I hang up the phone.

"What was that about?" My wife asks.

"Dr. Jonas is going to fly to Las Vegas with me." I tell her.

"That's good you'll be able to go then. You've been worried about this." She says.

I'm not saying anything because I'm really not sure.

"Nothing ever makes you happy." She announces as she walks out of the room in disgust.

She's right; nothing ever does make me happy. It's the reason that I am this way. It seems like I would rather be pissed off about something rather than happy and maybe in that twisted way this is what really makes me happy. I guess this is what I wanted. I just can't shake the feeling that this isn't going to be a smooth trip.

TWELVE

Dr. Jonas and I decided to meet at the airport at nine AM for our flight, which was scheduled to leave Pittsburgh at ten-thirty-five. My ass is really dragging this morning. I had trouble sleeping last night. When I finally did doze off I dreamed I was laying there tossing and turning and having trouble falling asleep. This sucks because it's not like being asleep at all even though you are. Because of this none of the sleep I did get actually counted so it's like I've been up since yesterday.

I get to the airport at about five until nine and I don't see any sign of Jonas. I can't check my luggage and get my boarding pass without my escort so I get into the back of the line and hope that Dr. Jonas will show up before I get up to the counter.

That's when I hear my name being called "John, over here, John!"

There's Dr. Jonas at the check in counter waving me over.

"Are you sure?" I ask "I don't want to cut in front of anybody."

"Come on over, you're all set." He replied.

As I reach the front of the line I can see that Dr. Jonas is looking way too happy for somebody that is about to experience the hell that is flying on a commercial airline.

"Good morning sir." He says.

I force out a mumbled, "Morning."

I'm not a morning person to begin with and my mood takes on an even darker tone on days that I have to travel. Add to that the fact that I didn't really sleep last night and this guy is just way too chipper for me this morning.

"I've been explaining our situation to the lovely Donna here," He says.

The Donna he's referring to is far from lovely. It's not that she's unattractive; in fact ten years ago she was probably a real knock out. It's just that she looks as though life has really beaten her down. It's perfectly understandable, a person working for a commercial airline after all. When she started here it probably all seemed pretty glamorous. Good pay and benefits, good retirement plan, not to mention the fact that you could fly free whenever you want. She had to have been thrilled the day she was hired. Of course that was before bankruptcies and restructuring and pay cuts too numerous to count. And there's the fact that she will almost certainly never be able to retire. Not if she wants to eat anyway. No, Donna looks like she quit giving a damn a long time ago.

Through her miserable expression Donna dead pans, "I'll need your picture ID."

I hand her my driver's license and she starts punching the computer keys.

"You're going to require special screening." She informs me and the day is off to a rousing start.

"That shouldn't be too bad." Dr. Jonas reassures me.

"Yeah it shouldn't be too bad because you don't have to do it." I say.

Now I'm on the watch list as a suspected terrorist. The guy traveling with me isn't. It just doesn't make any sense. We're traveling together, going to the same destination on the same flight and I'm a suspected terrorist but he's fine. I guess he's just a guy that likes to travel with suspected terrorists.

"Is there any chance that there are seats available in the exit row?" Dr. Jonas asks Donna.

She punches the keys and announces, "He's not aloud to sit in the exit row."

She's kind enough to say it loudly so that my fellow passengers are able to hear.

"Do you have two seats together?"

He asks and I add, "Can you see if you have two aisle seats across from each other?"

"That's good," Jonas says. "That way one of us won't have to be squeezed into the center, good thinking John."

"Thirteen C and D," Donna grunts.

"That will be fine." I say.

"I guess that you're not superstitious." Jonas comments.

"Why because of row thirteen?" I ask.

"A lot of people don't like that number." He says.

"That would be kind of a dumb superstition to have in this situation, don't you think? I mean if something is going to happen because I'm sitting in row thirteen, in this case it's also going to affect the guy seated in row ten and the people in first class and the lady in row twenty-nine and I hope they wouldn't be thinking we'd be OK right now if that jerk hadn't sat in row thirteen." I say.

"That's a healthy way to look at it." He says.

"We'll need your credit card." Donna tells me.

"For what?" I ask.

"It's twenty-five dollars for each piece of checked luggage." She informs me.

"This means that it won't get lost, doesn't it?" I ask as I hand my credit card to her.

The fact that she doesn't answer gives me no reassurance. You would think that for twenty-five bucks a pop the airline would give you a no lost luggage guarantee but that would mean that they actually give a damn about the passengers. There's no way that is going to happen. Donna hands us our boarding passes and luggage claim checks and we head down the escalator to the security line.

"I thought she was nice, Donna, don't you think?" Jonas asks.

"Are you kidding me?" I say. "If you would have asked her if she wanted to finish her shift or have you shoot her in the head, she would have answered, please give me sweet death."

"Yeah, maybe," He says. "But I still thought she was nice."

Jonas seems way too cheerful for a gloomy Monday morning in the middle of January and then I realize why. This guys on his way to Las Vegas, sin city, where what happens in Vegas stays in Vegas. He's going to be away from the wife and kids running amok in the dessert. Then again I can see this guy using his time sitting in his room and catching up on his reading. He doesn't seem like the usual Vegas tourist which is probably for the best. That town could pick a guy like this clean.

The line for security isn't too bad for a Monday and we enter the maze of ropes that will lead us eventually to the Promised Land. Jonas is looking around at the other people in the line with us.

"Would you look at how people dress to travel? Sweat suits, undershirts, some of them look like they just crawled out of bed to get here." He says.

"Some of them probably did." I answer. Dr. Jonas is dressed as if he's on his way to work, top coat, tweed jacket, corduroy slacks, and dress shoes. I on the other hand am wearing my standard flying uniform, comfortable button down shirt with at least one pocket to carry my cell phone, jeans and sneakers.

"People like to be comfortable when they fly." I say.

We arrive at the front of the line and hand our ID's and boarding passes to the security guard.

He looks at my boarding pass and gives me the once over and says, "Go to that line over there, we have to give you additional screening."

I'm instructed to take off my shoes and take my lap top out of its case and to remove any metal and cell phone from my pockets. I then have to stand behind a door in a sort of holding pen while I watch some security moron thoroughly going over an elderly couple that looks to be in their eighties with a wand while they stand spread eagled. Grandma and Grandpa look like they could be dangerous and thankfully this crack security team are here to keep us safe. It's all so ridiculous. I mean what could these geezers do even if they wanted to? In the meantime while this old couple is being harassed, people that look like they just escaped from prison pass through without so much as a second glance.

The elderly couple is cleared and I am finally released from the holding pen to be subjected to the same treatment that they just received. Although, maybe not. One of the security guys is putting on a pair of white surgical gloves and looking me over. I can't believe it, I'm about to be given an anal probe while everybody gawks at me. Not only that, but in this day and age where everybody is able to video record with their phone, I'm probably going to end up on YouTube. Finally I will be world famous, just not in the way that I had envisioned. I can see it now, people coming up to me on the street and asking, "Hey, aren't you that guy…" I'll be able to stop them mid-sentence, "Yes, that's me. I'm the guy getting an anal probe on YouTube." Then I can do the talk show circuit, "Ladies and gentlemen, please welcome suspected terrorist John Knight!" Oh, the humanity.

I feel a sense of relief as the guy with the gloves starts to poke around through my luggage, pulling through my socks and underwear. You wouldn't think that you would be relieved when somebody is rummaging through your under shorts but it's better than the alternative. It looks like I'm not going to be anally probed. That's when I realize that the dream is over. I was almost famous there for a second. In the world of reality television and the internet you have to take it anyway that you can get it. So what if you're known as the anal probe guy. At least they know who you are.

All the other passengers passing by look at me as if I'm some kind of criminal as I go through about ten minutes of careful screening. They go over me with the wand and swab my luggage and send it through a detector to check for explosive devices. Finally they clear me and I am given my freedom. Jonas has been watching all of this in amusement as he put his shoes and belt back on.

As I catch up with him he gives me a wry smile and says, "Maybe I shouldn't be seen with you, you could be dangerous."

At least he got a big kick out of me being randomly harassed. I'd hate to think that I went through all of that for no other reason than security putting on a show so the idiots that live in constant fear can feel safer as they board their flights.

We board the tram that will take us to the gate area and I feel like everybody is staring at me. Hopefully that terrorist will not be on my flight they probably think to themselves. None of them even taking the time to consider that maybe some poor innocent citizen may have just been hassled for no reason at all. It was all just to keep the fear factory going.

It's only about nine-thirty now and Dr. Jonas decides that he would like to grab some coffee. I don't want any caffeine because I'd like to try get a nap on the plane. There's a long line at the coffee place, I guess people like to be wired at thirty thousand feet, nothing like being more on edge when we hit some turbulence.

There are no Starbucks at the Pittsburgh airport, which you would think to be against the law. We are in line at Mayorga, which actually sells their coffee in small, medium and large sizes, not like the cutesy names that Starbucks insists on. Even at Starbucks I refuse to give them the satisfaction, I still order a large coffee, they know which one I mean. I've only had one person give me a hard time about it, an effeminate gentleman in Atlantic City that explained they had three sizes, "We have tall, grandee and venti!"

I said, "Give me the big one chief," and that's what he did.

We arrive at the front of the line and I grab a bottle of water to take on the plane with me. It costs two-fifty, which is more than a large coffee that is made with water. I should have just ordered the large and said, "Hold the coffee," but that would have surely caused a commotion and I've already been through enough this morning. I'm one of those people that still drink from the tap when it's available and since studies have shown that most bottled water is just tap water that they charge you an outrageous price for, I figure what's the difference. People are always looking for the next great billion dollar idea and most of us miss the boat on finding a way to charge people for something they can get for free. Those are the true innovators, the people that realize just how gullible the general public is. I'm currently working on a plan to sell breathing air to people and if that works I'm going to charge them for sunshine.

"That's all that you're having, water?" Jonas asks.

"I don't like to drink coffee before I take a long flight." I respond.

Dr. Jonas realizes who he's dealing with and what happened the last time I flew and says, "Yes, I guess that is wise."

Then he orders a large coffee, this surprises me. I had Jonas pegged as a latte guy. He also orders a bran muffin, which is a brave move I think.

"Coffee and a bran muffin should have you running for the rest room by the time we're over Dayton." I say.

"Why" He asks.

"What do you mean, why? C'mon coffee and a bran muffin, why not just order the enema special?" I respond.

He's giving me a look like he has no idea what I'm talking about.

"Just forget it." I say and he shrugs as if he hasn't a clue.

I figure I'll remind him about it when it hits.

There's a table open and we grab a seat as Jonas sips his coffee and picks at the muffin.

"Would you like some?" He asks, referring to the muffin.

"No thank you. I had some granola at home." I respond.

"I'm really looking forward to this. I haven't been out to Las Vegas in about five years." He says as he shovels a big piece of muffin into his mouth.

I've never seen Jonas eat before and it's really kind of disgusting. He chews with his mouth half open, making smacking noises the whole time. Then he makes loud sipping noises as he drinks the coffee. It's all a bit much at this time in the morning.

"They really gave you the business down there at security." He says.

"Yeah, me and that old couple in front of me, they're really keeping America safe aren't they?" I respond.

"They do what they have to do. You know since 9-11 we can't take any chances." He says.

"Oh, come on! Why would they be bothering that poor elderly couple? Do you think they were terrorists? It's all just a show to keep the public aware of the fact that they should be afraid. Be afraid while we harass you at the airport and attack countries for no reason. It's all just a bunch of shit!" I say.

Jonas is looking at me strangely as he sips his coffee.

"I would never have imagined you to be one of these conspiracy people." He says.

"I'm not one of those. It's just that it's all bogus, this idea that those security people are making us any safer. They're looking for the wrong things. They'll make you throw away any liquids that are over two ounces. Like it makes a difference if you are trying to bring on six ounce toothpaste instead of two, I mean it's not like terrorist are known for their grooming habits. But, do you know that I've gone through security here with my keys in my pocket on four different occasions, one time it was twice on the same day."

I remember something and reach into my pants pocket and pull out my set of keys with the alarm detonator attached.

"Make that five times."

Jonas looks at me as if he is shocked by this, "They even went over you with the wand!" He says.

I nod my head knowingly.

"Wow," he exclaims.

"Do you see this?" I ask as I wave my keys at him. "Look, you've got metal in the keys, the alarm system, which could just as easily be a trigger for a bomb and I went right through an extensive search with these in my pocket."

"I guess that they miss things on occasion." He says. "Did I mention that of the five times I went through security with these in my pocket, those were the only five times that I forgot to take them out of my pocket? They never set off an alarm, not even once."

Jonas is shaking his head in disbelief, "Wow." He says again.

Jonas takes a long sip of his coffee and seems to be concentrating on something.

"Even though it's not a perfect system, we still need it in order to protect our freedom." He says.

"Freedom, are you kidding me? How much freedom did I have down there, standing behind a locked door while somebody is digging through my luggage, pulling through my underwear? I think he was really enjoying it. It looked like the sick son of a bitch was getting an erection." I say.

"Really?" Jonas asks.

"No, I'm kidding." I say.

"This isn't going to be an issue with you? I mean what went on down there is not simmering somewhere deep inside of you, waiting to trigger a reaction later. I want you to just let this go, realize that it's all a result of your past actions. I have my reputation on the line here, not to mention that if you have another incident they probably aren't going to let you fly again for a really long time." He says.

"It's already forgotten." I assure him. "Don't worry I won't do anything to damage your precious reputation."

I notice an older couple seated next to us is listening in to our conversation. The woman has some sort of dyed bright red bee hive thing going on with her hair like she never let go of the sixty's. Her husband is wearing a rumpled jacket and tie and seems to have more hair growing out of his enormous ears than on his head. He also has a look about him like his elevator stopped going to the top floor a long time ago. It's her that seems overly curious about what's going on over here.

I look in their direction and say, "It's my psychiatrist. He has to travel with me because I'm dangerous. Where are you folks headed?"

In a stern southern drawl the woman answers, "Little Rock Arkansas."

"Hey, that's where we're going. I guess we'll see you on the plane!"

Bee Hive's mouth drops open and she grabs her goof ball husband by the hand. The couple gets up and walks away briskly, probably rushing to change their flight. Volunteer to take a later flight so they won't have to travel with the sick bastard that promises to make their life a living hell.

"Why did you do that?" Jonas asks.

"They shouldn't have been listening in. People need to mind their own business." I say.

He finishes his coffee and stands to toss his empty cup into the trash can.

"You really shouldn't have done that to those people. Who knows what they might be telling the gate agents."

"Don't worry about it. We're not really on their flight." I answer.

"Maybe so, but I still don't think it was right. We should start walking down to our gate." He says.

"Yes, let's get out of here." I say.

I grab my luggage and he picks up his brief case and we begin toward the gate.

"How do you feel?" He asks.

"I'm OK." I assure him.

"If you feel like you may have a problem I think we should discuss it now."

"I'm fine." I tell him again.

"Because if you are holding something back…"

I interrupt him, "I'm telling you that I'm all right, but if you keep asking me about it, then I might start to have some issues."

"I just want to make sure." He says.

We pass the newspaper vending machines.

"I'm going to grab a newspaper." I say and I put two quarters into the machine.

When I try to open it nothing happens. Then when I press the coin return again I get nothing.

"Can you believe this? The stupid machine just ripped me off!"

"Did you put in enough money?" He asks.

"It says right here, fifty cents. That's what I put in, two quarters and what did I get? Nothing!"

"Do you need another fifty cents?" He asks reaching into his pants pocket.

"I'm not going to put two more quarters in this stupid thing, then I'll be out a dollar. I'll grab one at that store over there." I say as I walk toward the newsstand.

"Do you need anything?" I ask.

"Maybe I should grab some water." He answers.

I pick up a copy of the Pittsburgh Post Gazette and Dr. Jonas grabs a bottle of water from the cooler and we get in line. There's only one woman in front of us, she's buying a magazine and a pack of chewing gum. The cashier looks to be about eighteen. She's got tattoos on her arms and neck and the piercing in her lip makes her look like a fish that broke the line and has to swim around with a hook stuck in its mouth.

"The total is five dollars and eighty-five cents." She announces as the ring in her lip bobs up and down.

The woman pulls out a credit card, I look at Jonas and roll my eyes and he doesn't seem to get what I'm trying to signal to him.

The pierced girl runs the card through the machine and stares off into space. Nothing seems to be happening, and then she runs the card through a second time.

We stand patiently waiting for the results and then she says, "There must be something wrong with your card, it's not going through."

The woman protests, "I just used it yesterday, it should be OK."

"Sometimes they become demagnetized." The pierced girl offers.

"I don't see how that could happen, like I said I just used it yesterday." The woman says.

"Maybe she held it too close to her face." I offer. "All of that metal in her lip might have done it."

The woman trying to pass off the bad credit card and the pierced girl are now giving me dirty looks as if I did something wrong. Dr. Jonas is shaking his head as if he's disgusted with me.

He grabs the paper from me and announces, "We can get this someplace else."

He puts his water back into the cooler and sets my paper back on top of the pile and I follow him out of the store.

"Why would you say something like that?" He asks. "You assure me that you're Ok and then you go and insult that poor girl who's just trying to do her job."

"Hey look, first of all, who is about to get on an airplane and travel to another city, maybe even another country and doesn't have six dollars in cash?"

"A lot of people don't carry cash anymore." He answers.

"Well if she's not going to carry cash, she should at least have a credit card that works." I say.

"She said that she just used it yesterday." He replies.

"Yeah, that's what she said." I answer sarcastically.

"So what do you think, this woman flies around the country passing off bad credit cards in order to stock up on magazines and chewing gum?" He asks.

"How do I know what she's up to?" I say.

"You don't have much faith in your fellow man, do you?" He asks.

"Not really." I answer.

"You have to think before you act, that's what we've been talking about in our sessions. Take a moment, analyze the situation, determine what it is you're getting upset about and if you do that I think you will realize that in most cases there is actually no justifiable reason for your anger." He says.

"Yes, but you're also telling me that I shouldn't hold anything inside, I shouldn't let it seethe inside of me and become an issue later." I respond.

"I'm not telling you to go around insulting people! What you did in there was nothing but a result of your impatience." He says.

"I never did get my newspaper." I respond.

I walk toward another newsstand. Luckily there are quite a few of them in this airport. Dr. Jonas follows behind.

"Did you listen to anything that I just said?" He asks.

"We're not having a session today. You're just here to hold my hand so I can get on the airplane." I reply.

"That's where you're wrong, this is an important session. I'm getting the opportunity to observe your behavior first hand, not dependent on what you tell me at the office and I must say, based on what I've seen so far, we have a lot of work ahead of us." He says.

"Did you want to miss the flight while we watched a girl with a fish hook in her lip try to run a bad credit card? We can go back if you like."

"Yes, I think that's a good idea. I think it would be a positive move for you to go back and apologize to that girl." He says.

"Do you still want water?" I ask as I move to enter the store. Dr. Jonas puts his hand on my shoulder to stop me.

"Let's go back to the other store." He says with a face like a puppy that wants you to pet him.

"Do I have to?" I ask.

"I think it will do you good." He says.

When we enter the store the girl with the pierced face is engaged in a conversation on her cell phone. I grab the paper and Jonas pulls out a bottle of water and we head to the counter.

The girl is so deep in her conversation that she really pays us no attention except to say, "Three dollars."

Dr. Jonas says, "I've got it."

And he hands her a five and she gives him two back. She turns her back to us and continues in her conversation, which from what I can hear is about a guy that she's been cheating on and how he's so dumb that he believes anything that she says.

Dr. Jonas taps her on the shoulder, "Excuse me, my friend here has something that he would like to say to you."

The girl seems very put off by all of this and says into the phone, "Hold on a second, there's a couple of creepy old guys here that I think are trying to hit on me."

Now, I'm the one giving Jonas the dirty look.

"Go ahead," he says.

"I think we should just leave." I say.

The girl is now looking at us like we're a couple of perverts and I can sense that she's about to reach for the pepper spray that she probably keeps in her purse.

"Go on." He urges me again.

Reluctantly I start, "I'd just like to say that I'm sorry for what I said before. There was no reason for me to act that way and I hope that you will accept my apology."

Dr. Jonas gives me a big smile as if he's just found a cure for cancer. The girl looks stumped by all of this.

"Why what did you do, were you guys in here before?" She asks.

On that note I pick up my newspaper and head out, Dr. Jonas follows.

"Yeah, I feel much better, not like an idiot or anything." I say.

He doesn't say a word.

Let's just say that I'm not exactly happy right now as we walk toward our gate. I'm walking at a pretty brisk pace and Jonas is beginning to fall behind. Of course I'm doing this on purpose because I'm really pissed at him right now for putting me through that humiliation. OK, I've got to calm myself down and show him I'm a bigger man than that and it's going to take more than embarrassing myself in public to set me off. I slow down and let Jonas catch up to me.

"Look, I'm really sorry about that. I didn't realize that the girl was going to turn out to be a…"

I can see that he's struggling to find some polite word to describe her so I figure I should help him out.

"What, a ditz? Is that what you're trying to say? That you're sorry that the girl was such a ditz?"

"There you go labeling people again." He says.

"Well what would you call her?" I ask.

"She was just a confused young woman." He answers.

"That's exactly what I said, a ditz!"

He has no response and we continue on toward the gate.

"Now I don't want this to become a problem." He says.

"You know what's becoming a problem? The fact that you keep dwelling on everything that happens to me and saying that you hope it doesn't become an issue or a problem, that's what's bothering me. If you're worried that I might be a little pissed off right now, well I have to tell you that I am. But I will get over it and move on with my life. What happened back there is not going to cause me to act in a way that will shame you." I assure him.

"That's a good attitude. Just know that I'm here if you want to talk about it." He says.

He's really starting to get under my skin and I feel like ditching him right now.

We arrive at our gate and I look to see that there's a plane parked there. The gate agents look as if they're getting ready to board us, which is a good sign that we will be on time.

"I'm going to use the rest room." I say to Jonas, who seems to be analyzing every move that I make.

"I really have to go." I assure him in case he's thinking that I have some ulterior motive.

"Go ahead, I'll wait here." He tells me.

"You don't have to go?" I ask.

"No." He answers.

"Are you sure? I mean you just had that large coffee and sometimes they don't turn off the seat belt sign for a good while after take off." I say.

"I think I would know if I had to go." He replies.

As I walk toward the rest room I realize that I was acting like a mother hen back there telling him he should use the toilet before we leave. Why should I give a fuck if he ends up pissing himself on the plane? At least that would take his mind off of me.

I really don't have to go either but I figure I should force one out, leak that is, before I get onto the plane. It's something I do every time I fly and if nothing else, I am certainly a man of habits. I finish and head for the sink. I know it's something that we're taught as children, wash your hands after going to the bathroom. The problem with this is there are probably more germs on the sink than what I just had in my hand. I don't care if people wash their hands in the bathroom, unless they're going to be handling my food. I remember one time, I was in a restaurant in Pensacola, Florida and I went in to use the rest room. There was a stench coming from one of the stalls that was so disturbing, I actually had to hold my breath while I was urinating. The toilet flushed, the stall door opened and out walked the chef. He went right for the door, never even came close to the sink. The fact that I had already eaten was no comfort to me. The person who had been touching my food was a disgusting pig! It may have been psychosomatic but I was nauseous the rest of the night.

The sink in the rest room here has the motion activated faucet. These things are great for people that don't want to touch anything for fear of germs. The only problem is that they seldom work right, like now. I'm holding my hands under the spigot waiting for the water and nothing is happening. I move my hands around, nothing, I walk away to try another sink, nothing. I'm beginning to think that I may be invisible. These motion activated devices in rest rooms never work right. You know this if you've ever been standing there with your hands dripping wet trying to wave your hand in just the right spot to get the towel dispensed and then walking out of the bathroom frustrated as you dry your hands on your pants.

And then there are the ones that work too well like the self flushing toilets. You know how annoying those things can be if you've ever gotten your seat protector situated just right only to have the toilet flush and suck the protector down before you are able to sit. Sometimes it takes four or five attempts before you can actually outmaneuver the stupid thing! Of course when you do this the people in the other stalls are wondering what the hell is coming out of you that has to be flushed four or five times. Outside I hear them calling my flight to board. Screw this, my hands are clean, I head on out to the gate.

People are lining up now to get on the plane. As I observe the motley bunch that I will be traveling with I have to wonder why I was the one that required additional screening. I can't believe that they would even let some of these losers into the airport let alone on a plane.

"We're boarding." Dr. Jonas says.

"I can see that." I answer.

This guy certainly has a grasp of the obvious. It's probably why he became a doctor.

"Las Vegas here we come!" He says and with that we hand our boarding passes to the gate agent and walk into the hallway that leads to our flight.

THIRTEEN

As we turn the corner into the hallway we find the long line of passengers creeping toward the plane. It's always like this when you are boarding. The first few passengers board the aircraft and then forget that they are not the only people flying today. No, they take their good old time trying to cram their over sized bag into the tiny overhead space. I can understand not wanting to check luggage, anyone that has ever arrived at their destination only to find that your luggage didn't make the flight with you can understand this logic. Especially today, when you have to pay an extra service charge to the airline for them to ship your luggage to the wrong destination.

What bothers me is the principle of physics. If the object that you are trying to fit is bigger than the space in which you are trying to place it, well, it's not going to fucking happen! I see it on every flight I take, at least one idiot turning their bag every which way as if that will make a difference. "Oh yeah, it's much smaller if you put the back end in first. Try it upside down, maybe that will work! Since both sides of the bag are exactly the same size what makes you think that turning it around is going to make a difference you stupid moron? What ever possessed your parents to think that breeding would be a good thing?"

These people are determined, they will not take no for an answer. Even though they have tried every possible angle to get the bag into the space without success, they don't stop. Usually they will go through the same cycle again, possibly hoping that their first attempt has actually succeeded in stretching out the space and thus now making it possible for the bag to slide into the overhead compartment. Usually during this second cycle, as we are being further delayed by this passenger's insistence (ignorance), the flight attendant will show up and suggest that the passenger check this particular piece of luggage.

This will usually bring about the response of, "But, I don't want to check it."

"If it doesn't fit in the overhead or under the seat it has to be checked."

"Is there anyplace else that I can put it?"

At that point I usually have a great suggestion and I'm guessing that the flight attendant is thinking exactly the same thing.

When Dr. Jonas and I finally enter the plane we have to pass through the first class cabin in order to get to our tiny cramped seats back in coach. Look at all the lucky bastards that won't have to go through the same hell as we will. Some of them actually smirk at you as you pass by on your way to agony.

I have to admit that there was a time I had so many miles on one particular airline that I flew nothing but first class for two or three years. That was back when the airlines had more than four first class seats on their planes. Back when they rewarded passengers for showing loyalty to their airline. Back before they started charging more for the special section of the plane that gives you an extra inch of leg room, back when they even fed you in coach, instead of charging you for disgusting airline food. I guess the thought is, if people get hungry enough they'll eat anything and pay handsomely for it. Back before the bankruptcy's and restructurings, back before the layoffs and cutbacks, back before pay cuts and concessions, back when the airlines actually treated you with dignity. I miss those days and I especially miss my days in first class, back when the flight attendant would pass around the cabin with a bottle of wine asking if you would like a refill. A couple of glasses of wine at thirty thousand feet can really take the edge off.

We arrive at our row and I'm surprised to find that there is actually still enough space for me to squeeze my small bag and jacket into the overhead and I slide my laptop under the seat in front of me. That's what they ask you to do when you're boarding, "if you have two bags, place one in the overhead and one under the seat," The thought here being that this will then leave space for everybody. Of course this suggestion doesn't apply to the special people that bring on two enormous bags and then jam them into the overhead. It doesn't matter if there's room for anybody else. They don't have to follow the rules. They're the special people after all. The sun shines out of their ass and they can do whatever the hell they want. Now, I may get easily annoyed and lose my temper on occasion, but one thing I am not is a selfish fucking pig!

As I take my aisle seat, there is an older woman seated in the window seat and the seat in the middle is empty. At this time I can still dream. Maybe this seat will stay open and the flight will not be unbearably uncomfortable. I'd like to at least try to get a short nap since what little sleep I had last night didn't really count. Of course this is also when I like to play a little game called, "who will be my seat mate?" What you do is watch as the other passenger's board and try to guess which one is going to sit in the middle seat next to you. Now in all my years of flying I can tell you that it's never a tiny person. It's never an attractive woman. No, I keep an eye out for the biggest, fattest, dumbest looking son of a bitch to turn that corner and nine times out of ten it will be, "Uh, I'm in there." "Of course you are I knew it the moment that I laid my eyes on you."

Since I fly quite a bit, at least I did before the incident, I know the drill. When you're sitting on the aisle you want to lean in toward the middle seat while the other passengers are still boarding. The reason for this is that people fling their luggage over their shoulders and when they walk by…BAM! Jonas just got whacked in the face by some guy's carry on. It was a pretty good impact and it actually knocked his glasses crooked.

"Are you all right?" I ask.

"Did you see that? That man didn't even apologize." He responds.

"What cave have you been living in? People don't apologize anymore. You're lucky if he doesn't try to sue you for damaging his luggage. Now you should watch yourself. I know that you don't fly that often so I'll tell you something, you should lean in a little, until everybody is past you."

Instead of listening to me he leans toward me and asks, "Did you say I should lean in?"

Right at that moment a girl walking by us turns to say something to the girl behind her and the bag over her shoulder…WHACK! Jonas takes another shot to the head. It looks like I can't take this guy anywhere.

There are no more passengers boarding at this time and the seat next to me remains vacant. Could I actually be so lucky? Jonas has an older couple seated next to him and the woman in the middle seat can't weight more than eighty pounds. He won't even notice her. I on the other hand may have the privilege of flying into Las Vegas with an empty seat next to me and lots of room to stretch out. I might even be able to squeeze in a nap, although the chances of that are slight even though I feel like I could pass out right now. It's almost impossible to find a comfortable position in one of these seats. There are of course people that can doze off anywhere and will be snoring before we hit the runway. The reason is that some of these people are heavily medicated when they fly, but others can sleep because they have the simple mind of a child. They can just make their minds go blank and fall asleep anyplace at anytime. They just don't know any better. Ignorance is bliss but I think I'd rather be heavily medicated.

It looked like the flight attendant at the front of the plane was going towards the door. Is she actually going to close it? Could I actually be this lucky? That's when I see him. He turns the corner and enters the plane. All light behind him is blocked. He's so big that he probably has his own atmosphere. I think I see not one, but two moons circling his head. He's headed in my direction, please don't stop. Keep on going, there are probably seats farther back.

"Can I squeeze in here?" He asks and hell followed with him.

Fuck! I want to tell him the truth, that there's probably no way for him to squeeze in, not without the Jaws of Life anyway. I can see Jonas looking at me, expecting me to cause a scene. I can't do that so I get up and let the fat bastard in. He wedges himself into that center seat and quite a bit of him is spilling over into mine. I can no longer see the woman seated near the window. This is going to suck!

The flight attendants are now closing the doors as we get ready to depart. Oh sure, close it now. Why couldn't you close it two minutes ago, before this cow waddled his way up the ramp and got on the plane? Why isn't he in the cargo area with the other livestock?

He's struggling with his seat belt, there's no way in hell that he's getting this thing around him.

He calls out to the flight attendant, "I'm going to need an extender for my seat belt."

She grabs one from the front of the plane, hands it to him and he snaps the two together like he's had a lot of practice which I'm sure he has. The days of one seat belt are just a distant memory for him now. It's a very close call, but he manages to snap it tightly shut around his waist. I can tell you there's not any seat belt left over. If this guy takes a deep breath that baby is going to blow and some-body's going to be badly hurt. Wouldn't that be a terrible way to get injured? "What happened to you?" "A fat guy on the plane sneezed and his seat belt exploded and hit me in the head." He's stuffed in there good right now. I personally believe that if you need two seat belts then you should also require two seats instead of taking up half of mine, but then what do I know?

Our flight attendant, she's been introduced as Barbara, is now in the center of the aisle demonstrating how to fasten a seat belt, just in case there's a total idiot on the plane that has never learned how to do this before. The other flight attendant, whose name I don't know, the one that got the extender for the fat fuck next to me, is giving the instructions as Barbara demonstrates. They do this procedure on every flight and I always look around to see if anybody is following along intently, learning as they go. I haven't witnessed it yet but if I ever see such a person I will put up a petition to keep this person from ever driving or operating heavy machinery. I was going to point out to my seat mate the fact that Barbara is only us-ing one belt in her demonstration, but he's too busy shoveling a handful of candy into his mouth. Now we can see how he keeps that willowy figure.

"Sit down back there!" Barbara shrieks toward the back of the plane. We all turn to see a visibly shaken man close the overhead and sit down without whatever it was that he was looking for. Barbara is a squat stocky woman, with short blonde hair. She has a piercing glare that goes right through you which she is using to stare the man down like a pit bull about to pounce and chew out a jugular and she's scaring the rest of us as well. I guess she's going to show us who the boss is here, in case we may have thought otherwise. From her demeanor I also imagine that Barbara probably spent some time as a Nazi prison guard in a past life.

I'm guessing Barbara is probably just some sort of stage name she uses. Her real name is probably Helga or Natasha or Hilda. She just doesn't come across as a Barbara. Barbara is the kind of name that a playmate would have, of course they would shorten it to Barbie or Barbi with an i. Barbie's don't look like they could reach into your throat, pull out your heart, and show it to you before you fall over dead, but this woman does. Usually during the safety instructions you will see most of the passengers reading or talking and just not paying attention. Not today though, all eyes are on Barbara, you don't want to piss off this broad.

We begin to push back from the gate and I look at my watch, we're right on time, which is good.

"Here we go." Jonas says excitedly as if he's a little kid riding the roller coaster.

I feel bad that I can't share his enthusiasm, but then he doesn't have this massive blob of meat pressing against my shoulder. I look out the window and notice that it's beginning to snow. The weather was calling for some but said it shouldn't be an issue. The first part of the flight may be a bit bumpy, which means this flab will be bouncing off me. I could end up with some bruises. Of course nobody will believe me when I tell them I was nearly fatted to death on the airplane.

We begin to taxi out to the runway when the pilot comes over the speaker. "Good morning folks, as you can see outside it's beginning to snow, so we're going to have to head on over to the de-icing station before we take off. It shouldn't take but a few minutes and

I don't anticipate any further delays, so we should be getting you into Las Vegas right on time. We'll give you an update on weather and our expected arrival before we take off. Now, sit back and enjoy your flight."

What does he mean he doesn't anticipate any further delays? Why does he have to give us an update on our expected arrival time? I look around and see that the other passengers seem calm, either reading or talking or starting to doze off. It looks like I'm the only one seeing a potential problem and I should probably just let it go. It's just that from my experience, if there is the chance for some type of problem, in all likelihood it will occur. Hopefully I'm wrong.

"It really doesn't look too bad out there, do you really think we need to de-ice?" Jonas asks.

"I think its standard procedure, if there's snow coming down they always do this." I respond.

"Better safe than sorry, I suppose. Is it just me or does it seem like these seats keep getting smaller?" Jonas asks as he fidgets around trying to find his comfort zone.

"Maybe you'd like to switch with me." I respond. Jonas looks my way to see me being crushed by the mounds of flesh that have invaded my space.

"I think I'm OK here." He responds.

The plane taxi's for what seems to be about ten minutes and I begin to wonder if the de-icing station is at another airport. We come to a halt and I glance at the newspaper for the first time. I put it back down. I'm not going to read it now. I want to save it for the time in the air. It takes my mind off flying when I read. If I start reading now chances are we'll be stuck here on the ground long enough for me to finish the whole paper and then what will I do for the rest of the flight, talk to Jonas? No, the newspaper is my excuse not to have to engage in conversation with this guy. He can just look out the window and count the clouds.

We haven't budged for a while now and I look at my watch and see that it's already fifteen minutes since we left the gate. It looks like we will be more than likely getting into Vegas late, but that's OK because I will still have plenty of time to get down to Laughlin. We were originally scheduled to get in at twelve-fifteen, so even if we don't get in until one it will leave me with plenty of time. It's about an hour and a half drive, so even with waiting for luggage and picking up the rental car, I should still get down there no later than three-thirty or four. The show isn't until eight so there's no need to panic.

The captain comes over the speaker. "Ah folks, it seems that they weren't anticipating this weather this morning and we only have one de-icing station available at this time. This is a busy time of morning and our current situation is that we still have about nine planes in front of us waiting to be de-iced. We apologize for the delay and will hopefully be underway shortly. I'll give you an update when I know anything further."

OK, we're going to be even later, but there is still no need to worry.

A woman stands and begins to walk toward the restroom. Barbara grabs the microphone, there's fire in her eyes.

"Ladies and gentleman, the fasten seat belt sign is on, this means that you must remain seated until we take off and get into airspace that the captain feels is appropriate to turn off the seat belt sign. Then and only then will you be permitted to get up from your seats! Is this understood?"

The woman sulks back to her seat. Either it wasn't all that urgent or she no longer needs the use of the restroom because old Barbara just scared the piss out of her.

I notice that Jonas is looking at me with concern.

"What?" I ask.

"Just wondering how you were handling all of this." He says.

"I'm OK, this is nothing. When you fly as often as I do you get used to it. The fact that we left the gate on time was almost a miracle of itself. This is why I don't cut it too close with my flights. I always give myself plenty of extra time because you never know what will happen." I say.

The way he's looking at me now, I know exactly what he's thinking.

"Yeah, I know what I did the last time. You don't have to say anything, I'm fine."

I pick up the newspaper and turn to the sports section. Again, I don't want to read it now I'm just trying to avoid Jonas.

Since it looks like we might be here for awhile, I decide to lean my head back and maybe catch a quick nap. Hopefully when I wake up we'll be half way to Las Vegas. This is of course wishful thinking on my part because there is no way to get comfortable with this mass of flesh that is pressing against my right shoulder and chest. I take a look around the cabin to see if there are any other seats available. At this point I would be better off with a middle seat in between two normal size people. I wonder if this guy would feel insulted if I left an aisle seat to take a middle seat because it would be more comfortable than sitting next to him. Nah, probably not, this guy probably got over being insulted about a hundred pounds ago.

The plane has been inching slowly forward now for about the last twenty-five minutes and we come to a stop. There is a sound of liquid hitting the plane and you can see the pink goo sliding down the windows now.

"I wonder what's in that stuff." Jonas says.

"I don't know." I say.

"Wouldn't it be nice to have some of that to spray on your car so it wouldn't ice up?" He asks.

"Actually that would be really cool." I respond.

"I wonder how I could get some." He says, hypothetically I believe.

I nod my head toward Barbara who is standing guard at the front of the plane. She has her hands clasped in front of her as if she's waiting to pounce at the first provocation.

"Why don't you ask her?" I say.

Jonas takes a quick glance toward Barbara and says. "I don't think so."

"Yeah, I wouldn't." I add.

"Do you think she's married?" Jonas whispers.

"She may have been at one time. I'm thinking that her husband is probably now in small pieces in plastic bags shoved into the back of her freezer." I say.

Jonas begins to chuckle and I laugh along with him. Barbara is giving us the evil eye. We're dead men.

The de-icing has stopped and we are beginning to move again. I can see out the windows that the snow is really starting to come down right now. At least I'm going to get a little break from this weather. It's been a long winter already and we still have at least two months left. Anyway, we seem to be rolling along at a pretty good clip right now. We should be almost to the runway and then we'll be off. The plane comes to an almost screeching halt and it feels as if we have pulled off to the side of the road and parked.

It's now an hour and five minutes since we've left the gate and we're getting nowhere fast. I don't think that most of the passengers are aware of the fact that we are no longer on our way to the runway. When you travel as often as I do, you can get a sense of what is happening. I always know when the plane has gone into a holding pattern when it's waiting for clearance to land and right now I am conscious of the fact that we aren't going anywhere, of course nobody is telling us anything.

"We seem to have stopped moving." Jonas says.

"Yeah, we're parked on the tarmac." I respond.

He looks out the window at the now heavy snow and says, "It's probably because of the snow."

"Probably, although it would be nice if they could tell us something," I say.

As if he heard me, the captain comes over the speaker, "Ah folks, we have some weather in the area right now and they're grounding all flights until it clears. Hopefully it won't be too long. We're going to be shutting the engines down to conserve fuel while we're here on the ground. I'll give you an update as soon as I know something."

I'm aware of the fact that I am now grinding my teeth and Jonas must be aware of it too because he's looking at me with the fear that I'm about to lose it.

"Let it go John, just take a deep breath."

I do what he says and take a long deep breath, it really doesn't help but I pretend for his sake. Not only that but it's hard for me to get a full breath with the girth pressing against me. I'm going to just have to accept the fact that there is nothing that I can do about this. It's out of my control. I just have to sit back and relax. Of course that would be a lot easier if I had a whole seat to sit back in. This fat bastard is crushing me!

The woman that had been attempting to use the rest room earlier rises from her seat and creeps toward the back of the plane. I see the veins in Barbara's neck tense to the point where they look like they are about to explode. For a moment I'm almost sure that she's about to tackle the woman and beat her to a bloody pulp just to set an example for the rest of us.

Instead she grabs the microphone and shrieks into it, "Sit down back there! The fasten seat belt signs are still illuminated, we could start moving at any moment! This is for your own safety! When the captain turns off the seat belt sign then and only then will you be aloud to move about the cabin!"

The captain must have heard this because at that moment the seat belt light went off. This seemed to piss off Barbara even further and I think I can see some blood flowing from where she just bit into her lower lip. The poor woman is now standing in the aisle and looks like she is too frightened to move. She is now using the procedure that one would use if confronted by a bear or some other wild animal, stand perfectly still and hope that it goes away. Barbara isn't going away though, it's now become obvious that we are prisoners here and Barbara is going to run a very strict camp.

Barbara is staring the woman down as she says into the microphone, "If you have to go, go. Do not block the aisle."

The woman confused by all of this, slumps back into her seat. It's probably the safe thing to do.

Jonas leans over and in a very low voice says, "This flight attendant is a little scary, isn't she?"

"Trying to run away from an angry bull while you're wearing bright red pants is a little scary. This bitch is downright frightening." I respond.

I notice that Barbara is staring at us and she must know that we're talking about her.

"Shh... she sees us." I say.

Like two frightened children we snap back into our seats in an upright position.

It is eerily silent on the plane. We are all in fear of this beast. Barbara has an evil smirk now, she is aware of the fact that she has gained the upper hand and she is thriving with authority.

"Psst…" Jonas is trying to get my attention.

I look his way.

In a whisper he says, "I really have to go."

I whisper back. "So, go."

"I don't know if I should chance it." He responds. I look toward Barbara and she is staring at the two of us with her arms folded across her chest.

"Do you think that I should try?" He asks.

"It's your life." I reply.

He takes a long hard look at Barbara and makes his decision.

"I think that I can hold it."

I notice that some of the other passengers are making calls on their cell phones, probably notifying loved ones about their predicament. "We're being held hostage by a terrible, evil woman. If I don't make it tell the world my story." Since others are doing it without being scolded I decide that I should probably call my wife and let her know what's going on.

"Hello." She says.

"Yeah, it's me" I say.

"What's wrong, why didn't you leave yet?" She asks.

"I don't know; something about the weather." I answer.

"Is your plane there?"

"I'm on the plane."

"You're on the plane, then you must be getting ready to leave."

"Not necessarily, we've been sitting here for over an hour now."

"Did they tell you when you would be leaving?"

"They're not telling us anything. We're just sitting here."

"Just make sure that you don't lose your temper."

"Yeah, I know. I'll just deal with it."

"Let me know if you find out anything."

"I might not be able to. If they come on and tell us that we're ready to go I'll have to turn off my cell phone."

"OK, then if I don't hear from you I'll know that you left."

"Then I'll call you from Vegas."

"Just don't cause a scene!"

"I won't. Love you."

"Love you too."

Outside it looks as if the snow is letting up. Hopefully we'll be able to take off soon. I can feel myself beginning to get extremely stressed about the situation here. I know I still have time but it's getting closer and closer the longer that we sit here. I've got to try to take my mind off of things so I decide to look through the crappy in-flight magazine they put in the seat pockets. As I try to reach forward I realize I can't move the right side of my body. No, I'm not having a stroke it's just that I'm weighted down by the bulk of this guy next to me. I struggle to free myself but he's not budging.

"Excuse me, could you lean forward a little bit so I can grab this magazine?"

He leans forward and my arm and shoulder are released from the weight that has been pressing against them. The only problem is they are still numb. This can't be good. I'd like to get up and walk around and stretch out a bit but I'm afraid that if I get up even more of him will spill over into my seat and I won't be able to get back into it. Some of the passengers have gotten up to use the rest room, but Barbara has made sure that they take their seats immediately so even if I get up I'm going to have to sit right back down. No loitering under her watch. We're currently living in a police state.

"I can't hold it anymore." Jonas says as he starts to get up.

Just then the Captain's voice comes over the speaker. "Hello this is the captain. I have good news and bad news. It looks like the weather is cooperating and we should have you out of here shortly."

The passengers begin applauding, which I think is stupid because he hasn't told us the bad news yet. Wait for the shot in the nuts before you get overly excited.

"The bad news is that since we've been sitting here for quite some time, we're going to have to go back and de-ice once again."

A consensus groan fills the cabin and with that the engines kick back on. Poor Jonas has to sit back down.

"You should have gone before." I say.

"I know." He answers.

I can tell by the way that he's sitting that it's going to be a struggle for him to hold it now. I'll bet you wish you didn't have that coffee and muffin now, I think to myself.

We roll along at a pretty good clip for a few minutes and then come to a halt.

"We must be back in line." Jonas says.

"You figured that out, huh." I say sarcastically.

"I hope it doesn't take as long this time. I really have to go." He says.

"If I were you I'd try to take my mind off of it. I'd imagine that this will take just as long if not longer." I suggest.

"How am I supposed to put it out of my mind? I really have to go."

"Why don't you picture yourself at the ocean, feel the breeze and listen to the waves. Listen to the waves, here's another one, listen to the waves."

I tell him and I know I shouldn't be doing this because now he's really squirming and I'm almost certain that he' going to piss himself and it will be my fault. It wasn't nice of me to talk about the waves when he's in this state but hey, I'm really bored not to mention anxious right now.

Jonas is raising his hand, as if he's a child in school that wants to ask for the hall pass. He finally has Barbara's attention.

"Excuse me, would it be possible for me to use the rest room?"

"I'm sorry but nobody can leave their seats while the plane is taxiing. You can go when we've reached a comfortable altitude and the captain turns off the seat belt sign." She replies.

The plane is currently moving about two inches every five minutes and I don't think that Jonas would have trouble navigating his way back and forth to the lavatory but rules are rules and Barbara really likes to enforce them.

"I'm sorry, but I really have to go." Jonas pleads as if it's going to make a difference to this Nazi bitch.

"You should have gone before." She answers coldly.

"I told you." I say just to rub it in.

Jonas doesn't find the humor in it and looks now like he's about to burst. I have to admit that his misery is actually helping me to keep my temper under control. Suffer you poor bastard.

By the time the de-icing fluid finally starts hitting the plane it's twelve-forty five. It's now two hours and ten minutes since we left the gate and yet we can still see it in the rear view mirror. I can see that the sound of the liquid hitting the plane is driving Dr. Jonas insane. Wouldn't that be ironic if the therapist flying along with me to keep me under control were to lose his mind? If nothing else it would make a great story to tell when I'm out having a drink. Then again it might make for a good movie on The Lifetime Channel since it would be based on a true story. They could get George Clooney to play me. Jason Alexander would play Jonas with Vin Diesel as Barbara, although he may not be masculine enough for that role.

My mouth is getting dry so I reach to grab my bottle of water out of the seat pocket in front of me. This time old lard ass leans with me. All of this irritation must be giving me strength. I pull the bottle out of the pocket and think for a moment that it would be really funny to offer some to Jonas. I'm beginning to realize that I have a real mean streak when I'm under stress. I'm not really going to offer him any because first of all I don't want his germy lips all over my bottle. He's already given me the flu once this winter. Also, I guess that I'm not really a sadistic son of a bitch although it does take my mind off of things to think like one. I take a small sip because I don't want to end up like the doctor over there since there is no guarantee that we will ever get to the promised land of a comfortable altitude.

The de-icing stops and through the pink liquid streaming down the windows I can see that it is beginning to snow at a pretty good clip. Hurry up, I think, let's get out of here before this gets too bad. We taxi toward the runway and I'm optimistic that we are finally going to take off, that's until we come to another screeching halt and pull off into the same spot that we left forty-five minutes ago. A chorus of groans fills the cabin and Barbara takes a stance that shows she's ready to go into battle and if things get any worse, she just might have to.

"Well, they've grounded us once again. Hopefully we'll know something shortly. We're going to be shutting down the engines while we are here on the ground." The captain says over the speaker.

The seat belt sign goes off and if it's exactly what he's been waiting for. Jonas makes a mad dash for the lavatory. Unfortunately a handful of other people seem to have had the same thought and it looks like Jonas is about number six in the line. At this time I am beginning to become concerned about making it down to Laughlin in time for my show. We've already been on the ground here for two and a half hours and there is no end in sight. The captain was extremely vague in his last announcement, as if to say he had no idea when or if we would be leaving, which is exactly the way it is. We could end up sitting here for another five hours and then wind up right back at the gate we started from. Eight hours on a plane and going absolutely nowhere.

There is some sort of commotion back near the rest room where Jonas is waiting and I can see from the expression on her face that Barbara will be having none of this. She pulls the microphone from the holster and makes her announcement.

"We can not have the aisle blocked this way. I am now going to ask everyone that is not currently in the lavatory to take their seat until the lavatory becomes vacant."

Nobody moves and Barbara is not going to stand for this.

"I said take your seats!"

Jonas begins to creep gently back toward his seat. Two women that were ahead of him also follow Barbara's orders. One defiant gentleman continues to stand waiting his turn.

Once again we hear from Barbara, "Sir, I need you to take your seat."

This is a big man. He stands about six-three and looks to be a solid two hundred and thirty pounds or so. He also has the pissed off look of somebody that is sick of being treated like a pawn by this airline. I think he could take Barbara.

We are all silent as we watch the scene being played out in front of us. The big gentleman is now facing toward the front of the plane where Barbara stands perched with the microphone at her side. They look like two gunfighters facing each other at high noon. The fat guy next to me goes for his M&M's, Jonas is not quite back to his seat and now stands frozen between the two combatants as if he knows he is in the line of fire. Barbara's eyes are now a glaring squint and if she was wearing a poncho you would mistake her for Clint Eastwood. The only question now is who's going to draw first.

"Look, I'm next in line here and it sounds like the person in there is getting ready to come out, so I'm just going to wait."

The man says loudly enough that all can hear, especially Barbara in the front of the plane. The door opens and an oblivious older gentleman emerges. He must sense the tension in the air as he shuffles back to his seat. The big guy enters the lavatory, locks the door and the occupied sign illuminates. You can almost see the steam coming from Barbara's ears.

"Ok then, as of this moment the lavatories are now closed. We can not have things getting out of control here, so until we are airborne, nobody is to leave their seat."

A loud groan goes through the cabin, Jonas is still in the aisle and is now about to try to become the voice of reason.

"You can't treat us like children! If somebody has to use the bathroom they are entitled to do so while we are stuck here on the ground."

Barbara is now walking toward Jonas angrily. She gets right up next to him and shoves her finger into his face.

"Look, you had better just watch yourself. I don't need anybody starting a situation here. If need be I will have you arrested as soon as we land in Las Vegas."

A man seated on the aisle near where the confrontation is happening can't help himself and asks, "And when exactly will that be?"

Barbara looks like she is about to explode as she marches off.

A woman on the aisle asks, "Why can't we go back to the gate and wait?" Barbara ignores her and disappears into the cockpit.

Jonas takes his seat.

"This woman has some real problems. I'd like to give her one of my cards. I really think I could help her." He says.

"She won't let you go to the bathroom and you want to help her. What's the matter with you?' I ask.

"That's what I do. I help people." He says.

"If you try to give her one of your cards she would probably insert it sideways into your ass!" I say.

"Maybe." He replies.

Hostility and anger are now rampant as we approach the three hour mark on the ground here. Barbara is afraid that Jonas might start something here and she doesn't realize how close I am at this point to violating my parole. Again, the problem is that nobody has emerged as a leader. Somebody willing to let the airline know that you can't treat people this way. You can't hold us hostage like this. If only I didn't have that prior incident hanging over my head I could really turn this plane on its head. What it is though is the whole thing is almost surreal. Just when you think that things can't get any worse, they drop another bomb on you. If I didn't know better I would swear that Jonas prearranged this whole thing to try to really test me. Of course that's not the case. In his wildest dreams, when he was trying to come up with sick and twisted new forms of torture, even a vicious bastard like Dick Cheney wouldn't have come up with anything this cruel. All I keep thinking is that if I were able to stir things up a little bit here I would have a riot going right now that would make Attica look like a day at Disneyland! That thought and the knowledge that I am surely capable of causing such a scene are keeping me going right now.

I grab my cell phone and call my wife to let her know the situation. She can see that it's me calling on her caller ID, she answers, "Are you telling me that you haven't left yet."

"That's what I was about to tell you."

"What's going on? Why aren't you leaving?"

"I don't know, they're really not telling us anything."

"Where are you?"

"We're still on the plane."

"If they're not going anywhere why can't you get off of the plane?"

"I don't know."

"You're all right, aren't you? Please tell me that you aren't going to start anything."

"I don't know."

"John, please!"

"I don't know."

"Tell me that you aren't going to do anything!"

"OK, I won't. I'm just numb right now."

"Just promise me."

"OK, I promise you. I'll call you if I hear anything."

"Just keep your temper. I love you."

"Love you too."

"Bye."

"I'll let you know if we ever leave."

There is sometimes a moment when you reach what should be the breaking point and you don't react. At that time you become numb, the outside world becomes a dream like state, a nightmare actually and you find yourself unable to accept what is actually happening. It must be some kind of defense mechanism that is built into our psyche's that keeps our brain from exploding like a hamster in a microwave. That is what I am going through right now. It's almost like I'm dead and experiencing hell firsthand. If this were a dream I would have woke up screaming a long time ago.

The passengers are definitely growing restless. The ones that didn't bring it with them haven't had food or drink offered to them for almost three hours. Then there's the fact that Barbara is threatening to take away our bathroom privileges. I'm starting to feel kind of hungry myself. I probably should have grabbed one of those muffins like Jonas. Although as I look at him now, maybe not. This poor guy had better get into a rest room soon. It's kind of cold on the plane right now with the engines shut down but Jonas is sweating profusely as he holds his legs together and rocks back and forth.

It's the fat son of a bitch next to me that has me really concerned. He seems to have sucked down the last of his M&M's and it seems like he is now looking around the cabin for his next meal. I've noticed him eyeing me up and down and what scares me is that he could probably swallow me whole like a python before anybody even noticed I was gone. He'd just let out a loud belch and ask for another seat belt extender.

In the back of the plane the lavatory door swings open and the big guy steps out. He's been in there quite a while and one can only imagine what just came out of him. I'd hate to be the one to go in there after him but I don't think Jonas can hold it any more.

"The bathroom's empty, why don't you go?" I say.

"I don't know if I should. She said that we weren't to leave our seats." He replies.

"To hell with her, you have the right to use the bathroom! It's not healthy to hold it in." I say.

"I suppose your right, but there were other people waiting ahead of me."

"Nobody else is getting up. They're probably afraid of that bitch. They need somebody to set an example, a leader, somebody that's not afraid to take charge. I believe that you are the chosen one." I say.

"You know what, you're right. Not only that, but I really don't think I can hold this any longer. I'm going to go for it."

Jonas stands to make his way back toward the lavatory and we all stare in awe at the brave man that will lead us.

Jonas is about half way there when Barbara emerges from the cockpit. Our fearless leader stands frozen in his tracks. As Barbara gazes toward Jonas it appears that she has been crying. Maybe she went in there to have some sort of emotional breakdown out of our sight. The captain's voice comes over the speaker.

"While we're on the ground feel free to use the lavatory. Let's just keep the aisle clear in case the flight attendants need to get through for any reason. As soon as we have an update I'll let you know."

Or maybe Barbara got scolded and was told that you can't keep people from using the restroom and now she is pouting like a child that didn't get her own way. Never the less, through her tear streaked eyes she is staring down Jonas like a cheetah about to pounce on its prey. It's obvious now that he's going to be dog shit for the rest of the time here. Not only that, but when the captain made the announcement, ten people in the back of the plane jumped up and are now lined up in front of him, poor bastard.

The right side of my body is now throbbing from the weight of this heifer pressing against me. I don't have to go to the bathroom, but I need to take a walk and get some circulation going. I unbuckle my seat belt with my left hand, I can't believe I've been buckled in this whole time and I can still walk back to the airport if I wanted to. We've never even been on the runway. As I stand I realize that my right arm is completely dead, just dangling to my side. Not only that but as I got up a mound of fat spilled over into my seat and I don't know if I will be able to squeeze back in there. I try to ignore Barbara's icy stare as I make my way to the back of the plane and get into line behind Jonas.

"I didn't think that you had to go." Jonas says as I take my place in line.

"I don't, I just needed to get up. That guy next to me is crushing me. I can't even feel my right arm right now."

A gentleman seated two rows ahead of where we are now standing raises his voice, "Is it possible to at least get something to drink?"

The other flight attendant, the nice one, the one that we haven't seen much of, whose name I don't know, comes down the aisle and tries to diffuse the situation.

"Sir, we can't bring the drink cart out until we take off."

"And just when the hell will that be?" He asks loudly.

"Sir, if you like I can get you some water."

On that note Barbara comes charging down the aisle.

"If you get him water then everybody is going to want a drink! There will be no drinks served until we take off and reach a comfortable cruising altitude!"

This seemed to snap her out of her funk and back into tyrant mode.

"Even prisoners are entitled to bread and water!" The man says.

"If you like that can be arranged. We can have you taken off this plane and arrested right now!" Barbara snaps back.

I wonder if I'm the only one thinking, that doesn't seem like too bad of an option.

There is some tingling in my fingertips and I can feel my arm coming back. I grab it with my left and maneuver it around until all of the feeling comes back. I lift both arms over my head and stretch and then bend and twist to loosen up my back. I might look like an idiot but I really don't care at this point.

A woman seated next to the thirsty gentleman raises her voice, "I don't see why we can't have something to drink if we want it! This is inhuman, the way we are being treated."

A woman next to her chimes in, "We've been stuck here for three hours now! We should either go back to the gate and be allowed to get off of the plane until it's ready to leave or you should at least give us something to drink!"

Barbara storms away as if she hasn't heard a word of it. The nice flight attendant says quietly, "I'll get you all some water from the back, as soon as I can get through." I don't know if it was an idle promise or if she would actually get them water as soon as this line was gone. Either way, it has calmed the passengers for now although I can still see a major riot happening if we don't take off shortly.

Jonas turns and says, "I wish these people would stop talking about water. If I don't get into the rest room soon I'm afraid that I might have a very embarrassing situation."

"If that happens I hope you know that I'm not changing you." I say.

"That's not funny." He replies.

"It is funny and if you weren't the one that was about to piss himself you would realize that." I say.

"Can we change the subject?" He says.

"I suppose we could discuss the upcoming riot." I say.

"What riot? You're not going to start anything, are you?" He asks.

"I'm not going to do anything except sit back and enjoy the

mayhem. These people won't need me to start it. I think they may have been pushed almost far enough now that they aren't going to take anymore and they will revolt."

"Do you really think so?" He asks.

"If not it's going to totally destroy my faith in mankind." I reply.

Everybody is certainly taking their good old time in the lavatory. I guess that nobody is in a big hurry to sit back down. I know now that I have the feeling back in my arm, I have absolutely no desire to wedge myself back under that pile of fat. Jonas looks like he is trying to somehow cross his legs while he is standing. I know he isn't enjoying the time away from his seat, the small amount of freedom that we are able to experience during our time in hell. If the captain would come on and tell us to take our seats right now, I am sure Jonas would fall to the floor and begin to sob.

Through the window I can see that the snow is coming down heavy, this means that even if we do manage to somehow get clearance to take off we will have to de-ice again. I look at my watch and see that it is now almost two o'clock which is eleven AM in Vegas. We should be landing in about fifteen minutes which would have given me plenty of time to get down to Laughlin, as it is now I'm going to be really cutting it close.

Jonas must have heard the grinding of my teeth because he turned to me with a look of concern, "Don't lose it now, you've been doing great through all of this."

"I'm OK," I assure him.

"If you don't make it there today it's not the end of the world. Remember we've talked about this attitude in our sessions. You've got to just roll with this, just like the rest of us. You're not the only one in this situation right now. We're all in this together." He says.

"I know." I answer.

We have continued to move forward in the line and Jonas is next. I look out the window and the snow seems to be letting up.

"You're almost there." I say.

"If I don't get in there soon I'm going to burst." He says.

"If you're going to be long, why don't you let me go first?" I ask jokingly.

He turns toward me with a look that tells me that's not going to happen. The captain comes over the speaker.

"I have some good news, the latest weather is telling us that the storm has now moved out of the immediate area and we are going to be able to finally take off."

Applause erupts through the cabin.

The captain continues, "The bad news is that we're going to have to go back and go through the de-icing process yet again. They've assured me that there is now a second crew available and it shouldn't be too long. If we could have everyone return to their seats we'll be underway shortly."

Jonas turns and looks at me and his eyes are almost crossing at this point in his agony.

"Sorry." I say to him as I start back toward my seat.

"I can't go back. Not now, I'm so close. I'll never make it." He says.

"What about Barbara?" I ask.

"She can kiss my ass." He replies.

It was the first time that I had ever heard Jonas swear. I turn and look toward the front of the plane and can see that Barbara is now rejuvenated. Her mission to make our lives as miserable as possible is on again. She reaches for the microphone.

"We need everybody to take their seats, NOW!"

I start toward my seat; Jonas says to me, "I can't go back. I can't hold it any longer."

I head back not knowing if I will ever see him alive again.

I reach the area where my seat used to be. My neighbor's body has now spilled over so far that only a tiny fraction of my seat remains visible. Not only that but he is fast asleep and snoring like a moose. Now I have never heard a moose snore before but I can only imagine that it's as loud and disgusting as the noise coming out of this blob right now. The other thing that bothers me is how can you sleep right now? The rest of us here are living through torture and there you are sleeping like nothing is wrong. He probably has visions of sugar and whole sides of beef dancing through his head right now.

I sigh and squeeze in as best as I can. I am now leaning forward at almost a forty-five degree angle as I am now pressed back against him. It's very uncomfortable but at least my arm won't go numb in this position. I try to get as comfortable as possible and hope to wake him. I know that's not nice but he's snoring right into my ear right now. I'm hoping that he doesn't in fact suck me in. That would be a hell of a way to die, sucked in by a fat guy. I can see Jonas struggling, trying to pull me free by my feet that are still dangling out of the elephant's mouth. Barbara of course would be telling him to take his seat not giving a shit whether I live or die. If nothing else I would be famous for a day or two once the story hits the news.

In the back of the plane the lavatory door swings open and Jonas rushes in. Barbara observes this and enters the cockpit. The captain comes back over the speaker.

"Ladies and gentleman, we need everybody to take their seats right now. I've been informed that we still have somebody in the lavatory. We have a window that we have to fit into in our routing out to Las Vegas. If we don't make it into that window we will have to wait to be released and we could be on the ground for another hour, so please take your seats."

Barbara has taken matters to a higher authority. She emerges from the cockpit with a look of evil satisfaction on her face.

In the back of the plane the door to the rest room opens, Jonas makes his way back to his seat through a sea of dirty looks from the other passengers. He sits down and looks extremely uncomfortable.

"You're going to make us late." I say kidding.

"I couldn't go." He says, grimacing.

"What do you mean you couldn't go? You risk your life to get in there and then you didn't go?" I ask.

"I couldn't, there wasn't time." He says.

"It shouldn't have been a problem. You said you really had to go so it should have happened as soon as you got in there." I say.

"You don't understand, if I did one I was going to have to do the other and then the captain came on and I didn't want to hold things up, so I knew I wasn't going to have time to do both." He says.

"What are you talking about? I ask

"I really don't feel comfortable talking about this, but if you must know, the situation was that I could tell if I started to do number one, well then number two was going to happen and there wasn't time." He tells me.

"Number one and number two? What are we children?" I ask.

"I told you I'm really not comfortable talking about my bath-room habits." He replies.

"You should have done the first one." I say.

"I'm telling you that if I started it was going to happen the other way and then he came on and..."

I interrupt and say, "You shouldn't have had the bran muffin."

"If I knew then what I know now." He replies.

In the meantime Barbara has been giving him a cold stare that lets me know she has it in for him now. Jonas your days are numbered.

We have begun to move again and there is a sense of calm in the cabin. Maybe our journey through hell is about to end. Maybe we will actually take off and then after four more hours we will finally be able to escape from this long narrow tube we've been held hostage in for the last three and a half hours. It's still a long journey ahead but at least now we seem to be able to see some light at the end of the tunnel. We come to a halt and I look out to try to see how many planes are now in front of us as we wait to de-ice once again. I can see there is no longer any snow falling which is a good sign anyway.

"I'm not going to make it." Jonas whispers to me.

"What are you going to do?" I ask.

"Maybe if I explain my situation I will get some understanding. It's not like we're moving along at such a pace that I would hurt myself. I think I should be able to go while we're still here on the ground." He says.

"And where do you think you're going to find that understanding? Barbara doesn't seem like the understanding type. If she's anything she is certainly a stickler for the rules." I say.

"Maybe if I talk to the other one." He says.

"If I were you I would try to put my mind on something else." I say.

I reach into the seat pocket in front of me and pull out my newspaper and hand it to him. "Here, try reading the paper maybe that will help." I say.

"What are you doing, trying to kill me? Do you know where I like to be when I read the newspaper?" He asks.

I guess that I didn't realize what I was doing or maybe subconsciously I'm fucking with the guy.

Barbara steps back into the cockpit and Jonas uses the chance to race back to the restroom. He has his finger over his lips as he moves along, as if he's a bad child in class hoping that none of the other children will squeal on him. I can see by the way that some of the other passengers are looking at him that they must be wondering what this crazy son of a bitch is up to. Wasn't he just in there? Is he up to something? In this generation of people that experienced nine eleven and then were continually manipulated with fear by the Bush administration, trust is a hard thing to come by. Everyone you see could possibly be a terrorist and it's much safer to turn in your fellow man than give him the benefit of the doubt. I can see Jonas being whisked off to some secret prison and water boarded until he confesses to something that he never had the intention of doing, all because he had to have that damn bran muffin.

Toward the back of the plane I see he is now being confronted by the other flight attendant, the nice one. He seems to be pleading his case and she must be very understanding because she lets him go ahead. Now we can only hope that Barbara doesn't find out that he's gone before he gets back, which could lead to an ugly situation.

We begin to move forward slowly and I look back for a sign of Jonas. The other flight attendant is now knocking on the lavatory door telling him that he has to get back to his seat. I hope he's able to accomplish the task at hand.

Barbara comes out of the cockpit and immediately eyes the empty seat. As she walks toward me I can feel my heart begin to beat faster. The look in her eyes tells me that she means business and I'm hoping that she doesn't just sink her teeth into my throat, tearing it out like a hungry tiger and then howling in triumph for all to hear.

"Where's your friend?" She asks angrily.

At this point I can feel my fear turning to anger and I'm thinking about decking this Nazi bitch. Just cold cock her, put her out long enough to let her know that there are some people you can only push so far. Maybe it would be the best thing that ever happened to her. Maybe if somebody would have knocked her out a long time ago she wouldn't be on this power trip. Then again, I am on airline probation, so I decide to lie instead.

"He's not my friend."

"I've seen you talking to him all morning." She says.

"He's sitting across from me, he seems like a decent enough guy and we just happened to strike up a conversation." I tell her.

In reality he's not really my friend, he's my therapist that was assigned to watch over me so I don't flip out on another flight and if ever there was a flight to snap on this would be it, but this is more information than she needs to know. Barbara's gaze now turns to the back of the plane where Jonas is now making his way back to his seat. I can tell by the calmness in his expression and the little bounce in his step that things went well in there. He doesn't even seem to mind the fact that he has to slip past Commandant Barbara on the way back to his seat.

"You were told not to leave your seat!" She blares out at him.

"Sorry, it was a decision that I probably made in error, but at the time it seemed like the thing to do. You see I was feeling quite uncomfortable and I probably made my choice in haste. It's a judgment that I now realize was unwise, but unfortunately I was not thinking clearly at the time. It's a decision that I will now have to live with for the rest of my life and I hope that you can find some place deep down inside of you that will allow you to forgive me." He says.

Barbara is left speechless and turns hastily and walks away. Jonas has really been showing me a side of him that I would never have imagined even existed.

I say, "Doctor, you can be a real bastard when you want to."

He just smiles and lets out a sigh of relief. He's a new man.

I look at my watch and it's now two-fifteen, almost four hours since we've left the gate. I think to myself that if by some miracle we can get out of here in the next fifteen minutes I can probably make it down to Laughlin and maybe even have time to grab a quick shower before the show. This way of trying to plan my life far in advance is part of the reason I have anger issues. I should just wait until we get into Vegas before I start worrying about how much time I have to do what needs to be done and maybe just change plans depending on the situation, but I just can't live like that. What would I do without stress in my life?

The plane is still inching slowly forward and I look toward Jonas.

"You know you took a hell of a chance back there. You're lucky if you don't get arrested when we get off the plane like I did the last time."

I obviously said this too loudly because the woman sitting next to Jonas is staring at me curiously.

"Don't worry ma'am, you see he's my doctor and he's here to make sure that I don't flip out again."

This poor woman now has to be wondering what she's gotten herself into and will have to live in the fear of not knowing what these two crazies will do next. Just then the sweet sound of de-icing fluid comes flowing over the plane for the third time today. Hopefully the third time will truly be a charm.

Right when all began to seem right with the world again a woman three rows back begins to loose it.

"I can't take this anymore. I've got to get off of the plane!"

Oh, this is all that I need. We're so close now and this psycho is going to make them take us back to the gate.

"Miss, we're going to be leaving now. We're on our way to Las Vegas. Don't you want to go to Las Vegas?" I say, trying to calm her down.

"I don't care I just want to get out of here. I can't take this anymore!"

The thing is, I can feel her pain, and I've been holding it back so far today but deep down inside of me I'm ready to explode. Nobody should be treated the way that we have during this long torturous ordeal but I have to make it out there. Unlike most of the rest of these people I'm not on my way to Vegas on a pleasure trip. I start an engagement tonight and I really need the money. If this woman makes us go back to the gate I'm totally screwed. If she was going to lose it why not an hour or two hours ago, not now when it looks like we might actually get off the ground.

I look at Jonas, "Can't you do something, give her a valium or something?" I ask.

"I can't just go around handing out prescription medications." He says.

"Why not, you tried to give them to me." I say.

"You're my patient." He says as if that justifies getting people hooked on narcotics.

"I just want to get off of the plane!" She cries out.

"Can't you do something to help the poor woman? I really don't want to have to go all the way back to the gate. Not now anyway, when we're so close to the finish." I say.

"Maybe I can talk to her." He says.

With that he unbuckles his seat belt and steps out into the aisle to try to talk some sense into the woman.

"Hello, I'm Doctor Amile Jonas. I'm a doctor of psychology and if you'd like to…"

BOOM! Jonas hits the floor. I had my eyes on the woman in distress and missed Barbara coming at him. She took him down with a single shot to the kidneys and now Jonas is writhing around the floor of the plane in agony. Barbara stands over him like a hunter standing over her trophy.

I rise from my seat to help Jonas.

Barbara starts screaming at me, "Get back to your seat! Nobody is to leave their seat!"

I have to admit that through all of the merciless torture I've been through today I've been able to remain relatively calm. I don't know if it was having Dr. Jonas here with me or perhaps it's the work he's been doing with me and of course the most logical reason was the fear of knowing that if I lose it today I can pretty much kiss my flying privileges goodbye. But now things are different, now I'm really pissed. Where does this evil bitch get her nerve? Knocking down a defenseless man when he's not looking and why, because he didn't adhere to her stupid rules? Because he was trying to help a person that was having a problem, or maybe because Barbara is such an insensitive self loathing piece of human garbage that she really gets a kick out of treating people this way.

"What the hell's the matter with you?" I ask Barbara as I attempt to help Jonas to his feet.

"We can't have people just wondering about the cabin as they please. He's been wondering around the whole flight. We can't be too cautious, we have to protect ourselves. The enemy is out there and if we become soft they will walk all over us. I wasn't about to let this man walk all over me. I've been watching him the whole flight. I've been watching you too. I know the two of you are up to something." She replies.

Now I'm beginning to understand. Barbara has become so delusional with paranoia that she thinks everybody is out to get her. She has just declared war.

"I'll ask you again, what the hell's the matter with you?" As I say this I realize that I now have my finger in her face, I'm grinding my teeth and my body is anxious as if I'm about to go into battle. Jonas must sense the tension from his prone position as he tries to diffuse the situation.

"Let it go John. It's not worth it." He says.

At this time I notice that the other flight attendant, the good one, is kneeling beside Jonas and making sure he's OK.

"Help me get him up." I say to her.

We manage to get him up to his knees. His face is twisted in pain and he lets out a deep groan.

"Are you all right sir? Can I get you anything?" The nice one asks him.

Jonas waves her off, "No, no I'll be OK. Just give me a second."

He manages to get to one knee. Barbara is looking over the circumstances like a vulture waiting for the carcass to stop moving. Now I don't know for sure if she was actually trying to kill Jonas but I get the sense that if he had died she really wouldn't have let it ruin the rest of her day. Jonas reaches back and puts his hand over his lower back, right where she hit him. He lets out another groan and I almost laugh when I think to myself that if this had happened before he used the lavatory we'd have a real mess on our hands.

I take time to look around at the other passengers. They are very quiet as they view the situation. Their looks are hard to distinguish. Is it concern for this unfortunate man that lies before them, or is it fear? I'm sure that it is a combination of both. Anyone that was close enough to see what was happening and anyone that's been subjected to Barbara for the last four hours has to know that we are in the right.

Then again, who knows what people are thinking anymore?

The woman that wanted off of the plane is no longer saying a word. Maybe she now realizes that sitting on the plane for another four hours looks a hell of a lot better than a shot to the kidneys. At least Las Vegas lies at the end of those four hours.

I look at the older woman seated next to Jonas. Even though I was just toying with her before, she looks like the type that takes everything literally. With her it's fear, downright fear. I can see it in her face. She's wondering what she has gotten herself into and why she has to be seated nearest to the two potential terrorists.

Then I begin to wonder how many of these other people are unable to understand that Jonas and I haven't done anything wrong. I mean Barbara is wearing a uniform. That gives her an air of authority after all. There are some people that just won't ever believe that an authority figure can do any wrong. They place them on a higher plane than the rest of us. These people don't believe in such things as corrupt policemen or thieving doctors and heaven help us a lying politician. OK, I may have gone too far with that last one. At this point in time it's probably harder to find anyone that believes a word that they are hearing from any one holding a political office.

Jonas is somewhat shaky as we manage to get him to his feet. He puts his hands on his hips and bends backward as if he's stretching. He closes his eyes as he tilts his head back. It's obvious that he is in extreme agony.

"Sir, would you like to be checked out by a doctor?" The nice flight attendant asks him.

"I think I'm OK." He answers as he takes his seat.

"Are you sure?" she asks him again.

"I'm OK." He repeats.

I make a feeble attempt at easing the tension in the cabin.

"OK folks, shows over! There's nothing more to see here, you can go back to what you were doing."

They stare at me as if I'm nuts, which most of them probably think I am and maybe they're right. Maybe I am nuts and that's why I have to have my psychologist fly with me to keep me under control and then the poor man almost gets killed. I look down at the remains of my aisle seat and push myself back into that mountain of flesh. If I'm not insane now I probably will be at the end of this flight. That's if we even take off now. I'm sure that Barbara has already turned us in.

I haven't been paying attention, what with all of the commotion, but we seemed to have been moving the whole time. I'm assuming that we are headed back to the gate where Jonas and I will be arrested. We'll be able to plead our case and maybe if the nice flight attendant takes our side we'll get off with a warning. That will work out fine for Jonas. It's his first offense after all. I'm the one that will be screwed here. I think they look down on people that get arrested on two consecutive flights. The thing is, this time I really didn't do anything. It doesn't matter though, I was in the vicinity. I think to myself that if I lose my flying privileges and am unable to work, I'm going to get Barbara somehow. There is just no way I can let her get away with this.

I look toward the front of the cabin and Barbara and the other flight attendant are locked in a confrontation. I can't make out what they are saying but I can see that Barbara is having none of it. As I glance toward Jonas he is squirming in obvious pain. It'll be over soon, I think to myself. The authorities will be dragging us off of here in a few minutes. Outside the snow has stopped and it looks like there is even the faintest hint of sunshine coming through. The captain comes over the speaker.

"Flight attendants, prepare for departure."

We weren't going back to the gate! They must not have heard all of the commotion up there in the cockpit. Either that or after this much time they just assume we are going to get restless back here and could really give a shit. They've put in as much time as we have and they aren't giving up now.

The plane begins to roll, we pick up speed and we are in the air. I look out the window as the ground below becomes more and more distant. There is what can best be called a smattering of applause. Most of these people are probably too numb by now. Either that or watching a man being taken down by a flight attendant has given them a new outlook on life. The fact that they are now on their way to Las Vegas is not giving them the sense of joy they probably thought it would when they booked the trip. No, now that bliss they were expecting has been replaced with a longing to survive. I look at Jonas. He doesn't seem to care that we have taken off and has his head back against the seat. His eyes are contorted in agony. I lean back into the pile of fat and try to relax.

FOURTEEN

The air is rough flying out of Pittsburgh and we bounce around quite a bit. I've been thrown back against my seat partner on more than one occasion and the son of a bitch actually had the nerve to let out an indignant "OW" at one point. Hey I'm sorry, but the reality of the situation is that I've paid for a whole seat which I no longer have so if you're going to invade my space you may leave a little bit bruised, fatty. Maybe the next time you can look into flying first class or in the cattle section or wherever a person of your size can fit. Luckily I figured out that it was best to sit down after him so that he is not pressing against me. If not I may have lost my right arm.

Jonas hasn't been looking too good since we took off. He's had his eyes closed and his head pressed back against the seat but I can tell that he's not sleeping because every now and then he lets out a sort of groaning sigh. He hasn't said anything and I've chosen to let him alone in his misery. Hopefully there is no internal damage. He's such a soft man when you look at him. Then again even the toughest of us could suffer damage from a shot in the kidneys like that tyrant delivered. I think if he wanted to he might have a hell of a law suit on his hands. Of course with the state of the airline industry, he could win the suit and they would just hand over the reins of the company, then he'd really be screwed. Here you go, you win so were giving you a bankrupt company full of disgruntled employees. Of course the CEO comes along with it so make sure that you can pay his salary which is one zillion a year before bonuses.

The captain comes over the speaker.

"Hello folks, this is the captain. First of all I'd like to apologize for all of the delays back there. Unfortunately it was a weather situation and we have no control over that. We are going to try to make up as much time as we can in route and we will give you an estimated arrival time as we get closer to Las Vegas. We are currently at thirty two thousand feet which is going to be our cruising altitude. They are reporting that the air here is smooth, so I'm going to go ahead and turn off the seat belt sign."

DING! The seat belt sign goes off.

"We never know when we're going to hit some bumps up here so we ask that you keep your seat belt fastened while you are seated. Also if we could keep the aisle clear so our flight attendants can get through with the service cart it would be appreciated. Again, we apologize about the delays. Now sit back and enjoy the rest of the flight. I'll be back with an update later."

We've reached a comfortable air space! It was promised to us for hours. Barbara said that we could get up as soon as we got here and now we are there, the Promised Land. I think it would be appropriate if we all got up and danced the jig in the aisle. Of course the rest of these passengers look like a bunch of wimps and I think they already have the wrong impression of me, so I guess there will be no dancing today.

The nice flight attendant, the one whose name I can't remember comes over the loud speaker. Barbara hasn't had much to say since she took out Jonas and I'm wondering if her job might be on the line.

"Ladies and gentleman we will begin our drink service now. We will be coming through with juice, water, coffee and soda which can be purchased for two dollars. Cocktails are available for eight dollars and beer and wine can be purchased for seven dollars. There is also a variety of snacks available and you can find a listing on the menu page of the in-flight magazine. Prices vary between five and twenty dollars. We would appreciate it if you could please keep the aisle clear until we have completed the service."

I can't believe that they are going to charge for drinks. There was a time when if the flight was delayed for twenty minutes that would mean cocktails, beer and wine were free. That was back in the good old days when you could still get a free drink of water. Now, they charge for everything and overcharge at that. I guess they figure we can't walk to the store across the street where we might get a better price. No, we're trapped here as we have been for the last four hours and by charging for something to drink the airline is showing us how little regard that they have for us. I have my water with me that I have been rationing throughout the morning. I would love a beer about now but I have too hectic a schedule once we land. I have to get a rental car, fight rush hour traffic and try to get down to Laughlin in time for my eight o'clock show. I know that after my show tonight there are at least a couple of cold ones with my name on it waiting, but right now Jonas really looks like he could use a belt.

"How are you feeling doctor?" I ask.

He opens his eyes slowly and glances my way. He looks to be in a daze as he answers, "My lower back is really sore. She gave me quite a shot."

"I think that you should deck the bitch. It would make you feel a lot better." I say.

He lets out a quiet laugh and lays his head back in pain.

"Look, I know you're not the confrontational type, you're a lot like me in that way."

I say this and have gotten his attention because he has opened his eyes and is staring at me like I must be crazy. There's been a lot of that going around today.

"I thought that would get you. I just think that you should say something to her, let her know how you feel." I add.

"I think I've had enough discord for one day, thank you."

With that he closes his eyes and puts his head back against the seat rest.

"If you just let her get away with this she's going to keep going around bullying people." I tell him.

His eyes pop open again and he seems a bit agitated this time.

"Listen, I don't know the full extent of what is causing her to act this way. It could be an anger issue like you. It could be anger brought on by depression. It could be either of these things brought on by PMS. From the looks of her she's the right age to be going through menopause. It could be any of these or something completely unrelated. Now as I've discussed with you it takes time to come to an understanding of and dealing with an issue. Unfortunately we do not have that kind of time at our disposal here this afternoon. If she were interested in seeing me on a regular basis, then I would have no quandary. On the other hand, I am in quite a bit of pain at this time and really don't care to get involved."

He says as he closes his eyes yet again.

"I've got news for you. You are involved." I say.

As we await the arrival of the drink cart I have a thought.

"Say doctor, I hate to disturb you again, but I was just thinking, is it possible that you might have something in that bag of yours that might ease your pain a bit? Maybe some percoset, or vicodin, surely you at least have some valium in there?"

"Yes, I believe that I did put my pain pills in there, just in case." He replies.

"I would say that this is a case." I respond as I get up to retrieve his bag from the overhead.

I hand the bag to the doctor and he pulls out a bottle of pills and pops one into his mouth and swallows. He puts the bottle back into his bag and hands it to me.

"What you're not going to offer any to me?" I ask only half jokingly.

"They are my prescription, from my doctor for occasional back pain which of course I am now experiencing. They are not something that I am going to pass out like candy." He tells me.

"I don't see why not. I mean if you need more you can write your own prescription." I say just trying to ease his tension a little.

"When I tried discussing anti-depressants with you, you would have none of it. Now, you're surprised that I'm not some sort of walking drug dispenser." He says sternly

"I don't want to have to take them all of the time, but if they were available for occasional recreational use…"

He interrupts, "I'm sorry, I'm not that kind of doctor."

He's not that kind of doctor. There are enough of them out there. Writing illegal prescriptions, passing out drugs like they are candy, getting hooked on the junk themselves, totally ignoring what is right and wrong. Dr. Amile Jonas is not like that, as I look at him now I realize that he truly is a good man. I know that when I first started going to him I really thought it was nothing but a load of bullshit, but he really cares. That's an important quality in a person. If he didn't care he wouldn't be making this trip with me and because of that compassion look at what happened to him. He had to endure four long hours trapped here before we even took off. He was unable to use the rest room despite the fact that he was damn near ready to explode and then he was trying to calm down a frantic woman. And what does he get for all of his troubles? A fist to the kidneys!

When the drink cart nears I am seething inside. Barbara is just going about her business as if nothing happened. Look at the way she has that fake smile painted on her face as she charges for the tiny, pathetic, half filled plastic cups of soda. I notice that quite a few of passengers are shelling out the money for alcohol to calm their frazzled nerves. I wish that I could join them, but as I said I have a frenzied day ahead. I decide to make Jonas an offer.

"Doctor, I'd like to buy you a drink."

He opens his eyes and notices the drink cart nearing our vicinity. It is the first time that he has laid eyes on Barbara since she hit him. I sense a bit of anxiety, not to mention a bit of anger in his eyes. Why shouldn't he be pissed? I mean he can talk all he wants about understanding people's problems but that's all left behind when one of them knocks you out.

"I think I'll just get some water, but thank you anyway." He says.

"You can get water. Get it on the side. I really think that you could use a drink." I say.

"You saw that I just took a pill. I really don't think that it would be wise to mix alcohol." He says.

"One little glass of wine isn't going to hurt you. If anything it will help to calm you down and you can get some sleep, maybe a little nap will help the pain in your back." I say.

The drink cart arrives at our row and the woman that shall forever more be known as the nice flight attendant will be taking our orders. Barbara won't even look at either one of us. She doesn't look like she's embarrassed by her actions but more that she is put out by the fact that we are still here. If she had her way she would have just finished the job. Dismember Jonas and flush the parts out into space. Then she would make sure that I would never tell a soul what I saw happen on that airplane and now she has to serve us drinks.

As the drink cart pulls up beside us I begin to fantasize about Jonas getting up and knocking Barbara into the middle of next week. Witnessing something like that would surely make up for everything I've been through so far today. But it's not to be, Jonas just isn't that type. It's a pity really.

The enormous creature in the seat next to me has woken from his nap and it must be feeding time. He reaches for the bag he deposited under the seat in front of him when he sat down. As he leans forward he thrusts me almost into the seat in front of me. From his bag he grabs a package of barbeque chips and a diet coke. Diet coke, are you fucking kidding me? Are you suddenly counting calories? Hell if you keep this up I might be able to fit into my seat by the time we reach Las Vegas.

I just don't get it. It seems to happen all of the time. If you ever witness fat people ordering at a fast food restaurant, they will always order the biggest size of the most disgusting foods on the menu and a diet soda. I guess that you have to draw the line somewhere like it makes a difference. I imagine that the rationalization behind this is if you order the diet soda, then you can super-size your fries because of the calories you're saving.

"Would you like something to drink sir?" She asks me.

"No, I'm all set." I answer indignantly.

I just find it appalling that they would have the gall to charge for drinks after all we've been through today.

"I would like to get something for this gentleman." I say as I point toward Jonas and ask him, "What would you like Doctor Jonas? Some wine maybe?"

"Jack Daniels. Make it a double." He blurts out.

Jonas has apparently reconsidered the notion of mixing alcohol with his pain pill. Barbara seems reluctant as she reaches down and hands the two bottles to the other flight attendant.

"Would you like some ice with that?" She asks.

"Yes, please." He answers.

She places the bottles on Jonas tray and then fills a plastic cup with ice and hands it to him.

She then hands us both a small package and says, "This is compliments of the airline."

Oh boy, it looks like we're getting a free bag of pretzel dust! I guess it's the least they can do for jerking us around for four hours.

I attempt to reach for my wallet and realize that I will not be able to get at it without getting a bit more acquainted with my seat mate than I would care to on the first date. The flight attendant shakes her head as if to say don't bother and waves her hand in the same motion. I guess they figure Jonas can have a free drink. It's the least that they can do.

As she passes I notice Barbara give Jonas a dirty look as if he is the one that is wrong here. I think to myself that she's lucky that he doesn't knock her teeth down her throat and then consider doing it myself. Jonas is oblivious to the whole thing and is too busy twisting open the Jack Daniels and pouring them over the ice.

"Ahhh." He lets out as he takes the first sip.

"That'll help your back." I say.

"It may not help the pain but it should at the very least make it more tolerable." He says.

"Did you notice the way that bitch was looking at you?" I ask.

He waves his hand and shakes his head to let me know that he really doesn't want to talk about it. He takes a look over and out of the window.

"I must admit that there was a time today when I was quite doubtful that we would ever actually take off." He says.

"You're not the only one." I say.

He takes a look at his watch and then at me.

"You're going to be cutting it kind of close aren't you?" He asks

"Isn't it your job to keep me from stressing out?" I ask him sarcastically.

"I'm sorry you're right, that was insensitive of me. I guess I'm not myself right now." Jonas says apologetically.

"Well, that's to be expected. You took one hell of a shot back there." I say.

Jonas rubs the sore spot on his back and nods his head knowingly.

"Just remain calm, you've done a terrific job so far today and the worst part is over." He assures me.

I won't argue with him because we really don't know what lies ahead and I've trained myself to always expect the worst. That way it won't hurt as much when it happens. Even though I know deep down in my soul that this adventure is far from over and that things can get even more treacherous down the road, there's no sense in relaying this information to Jonas. He's suffered enough already.

"If there are no other problems and if the luggage doesn't take too long, which would be a miracle with this airline and if the line isn't too long at the rental car agency, and then if traffic isn't too hideous getting out of Vegas, if and only if all of these things work out for me, then I may get down to Laughlin about half an hour before the show." I say.

"And if the seas part and the angels fly down from heaven..." Jonas laughs as he says this and I know that he's just making light of the situation to try to keep me composed but deep down inside right now I'm really stressing, I'm just doing a really good job of not letting it show.

I open my package of pretzel dust, four of five tiny pretzels, each one smaller than a thumbnail.

"Can you believe this?" I ask as I show the contents to Jonas.

"Is that all that's in there?" He asks.

"That's it. Four hours on the ground, another four or five in the air and this is supposed to sustain us! That is unless I want to pay some ridiculous amount for a stale sandwich." I answer.

"Would you like something to eat? I'll buy it for you." Jonas offers.

"No, thank you anyway. If I really wanted something I would buy it myself. It's just the principal of the whole thing. I mean I paid my air fare, then it's twenty five more dollars for my luggage and now they want money for food. What's next, pay toilets?" I say and I can see that the thought of the last one gives the doctor a shudder.

I notice that my seat mate has already finished off his entire bag and is now staring at the contents in my hand. I see what appears to be a puddle of drool falling from his lip. I shove the pretzels into my mouth, chew a few times and they are gone. I wash it down with some water.

"I probably should have saved some for later." I say sarcastically.

"Would you like mine?" Jonas asks as he holds the bag out toward me.

"No, I'm full. I really made a pig of myself. I should have never eaten the whole bag like that." I say mockingly.

"I really don't want them." Jonas says as he waves the bag at me.

"I'll take them!"

My seat mate says as he snatches the package from Jonas in a swift motion that reminds me of a frog eating a fly. He rips the bag open and dumps it right down his throat. I don't think there was even any chewing involved. I guess he deserves a second bag; he is having the diet coke after all. Not only that but he is a growing boy. The problem is that if he grows any more I'm going to have to sit on the armrest!

Jonas takes a long swig of his Jack Daniels and says, "I think that I'm beginning to feel better already. I'm really not much of a drinker you know."

"Remember you had the pain pill with it. You just needed something to relax you. It's been a hell of a day for all of us. I wish I could join you but I still have a long road ahead of me" I say.

"I guess you're right." He says and then he downs the rest of the drink. "Damn, that was good." He says.

I look up and see the woman that was causing the commotion that led to Jonas getting knocked down is now approaching him.

"Excuse me, I don't want to interrupt, but I'd just like to say that I'm sorry about what happened back there." She says to him.

"Why should you be sorry? You didn't have anything to do with it." He says to her.

"I just feel that I'm responsible. I mean I was the one you were trying to help. Are you really a psychiatrist?" She asks.

"Yes, I'm Doctor Amile Jonas." He responds as he holds out his hand.

She shakes his hand and says, "I'm Julia. I just feel so terrible about what happened. It's just that at the time I felt like I was going to lose it if I didn't get off of the plane."

"Are you all right now?" He asks.

"Yes, since we've started actually moving I don't feel quite so trapped." She answers.

"Well, just know that I'm here if you need me." Jonas assures her as she walks away. "I think that I could use a refill." He says as he holds up the two empty Jack Daniels mini bottles.

There was a moment when I thought to myself that the doctor probably didn't need the second drink, not to mention the third.

Not on top of the pain medication anyway. It's just that I've never been very good at being the voice of reason. Then again you would think the flight attendants might have cut him off instead of giving him all of the free booze he wanted. Maybe they were just trying to make amends for the way he had been treated. Either that or they were hoping maybe he would get drunk enough to either forget what had happened or maybe cause an incident that would justify Barbara taking him out.

"Just look at him he's out of control, he's lucky that he only took that shot to the kidneys. We should have kicked his drunken ass off the plane before we left Pittsburgh."

About an hour outside of Las Vegas it was obvious that Jonas was no longer feeling any pain. It also occurred to me that we had now reversed roles. The original plan was that he would act as my guardian, making sure I didn't once again lose control and lose my flying privileges for good. Now however the tables had turned and I would have to do all that I could to prevent him from causing a scene and making a total ass out of himself.

"You know...muh back duzn't hurd at all. Ash a mattuh a fact, I'm feelin pretty good rie now, yezzir, pretty damn good rie now."

He's beginning to slur his speech and I'm hoping that he won't become a violent drunk. I can't drink hard liquor myself because I become very confrontational. I'm one of those people. I also know people that become very happy and loving when they drink. There are also those that can drink alcohol all day and it doesn't seem to affect them at all. They have built up such a tolerance through years of abusing themselves that it's just another day another drink. Jonas on the other hand said that he's not much of a drinker and the pain medication that he took with it can't be a good mixture. My only hope is that we can make it out to Las Vegas before he gets out of hand. A stumbling drunk out there won't even get you a second look.

"Boy um really hungry. Wha huppined to muh prezels?"

He says this loud enough that people below us on the ground are probably looking around to see where the drunken babble is coming from.

"You're talking too loud. Try to speak softly." I tell him.

In a loud whisper he says. "Oh, um sorry, I wone do it again. I wuz jus wunderin what huppined to my prezels."

"You gave them to this guy sitting next to me." I say.

Jonas looks over at my seat mate who's been snoring like a cow now for the last hour or so. I know that before I said he was snoring like a moose, it's just that his snoring now is in a completely different even more disgusting pitch and by the sound of it I swear that you could milk the fat bastard right now.

Jonas looks over at this revolting creature and says, "He ay my prezels."

"Yes, you gave them to him." I say.

"Sonfabich, I'm really hungry. I can believe he ay my prezels!"

He's beginning to get loud again.

"Shhh, quiet, you've got to keep your voice down." I tell him.

"Why you let em e my prezels?"

"You said you didn't want them." I tell him.

"I wun em now!"

"Maybe they have some more. I'll ask the flight attendant when she comes around. Just try to keep your voice down." I tell him.

"Sonfabich ay my prezels. He dudn't need em, look at em he's fat enough."

I've got to keep this from turning into an ugly situation.

I see the good flight attendant wandering about in the front of the cabin.

"I'm going to go up and see if there are any pretzels left. I want you to promise me that you will stay here and remain quiet. Do you think that you can do that?" I ask.

"Yur gonna git me sum prezels. Yur sush a nice guy."

"You're going to stay here and remain quiet, right?" I say, he puts a drunken finger over his mouth in a shushing motion.

I get up and start toward the front of the cabin when Jonas pulls on the back of my shirt. I turn to see what he wants.

"Shee if ay have any peanus. I could really go for some peanus."

Now I know that he meant peanuts but in his drunken state he has gained the attention of quite a few passengers who are looking back to see who the guy is that just loudly declared that he could really go for some penis. One guy has a look on his face like he would be more than happy to oblige this request. I'd better keep an eye on this guy.

When I get up from my seat I realize that my neck is quite stiff and my right shoulder is in a great deal of pain from sitting in such an awkward position for so long. I try to work out the kinks as I walk but this feels like it might be with me for a while. When I reach the front of the cabin I see that Barbara is seated and reading a magazine, she looks up at me and says.

"You can't be up here."

I really didn't want to deal with her but since she started it I say, "I just wanted to see if there might be any pretzels left, maybe some peanuts. My friend didn't have any before and he's kind of hungry."

"We already did the service." She blurts out in true Nazi fashion.

I really don't want to get into it with her, not this close to finally getting released from this prison in the sky. I turn and begin to head back to my seat when the nice flight attendant reaches down and pulls out about four or five bags of the pretzels and hands them to me.

"Thank you," I say, making sure to give Barbara a look that tells her that she can go fuck herself.

Before I can get away and head back to my seat I see Jonas stumbling his way into the passageway where we are.

"Come on, I've got your pretzels." I say, hoping that he will follow me back to our seats without doing anything.

I'm thinking that Barbara shouldn't look at him the way she is right now because at this time he's in no condition to be expected to act rationally.

I put my arm around his shoulder and say, "Let's get back to our seats and you can eat your pretzels. They have work to do up here."

I can see by the way that he is looking at Barbara that it won't be easy to get him out of here. I show him the pretzels.

"Look at all of the pretzels they gave you. Let's get back to the seats."

He attempts to adjust his posture so he is standing as straight as possible as he looks down at where she is sitting. I am sure they are about to come to blows. I'm also sure that she is going to kick the living piss out of him. She already took him when he was sober, in his current condition she'll pulverize him.

"Come on doctor; let's get back to our seats." I say, he'll have none of it and bats my hand away as I try to get him to follow me.

"Madam, I think you owe me a apology." He slurs.

"A what?" She asks. "Apology." He responds.

"Look, I owe you nothing. It's my job to make sure that we have order on this flight and you were told to take your seat because we were moving, but I guess that you think you're special and you don't have to listen to instructions because you went wandering around the cabin. Now when you do something like that I can't be sure what you are up to. My job first and foremost is to maintain the safety of the other passengers!" She responds.

"I aszure you my good lady that I wazzin tryin to cuz any problems. Ish my job to help people wif problems. I am e'fact a doctor, a doctor of psychology!"

I really thought that he was going to get stuck on psychology but he spit that one out clearer than any of the rest of his drunken babble, I guess it just goes to show what you can accomplish when you take pride in what you do.

What we have here now is a stand off. He's not going to accept anything short of an apology and I can't imagine that she's ever said "I'm sorry" in her life. I'd like to just grab him by the collar of his shirt and drag him back to the seat but I know that he's not going to come along peacefully. I can't have another scene. If my future of flying wasn't hanging by such a thin thread I would really be egging him on right now. After a day like we've had I think my fellow passengers and I could really use some entertainment. There wasn't even an in flight movie so a good old fashioned brawl might do us all a world of good. I'm also thinking that I should just go back to my seat and let the drunken son of a bitch fend for himself. I can't do that though, he's helped me through some tough times, and I suppose that I can do the same for him.

"Why don't you just tell him that you're sorry?" I find myself asking Barbara.

"Why should I?" She asks.

"Becuz, youuu jus should, thas why." He babbles.

Looking at him now he's full of all the confidence and swagger of a drunk. He's ready to take on the world right now. The only problem is that he's going down if she blows on him hard enough.

"Look, he was just trying to help that woman back there." I say.

"What woman?" Barbara asks as if this is all new to her.

"You know, the woman that was throwing the fit, right when we were ready to take off. If it wasn't for Doctor Jonas here we probably would have had to go back to the gate and you would have had a real riot on your hands." I say this knowing that it is total bullshit, the only reason that woman stopped whining was the fear that if she didn't shut up Barbara would take her out the same way that she did with Jonas

The other flight attendant chimes in, "You know Barbara, I'm thinking that if all that this gentleman requires of you is an apology, he may be letting you off easy."

I'm thinking the same thing myself, but then again he's not going to be in any condition to file a report once we land. He'll be best served to go and disappear into the Vegas night.

"Carrie, I don't think that I owe anybody an apology." Barbara responds.

Carrie! That's her name; the good flight attendant is named Carrie.

"Do what you want, it's your head." Carrie says and as she does Barbara storms off like a spoiled child that doesn't like being scolded.

Jonas looks as if he's about to go out on his feet. I stand next to him and brace my hand on his shoulder to keep him from falling backward and will also be able to stop him if he begins to go forward. At this time he's kind of rocking back and forth and his legs are wobbling beneath him. He could go either way but at the same time he's being very stubborn in this drunken state.

"I wanna apolojy. Why wun sheee apalijize?"

If you've ever dealt with a drunk you know that they will go on and on about the same thing until it really starts to get on your nerves. Dr. Jonas is doing that to me right now.

"She did apologize. She said that she was very sorry for hitting you and that she hopes that you'll forgive her." I tell him knowing that even though I'm lying he's probably not going to be able to recall any of this when it's over anyway.

"I didin hear her."

He's getting really loud now and I need to get him back to his seat.

"I don't know why you didn't hear her. We both did, isn't that right Carrie?" Carrie shakes her head in agreement with me knowing well that all we are doing is consoling a drunk.

"Sum fa bitch, I don't remember." Jonas says in a way that I can see that he's starting to buy it.

"Probably because you had a little too much to drink," I say. "C'mon, let's go back to our seats."

Jonas follows me like an obedient child.

On the way back to the seats I see Barbara headed in our direction from making her rounds. She is charging toward us like a cheetah going after an antelope.

She's almost upon us when Jonas says it, "I wanna thak you. I really didin think you were the kine a person thaaa wud apolojize an you prove me wrong."

Barbara looks as though she's about to chew off his face.

"I didn't apologize to you, you drunken ass!" She blurts out. Jonas is oblivious to the insult that has just been hoisted upon him.

"You know wha I think. I thin we need a hug."

Jonas opens his arms and moves toward Barbara.

The fact that she is extremely annoyed by all of this makes this moment all the more enjoyable.

"This flight attendant apologized to you, isn't that enough? Do you really need a hug?" I ask.

"She apoljized? Why whadda she do?"

At this moment in time all the irritation that I've experienced today is worth it. I'm able to guide Jonas back to his seat. Carrie covers her mouth trying in vain to stifle a laugh. Barbara's face is so red that I am sure she's going to set off the fire alarm. I'd like to thank Jonas for this amusement but I'm sure that he will never remember.

I'm surrounded by stereo snoring as we make our descent into Las Vegas. My seat mate's eyes pop open as the wheels touch down. It's good to see that he was able to have a nice restful flight while inconveniencing those of us around him. I don't know how long it will take for my neck and right arm to recover if they ever do. Nobody should be forced to sit against a pile of fat for eight and a half hours the way that I was. Jonas is still out cold as the plane slows down and rolls toward the gate. I can only pray that there is a gate this time. I've been able to control my emotions thus far and I think Jonas would be very proud of me if he knew what the hell was going on. It's just that if they come on and say we're going to have to wait for a gate to open up I'm probably going to snap and Dr. Jonas won't be able to help.

The plane rolls along and I can feel that we are actually pulling toward a gate. Sweet freedom is so close now that you can almost taste it. I turn my cell phone back on as I feel the plane pull to a stop. I need to call my wife to let her know that we've finally made it but I've got the doctor here to deal with. He doesn't look like he's going to be coming to any time soon and it's going to be up to me to get him up and moving. The thought crosses my mind to just leave him here. Let him deal with whatever city he might have landed in when he finally comes around, which could be days from now. Hell he could actually end up back home and outside of a few missing days it would all be just a bad dream, but that would be really mean now wouldn't it?

Shaking him is doing me no good because he's resisting. He just keeps trying to brush me aside and go back to his golden slumber. This is going to be a real pain. I'm going to have to physically drag him from the plane and through the airport. I can't imagine he's going to be feeling too good either. He was having the kind of drunk that only a good ten or twelve hours of sleep followed by dry mouth and a throbbing headache, not to mention a day or two of feeling really bad, can cure. No, he's only been out for about half an hour, he's still going to be half in the bag only now with the headache and dry mouth to go along with it. The best thing for him would be to have a couple of more drinks and then crawl into bed and face the consequences tomorrow. Unfortunately I won't be able to help him. I've got to get down to Laughlin so I've got to ditch him and hope that he's able to survive on his own.

It's now four-thirty five Pacific Time. So we made decent time out here, once we actually took off that is. Hopefully there isn't too much of a delay with the luggage and no lines at the rental car terminal. I must be dreaming to think I could actually be in the car and on the road by five-thirty. I tell myself that even if I'm on the road by six as long as I really haul ass it will still give me maybe twenty minutes to jump into a quick shower before the show.

Jonas is a lot heavier than he looks. I realize this as I have to physically pull him from his seat. I have to do this with only my left arm since my right arm has been turned into an ineffective piece of equipment. If my right arm never recovers who can I sue? The airline? The fat guy next to me? Or maybe the hostess company for making those treats so tasty that the man was unable to resist them and as a result he's now the fat tub of goo you see before you today.

The fat tub that has rendered my right arm completely useless. In this land of frivolous law suits I should be able to sue somebody.

I can see that Jonas doesn't really know where he is right now and is having trouble maintaining his balance. Not only that but I am going to have to carry both of our bags over my bad shoulder while trying to keep him upright with my good arm. This is going to be interesting. I've got to make sure that he stays upright, at least until we get out of the plane. If he falls over they're probably going to be calling the authorities and then I'm going to have to stick around to make sure that Barbara doesn't give some false testimony and poor Jonas winds up in jail. It does occur to me how ironic it would be if he was here to keep me out of being arrested and then wound up there himself, but Nah.

As we head toward the mandatory bye-gauntlet, if you've ever flown you know what I'm talking about. The flight attendant stands in the front of the plane with a big painted on smile and says bye to each passenger as they exit. I find it to be quite an annoying thing to have to do and I'm sure that the flight attendant aren't too crazy about it, but up until now no airline has had the balls to put an end to this moronic procedure.

Barbara is acting like she is busy and has her back to us. It's probably best for all. She won't have to pretend to act pleasant and the rest of us won't have to hold back the temptation to spit right in her face. Carrie, who else, has been elected to do the honors. As can only be expected, most passengers aren't too polite as they try to put the journey through hell behind them. I can see her looking our way as we approach and can only hope that Barbara doesn't spot us and start some shit. "Is he all right?" Carrie asks as we pass by. "I'll take care of him. And thank you, you were very nice." I reply and make sure to put the emphasis on you. Just one last little jab at

Barbara as we exit and then we pass through the door and into the jet way and we're free!

Jonas certainly isn't getting any lighter as we enter the corridor of the airport in Las Vegas. His balance is getting worse by the second and it's becoming quite difficult to keep him upright as we navigate through what is always a large crowd.

I'm surprised to see this many people here right now what with the state of the economy and all. I've heard that the numbers are way down here but I'm seeing no indication of that here at the airport. Of course these could just be people that lost everything going for broke and now they can't get home. Now this is their home, McCarran Airport in Las Vegas.

Well it's a big house anyway and that's how we got into this financial mess in the first place, people that didn't have the money to afford bigger homes but purchased them anyway with the money that was loaned to them by the greedy pigs on Wall Street. It was all a big scam. The mortgage brokers knew that these people would never be able to pay back these loans but they gave them out anyway. Then they took out insurance against the fact that these people would not be able to pay off the loans. Then a handful of people that already had all of the money that they would ever need made another bundle. In the end that money came from the taxpayers. It's like some kind of game at that level. Whoever has the most wins! It's just that nobody won and now we're all fucked.

My cell phone begins to ring and I know that it has to be my wife. I don't know how she lived before the internet was invented. She likes to track my flights on line and if I don't call her within five minutes of landing she will call me. I never seem to have a free hand when she calls. She has a knack of catching me mid-urination or in this case, struggling to keep a drunken doctor upright.

I prop Jonas against the wall and lean up against him in an attempt to keep him standing as I answer the phone.

"Hello."

"John, you're there?"

"Yes, we finally made it."

"Weren't you going to call me?"

"Yes, I just got off of the plane. Not only that but I have something that I'm kind of dealing with here."

"You didn't do anything; you're not in trouble again are you?"

"No, nothing like that."

Jonas begins to slide down the wall.

"Listen I'll call you and tell you about it on my way down to Laughlin."

"All right, go ahead."

"Love you."

"Love you too."

I hang up the phone and try to stop him but it's too late. He's going all the way to the floor. I don't know if you realize this, but when a grown man slides down a wall and ends up sitting on his ass, ready to pass out in the middle of an airport, people tend to stare.

So now I've got a crowd of people gathering around staring, a drunken doctor that doesn't want to get up off of the floor and just a little over three hours to get our luggage, hopefully get his drunken ass into a cab, get to the rental car terminal, rent a car and make an hour and a half drive. Oh, did I mention that I have a show to do at the end of all of this. That was the whole reason for this trip after all.

"Come on Dr. Jonas, we have to go. You're going to have to get up." I try to reason with him.

"Uh staying here." He babbles.

"People are looking at you. Listen you didn't come all the way out to Las Vegas to stay at the airport. Let's get you to your hotel and you can take a nap."

"Uh fine."

This is going to be tough. Again I consider leaving him here only now the feeling is genuine. I'm really not in the mood to deal with this.

"Gonna be sick." He blurts out and I can see that he means fast.

I can't let it happen right here in the middle of the airport so I struggle to get him from the floor as he is fighting with me and we head for the nearest men's room, which luckily is right across the hall. It's a battle all the way and I'm waiting for the sounds of sickness but somehow we make it into the men's room.

If you've been in a men's room before you realize that the best place to get sick would be in the stall. Everybody will hear you but at least they won't be able to see you. If the stalls are all taken and it's a real emergency, you may be forced to use the trash can. They are always lined and won't be too hard to clean up. In an extreme case you may want to use the sink, but do the best you can to clean it before you leave. Jonas on the other hand has decided to vomit into a urinal in between two guys that are taking a leak.

"What the hell's the matter with you?" The biggest one asks.

Big guys always tend to be more confrontational. That's probably because they can be. This one might be a little pissed because Jonas just splashed some puke on his leg. Man for a guy that hasn't eaten since early this morning, he's certainly gushing. Now come the heaves and…what do you know, there's more in there. If he keeps going like this he's bound to hack up an organ, something important, his liver maybe, then we will have a real problem.

It seems like he's finally got it all out and I feel that it might be safe enough to go in.

"Are you all right?" I ask.

He begins once again.

"I guess not."

"Hey!" The big guy yells at me.

He's now at the sink wetting a paper towel and attempting to get the vomit off of his pants.

"What's the matter with your friend?" He asks.

"I think he got a hold of some bad shell fish." I answer.

"Like shit!" He says. I wouldn't have bought that one either.

"Why didn't he go into the stall?" He asks.

I look over and see that the doors to all are open so I can't tell him that they were occupied.

"He's claustrophobic." I say.

"Like shit!"

He finishes wiping his pants, disgustedly slams the paper towel into the trash and storms out. Like shit, yes it is like shit. What kind of shit have I gotten myself into?

After helping Jonas clean himself up and splash some cold water onto his face, he seems like he may have sobered up a bit. At least I think he will be able to walk now without total assistance.

"Are you OK?" I ask.

"Yesh, fine. Jush a little embarrassed."

He's embarrassed which is a good sign. Drunks tend not to give a damn. Then again, the fact that he's still slurring his speech let's me know that he's actually just a rare embarrassed drunk. This isn't going to get any easier.

"We've got to go down and get our luggage now. Do you think you can make it on your own?"

"Yesh, fine." He says as he staggers out of the men's room and back into the corridor.

I can see that he's having trouble keeping his balance as we continue on through the crowded airport. I'm having enough trouble carrying the two bags with my stiff arm and shoulder. I'm trying to let him make it on his own as best that he can. We reach the escalator that leads down to the baggage carousels and I grab him by the back of the shirt. The last thing we need right now is for Jonas to go head first into the crowd. That would be a hell of a way to begin a vacation in Las Vegas for anybody, being taken out by a drunken psychiatrist that took a header on the escalator.

There are a lot of superstitious people out there and they would surely take that as a premonition that this probably isn't going to be their week. "We got into town feeling very lucky and then we got bowled over by some son of a bitch on the escalator! After that we were afraid to even put a quarter into the machines. It just seemed like really bad mojo."

You would think that after the vomiting delay and the fact that one of us is really having a hard time walking, that surely our luggage would be waiting for us on the carousel when we arrived. Also after the four hours that we were held up in Pittsburgh, perhaps the airline would consider this flight to be kind of a priority, but that was not the case. The other passengers from our flight were waiting impatiently when we walked up. I could see some of them looking at us strangely. I suppose because we were the ones that caused such a commotion on the flight not to mention that one of us has to hold the other upright.

It's five o'clock now and I should have been to Laughlin hours ago. There is no sign of our luggage and I'm beginning to have second thoughts about just shoving Jonas into a cab. There are a lot of desperate people out there and he would be a prime candidate to get rolled. I'm thinking that I am probably going to have to make sure he gets to the hotel safely and that will mean taking him there myself. I know I can lose my temper and be a real bastard at times, but deep down I have a good heart and care about people, which is a real pity right now because it's only going to make me even later.

"What are we waiting for?" Jonas asks.

"We need to get our luggage." I reply.

"Diddin we already get it?" He asks.

"If we did we wouldn't be waiting here, now would we?" I respond.

"Whassat you're carrying?" He asks.

"These are the bags that we took on the plane with us." I answer.

"I think thashall we need."

I just ignore him this time. I'm really not in the mood to get into a debate with a drunk. The best way to deal with a drunk is to be in the same condition. Everything makes more sense that way because you are both looking at life in the same manner. It can be very annoying to deal with a drunk when you are perfectly sober, not to mention the fact that there are more important things that I have to deal with right now other than repeatedly answering the same questions. It must be hell to be a bartender and be put into this situation night after night. It's a wonder that you don't see them go off on a killing rampage like a postal worker every now and then.

The red light on the carousel begins to beep, which means that our luggage will be coming. I don't get too excited because my bag is usually one of the last to appear if it does at all. I have no idea what Jonas' bag looks like so I have to ask.

"What color is your bag?"

"Black." He answers.

Oh good, black. Ninety percent of all bags are black so things just keep getting better and better.

"Will you recognize it if you see it?" I ask.

"Of coursh I will. Here eh comes right now."

Jonas reaches out to grab a piece of luggage and a woman grabs it out from underneath him. He stumbles and almost falls face first onto the luggage carousel. For a moment I think that I should just let him go for a ride. Maybe somebody else will grab him and I won't have to worry about him anymore.

"Here comes our psychiatrist, thank goodness the airline didn't lose him. Grab him and let's head to the hotel."

Maybe I'll just let him go around once and if nobody else takes him then I'm stuck with him. It could be worth a shot.

"Ok, here it comes."

Jonas reaches out and tries to pull the bag off of the carousel. An elderly man grabs the other side of the handle and he and Jonas have a bit of a struggle before the elderly man is able to pry it away. He gives Jonas a cold stare as he leaves with his bag.

"Thaa guy jush stole my bag!" He says.

"Um, that bag was red. You told me that your bag was black." I say.

"It is black." He replies.

"Then that probably wasn't your bag, now was it?" I ask.

"It looked like mun." He says.

This is going to be a real chore, not just finding his actual bag but keeping him from getting his ass kicked again!

Miracle of miracles, I see my bag coming toward me. I grab the bag and pull it from the carousel.

"Thas not muh bag." He says.

"It's mine." I reply.

"I knew it wassin mine because ish brown. Mun's black." He says.

"Then why did you just try to grab a red bag?" I ask.

"Muh bag snot red, ish black I toll you."

Again, I should know better than to argue with a drunk.

I notice a black bag that is coming around for its third trip around. On a hunch I grab it and read the name tag. "Dr. Amile Jonas."

I pull the bag from the carousel and ask, "Does this look familiar?"

"Of coursh, tha's my bag." He says.

I pull up the handle and ask, "Do you think you can manage this?"

He takes hold of the handle, pulls it a few steps and it slips from his hands and falls behind him. He is now staggering and fumbling with the handle, trying desperately to get it back upright. There is no way that I am going to be able to handle the two carry-ons, pull the two checked bags and keep the doctor upright at the same time. I think for a moment and come up with a solution.

"Do you think that you can stand here for a minute while I go over and grab a luggage cart?" I ask.

"Yesh, I think I cun stan fur a minute. I've been standin since I wash one years old."

Right now I would probably have an easier time dealing with a one year old but I have no choice in the matter.

The rack where you can get a luggage cart is halfway across the airport. There's no sense in me dragging all of these bags over there with me just to lug them all the way back.

"I'm going to leave these here with you. Do you think that you can keep an eye on them while I'm gone?"

"Yesh." He slurs.

Although I know that I'm taking a big chance here, I have no other choice. I suppose I could ask somebody to baby sit him while I'm gone but that's probably too much to ask of anybody. I decide to go for it. I leave everything except my computer. That would be too easy for somebody to snatch right out from under his drunken nose.

He's not looking too stable as I hurry across the airport. I'm trying to keep an eye on him to make sure that he doesn't fall over or walk away or do anything else that a normal adult wouldn't do. I should be paying more attention to what's in front of me than what's behind and I accidentally bump into a guy. The guy looks to be about twenty-five to thirty, about one hundred and sixty pounds with a head shaved down to stubble and he's giving me a look like he's ready to go.

"Excuse me, I'm terribly sorry. I should have been paying attention." I say. Thinking that I have calmed the situation, I begin back on my way.

"Asshole!" He utters. Now, under normal circumstances this would have led to an altercation. Right now I would be explaining to him, probably with a finger in his face, that I had apologized and if he wasn't such a stupid piece of shit he would realize that should be good enough, or something to that effect. However these are not normal conditions, so I just let it go. I don't feel good about it, but it's what I have to do.

When I reach the luggage cart rack I see that is one dollar rental and you can get twenty-five cents back when you return it. Cost is of no importance right now, it's just a matter of getting this and getting back to Jonas before he does something stupid. I reach in my pocket and find that I only have fifty cents. I could have sworn that I had at least a dollar in change. That's when I remember the newspaper machine that stole my two quarters back in Pittsburgh. Son of a bitch! I see that there's a slot that takes dollar bills so I can use that.

I slide a dollar into the slot and it just sits there. This isn't working. I take the dollar out and try to smooth it out and give it another shot. Again it just sits there. At that moment a short dumpy woman in a uniform that indicates she is an airport employee walks by.

"That machine is broken. It won't take dollars. You'll have to use exact change." She says.

"Would you possibly have change for a dollar? I ask.

"No." She says and walks away.

You were a big fucking help, I think to myself. Now I've got to find change. I glance over at Jonas and can see that he's staggering and looking around everywhere except at the luggage. I've got to do this fast. I look around for a solution, someplace that I would be able to make change. There's a Starbucks, of course, isn't there always, but the line is too long. I don't have time to wait behind a group of people that are trying to fuel up on lattes for a long night of heavy gambling. This is something that I've got to get done quickly. I decide to go to the general public. I see a guy around my age, wearing glasses with thinning hair approaching. He looks friendly enough so I give it a shot.

"Excuse me sir, would you possibly have change for a dollar? I need quarters."

He digs into his pocket and pulls out two quarters.

"I only have two."

"I'll give you a buck for them." I say.

He's thinking about it. What's there to think about? You're making fifty cents, you just got into town and already you're ahead.

"Make it two." He says.

Reluctantly I pull out another dollar and we make the exchange as I think to myself, "I hope that you lose your ass this week you cheap son of a bitch", which manages to take some of the sting out of it.

On my way back to Jonas, with the luggage cart, I can see that he is now seated on top of his bag.

Things get much worse when I reach him, "Hic!"

Now he has the hiccups and they are coming in steady intervals, about thirty seconds apart.

"Hic!"

Thirty second pause, "HIC!"

Oh good now they're getting louder. It's now five-fifteen and I've got way too much to deal with. I get the doctor upright and load up the luggage cart with our bags. The easiest thing to do would be to just throw him on here too but I'm afraid that he would probably keep falling off which would further delay me.

"Come on." I say as I try to get him to stay next to me as I push the luggage out to the curb where we can catch the shuttle to the rental car center.

We have to cross through a steady stream of cabs and limos to the other curb where we can get onto the rental car bus. Luckily there is a crossing guard that stops traffic every few minutes when there seem to be enough people waiting to cross. Maneuvering the luggage cart and keeping Jonas upright in this sea of people is quite a chore. His hiccups are now becoming louder and more consistent, not to mention very annoying. We are now in line waiting for a bus. There is what looks like at least fifty or sixty people ahead of us in the roped off line. One bus after another comes along to haul the herds off to get their rental cars. There is no other airport in the country where I have seen an assembly line operation like this to get a rental car. At most airports the cars are either available right at the airport or there are shuttles for each individual agency that will take you to their hub, usually within the airport grounds. The sheer volume of constant tourist traffic has led Las Vegas to come up with this unique system.

There is a young couple in line in front of us and they are well aware of our presence, due to my companion's constant hiccupping. "Hic, Hic, Hic." The young woman, an attractive blonde that is well dressed and looks like she probably comes from a privileged upbringing, turns and gives a look like this is not something that she should have to tolerate. You've all seen the type, good looking, dressed to the nines, giving off the impression that they've had their ass kissed their whole lives and no compassion whatsoever for anyone that is not like them. This is when I begin to wish that Jonas had not gotten sick already. What a sight that would be to see him puke all over "little miss nothing bad should ever happens to me." She'd never recover from a thing like that. No matter how good she tried to feel about herself there would be that deep down fear that at any moment a drunken psychiatrist was going to come along and lose his lunch on her. Her life would become a downward spiral of dread and depression and nobody would be able to help her, especially not a psychiatrist, since that was the root of her problem in the first place. Hey, I can dream can't I?

The line is moving at quite a fast pace, they really have a hell of a system here, and I'm doing all I can to get Jonas to keep up. There are only a few people in front of us now so we will be getting onto the next bus. The bus pulls up and I see that the shuttle driver is helping people with their luggage, expecting a tip of course, but hey I need all of the help I can get. The first few passengers at least make an effort to hand their bags up to the driver, but not our little princess, she just leaves it on the curb and makes her way onto the shuttle. I kind of wish that the driver would just leave it there, but he probably knows that a bitch like that would go after his job if he did a thing like that to her.

"Hic!" It's our turn to get on now and I grab the first bag from the cart and hand it up to the driver. He's a big burly Hispanic and is working at a hectic pace to load up the bus. He grabs the first bag and positions it into a holding rack. "Hic!" I hand him the second bag and then grab Jonas by the back of his jacket because he's about to wonder away.

"Is he all right?" The driver asks me.

"He's fine." I assure him. "He just has this terrible case of the hiccups. Can you believe that he's had them constantly for three years now?"

The driver gives me a stare that tells me that he knows that I'm full of shit, but I also realize that there's no way this is the first drunk he's had on his bus. With the two bags on board I grab the carry-ons and take hold of Jonas to steer him up the steps of the bus. I notice an empty seat right next to the little bitch and plop Jonas down right next to her. Did I mention that I can be a real bastard sometimes?

It's only about a five minute trip to the rental car terminal but I'm concerned that Jonas might end up suffering from motion sickness and we're going to have a real mess on our hands. "Hic!" Jonas is hiccupping at a relentless pace now and I notice the other passengers staring at us. I just give them a shrug. On this day I'm really getting used to people staring at me.

When we arrive at the terminal I make the decision to let the other passengers disembark first. Even though I am really pressed for time I figure this is best for everybody. The driver is unloading the bags and lining them up on the walkway outside of the terminal which will help. The only problem is that I won't have the luxury of a cart here. I'm on my own with four bags and a drunken, hiccupping menace. The bus is empty now except for us and I help Jonas to his feet and we make our way to the front. Even though I have him by the jacket Jonas slips and almost takes a header down the steps. Luckily the driver is there and catches him and takes him out and leaves him next to the rest of the luggage. I get off and slip the driver a ten. Normally for a service like this I would only give them a buck, maybe two, but this is different. Here's a little etiquette advice, when somebody helps you to take two pieces of luggage and your drunken psychiatrist off of a shuttle bus, tip them well.

There is a short flight of steps that leads up to the entrance of the terminal.

I look toward Jonas and say, "Look, you're going to have to help me out here. I'm running really late and I can't take you and the luggage up the steps here. Do you think that maybe you would be able to take your own bag?"

"Hic!"

That's not the answer I was hoping for. The only way that I'm going to be able to get this accomplished will be to treat Jonas like a child. I take the handle from his bag and place it in his hand.

"Now follow me." I instruct him.

I start toward the door when I realize that I should have probably had him go first.

BOOM! I turn expecting to see Jonas down for the count but am relieved to see that it was just the bag that slipped from his hand. Once again he's bent over the bag, fumbling desperately to get it back upright.

"Shit!" I utter as I head back toward him.

I get the bag back upright and put the handle in his hand.

"Go ahead of me this time."

"Hic!"

I'll take that as a yes.

It's not the most graceful thing I've ever seen but he manages to make his way up the three steps without dropping his bag. We enter the rental car terminal; it's bigger than some airports I've been in. It's complete with newsstand-gift shops, food court and every rental car agency. I steer Jonas toward the Alamo counter and we get into line. There are only two people in front of us and they seem to be together. Hopefully this won't take very long.

"Hic!"

I'm thinking that maybe I should have left him out on the curb and come around to pick him up. It's just that I don't think he's in any condition to be left alone right now.

"Next." The short heavy set Hispanic woman behind the counter barks.

The couple in front of me is engaged in conversation and totally oblivious to the fact that they've been called.

"Next." She says again and again they do not respond.

"Excuse me, she's calling you." I say politely. They turn and look at me as if that was the rudest thing that anyone could have ever done. Like, how dare you interrupt our conversation just because you might have someplace that you need to be. Don't you realize how special we are? We'll get to the counter when we are darn good and ready and you peasant; well you'll just have to be patient. They reluctantly head up to the counter. Sometimes I really fucking hate people.

We're up next. I don't know whether I should tell Jonas to go over and take a seat or keep him next to me.

"Would you like to sit down? You can relax while I get the car."

"Hic!"

This time I don't know if that means yes or no.

"Next."

We're being paged. I walk over to the counter and Jonas heads over to the chair. I guess that was a yes. The woman behind the counter looks to be in her early to mid-sixties. Her hair is a sprayed mass that looks like some sort of helmet. The black is an obvious bad dye job that looks like it would run if she were sweating. Her face is way too pasty white to survive in this desert sun and the circle of bright red lipstick only makes it look worse. Then, on top of all of this, is the way that she's drawn on her eye lashes. They make her look like she's in a state of constant surprise, or she's some sort of deranged clown. This old girl would definitely scare the shit out of you if you ran into her in a dark alley.

I already have my driver's license and credit card in my hand when I reach the counter. I've gone through this procedure many times so I know the drill. I'm sure that a lot of the other idiots I've stood in line behind in these places had done it before but still they have to be reminded. "Driver's license and credit card please." They hand it over like they've never had to do it before and by the time they get out to the car the process has already been eliminated from their memory bank. The next time they'll have to be reminded all over again. "No need to hold on to that one, there's always somebody there to remind me what to do." I don't think that most people are stupid, just too lazy to retain knowledge.

Jonas has taken a seat for now but I know that I had better keep an eye on him. The luggage remains at the spot in front of the line where we were standing, everything is within sight range including the drunken doctor, and I can deal with getting my rental car.

"Reservation for John Knight," I say as I hand my license and credit card to the frightening woman.

I'm getting the feeling that she's going to stay with me for a long time, somewhere in the dark recesses of my brain. She'll probably pop up in a nightmare somewhere down the road. Who knows, it could be tonight. After a long, sleep deprived, stressful day, at some point I will fall into an almost coma like state and that's when she'll appear. She'll come at me with those hideous red lips in pucker stage and who knows how I will react. The thing with dreams is that you have no control over your actions. I could end up sucking face with this circus whore in a ghastly dream that will scar me for a long time. I should have rented from Avis.

"I see that you've requested the economy class. For five dollars a day more I can upgrade you to a mid-size which will give you more room." She says.

"No thank you." I reply. The old upgrade scam. What I have found is that they rarely have the economy cars on the lot so they have to upgrade you anyway. Trying to get more money out of you for something that they are going to do anyway should be against the law but instead these counter agents actually get bonuses for conning you into spending money that you didn't have to. If you rent cars often you will know this to be the case, but then again you could be a fucking idiot.

"Hic."

I didn't hear him sneak up on me, but Jonas is now standing by my side.

"I hava go to da bafroom." He mutters.

"Hold on a minute. I've got to get the car." I say.

"Will you need any additional coverage?" She asks.

"No." I answer and I decide to speed things up. "I don't need any insurance and I'll bring it back full." I say to keep her from asking me that one.

"Will there be any other drivers?" She asks.

"Hic!"

I can't resist this.

"Hic!"

He's going at it like a machine gun now.

"Hic!"

"Yes, as a matter of fact Dr. Jonas here will be driving down to Laughlin. That's where I'm headed. That's not a bad drive is it?" I say.

She takes a long frightened look at Jonas and if I didn't know better I would swear that her eye brows actually changed position and were now showing fear.

"Hic!"

"You know what, on second thought maybe I had better get that coverage." I say.

"Sir, I can't...He doesn't seem like...I mean..."

She is now in a state of panic. She's wondering what will happen to her if she let's this drunken psychiatrist leave here and take the wheel of a car that she rented to him. Two die on the way to Laughlin, Rental Car counter agent held on murder charges, news at eleven.

"Hava go to da bafroom." He mumbles.

The clown woman has actually gone a shade paler, which I wouldn't have believed humanly possible. If she gets any lighter she'll be transparent.

"There's a...there's a charge for an extra driver. I'll also have to see his driver's license." She quivers.

I should probably stop right now, but it's been a long grueling day. I need a laugh.

"Dr. Jonas, she's going to need to see your driver's license." I say.

Jonas looks at me like this is an odd request and then he reaches back for his wallet. Somehow, just trying to reach his arm behind his back has thrown off his entire equilibrium and he falls on his ass.

"Oh God." She says from behind the counter.

I see the look of horror on her face and I begin to feel bad. I guess that I can stop now.

"An extra charge you say. Do you know what, I think I'll just drive down there myself." I say.

She lets out a gasp and hands the paper work to me.

"Initial the circled areas and sign the bottom of the agreement." She instructs.

"Hic!" Jonas lets out from the floor.

I sign as quickly as possible. I've got to get him the hell out of here.

She hands me my copy and says, "Take this up the escalator out to the garage and show it to the attendant. They'll tell you which car to take."

Those are simple enough instructions but not when they include hauling two pieces of regular luggage, two carry-on bags and an inebriated shrink that is currently face down on the floor getting ready for a long winter's nap. No, this isn't going to be simple.

"Come on, get up!" I say as I attempt to get Jonas back on his feet.

"Tired" He slurs.

"I know that you're tired but you can't sleep here at the rental car terminal. If you get up I'll take you to your hotel and you'll have a nice comfortable bed."

We are now holding up the line because Jonas is trying to take a nap on the floor in front of the clown woman's counter. I notice two guys that are next up and they are finding the whole thing amusing, which is better than getting pissed about it. Hell, you're in Las Vegas. This whole town is one big freak show, why should the car rental terminal be any different?

I grab Jonas by his belt and pull his waste up. He's a dead weight right now and his feet and head are still on the floor. All that I have done is pulled his ass up a couple of feet.

"Get up! You're going to be arrested." I say as I give him a little kick in the shoes.

He is unenthusiastic about the whole thing but he manages to stand. The two guys waiting applaud mockingly and I just smile and wave at them.

"You're going to have to help with the bags." I tell him.

"Bafroom."

"All right, that will be our first stop." I tell him.

I can see the way that she is looking at us as we go away. We're not her problem anymore and if I'm stupid enough to let this drunk take the steering wheel it won't be on her head.

"Next." She says and the two gentlemen walk over to the counter, still laughing.

I see a men's room located right next to the escalator. I steer Jonas that way and lead him in. When we enter he stares at me and then at the urinals.

"You're on your own in here doctor. I'll watch the luggage while you go."

He stares at me some more.

"Could you hurry this up please? I'm really pressed for time!"

Jonas walks over to the urinal and I look at my watch. It's now five after six. I have an hour and a half drive and a drunk on my hands, not to mention that we are not even in the car yet. Jonas is fumbling with his pants now, trying to get them zipped back up I think.

"Come on, we have to get going." I tell him. He turns toward me and I notice that he has part of his shirt hanging out of his zipper

and the front of his pants is soaked, what little hair he has is messed
and he still has the hiccups. If only his other patients could see him
now I think to myself. I should take a picture of this, I mean it's not
everyday you can get a shot of your psychiatrist right after he pissed
himself.

I put the handle of his bag in his hand and lead him out. I notice
an elevator right outside the door and determine that this will be
the easiest means of transportation up one floor to the garage. I
certainly don't like the odds of Jonas on an escalator with a piece of
luggage right now. I hit the button and the doors open. What luck,
the elevator was right there. I coach him in and follow. I hit the button to go up and away we go. We reach the garage floor and the door
opens. Jonas walks out and begins to vomit violently. I guess the
motion was too much for him. I see that we are in a somewhat iso-
lated area so I try to stand in front of him to block everybody's view
while he looses whatever is left in him. He finishes and wipes his
hand over his mouth. He's sweating pretty badly now, on top of all
his other problems. His messed hair, his shirt sticking through the
zipper of the pants that he just pissed and the spot of dried vomit in
the corner of his mouth. Sorry ladies, he's taken.

"Oh God." He utters as he staggers forward.

"Are you all right?" I ask.

"Yes, I think so." He replies.

I listen for a minute. If nothing else this latest sickness seems to
have cured his hiccups.

"Come on, let's get out of here. Can you handle the bag?" I ask.

"Yeah." He groans as he grabs the handle.

We walk over to what appears to be the lot attendant, a twenty
something black guy that is wearing the Alamo uniform. I hand him
my agreement and he looks it over. .

"You can take any one of those over there." He says, handing the paper back to me and pointing in the direction of three Chrysler convertibles.

I'm guessing that these do not qualify as economy and I've saved myself five dollars a day by not being a sucker.

There's a choice between the ugly green, silver and red.

"Which one do you like doctor?" I ask of Jonas.

He points to the red one, which is actually the best looking of the three and I'm tempted to grab it and then the thought crosses my mind that you are more likely to get a speeding ticket in a red car. This is probably just another myth that has no facts to back it up, but I'm not willing to take the chance. By the time I get Jonas to his hotel I'm going to have to really kick it into high gear to get down to Laughlin on time. The last thing I need is to get stopped for speeding on this day.

"Let's go for the silver." I say as I open the front door and look for the trunk release.

I find it on the keychain hanging from the ignition then pop the trunk and load our bags. Now I open the passenger door and guide Jonas in. He's still fumbling with his seat belt when I get into the driver's side and I have to buckle him in as if I'm dealing with a child, which he pretty much is right now. I start the engine and pull out of the space and drive over to the exit.

As I hand the agreement to the gate attendant he asks, "Did you look over the car to make sure that there was no pre-existing damage?"

I reply, "Yes I did," even though it's not true.

I am in a hurry and I probably should have looked it over but from what I've seen there was nothing that stands out, nothing that they are going to hold against me anyway. The attendant hands back the paper work and we cruise down the ramp to the exit and I head toward Las Vegas Boulevard.

When we exit the rental terminal I realize that I've forgotten which hotel Jonas told me that he was booked into.

"Which hotel are you staying at?"

"I'm not at a hotel. I'm in a car." He answers.

"Yes, I realize that we're in a car right now, but you made plans to come out to Las Vegas and you made a reservation to stay at a hotel. What I need to know is which one."

Jonas begins to laugh. I strain my painful neck to look his way. I realize that this pain is much worse than I thought and it's still lingering an hour after leaving the plane. I may never be the same again.

"What's so funny?"

"You thaw this wash a hotel. Issa car!" He answers and then laughs some more.

We make the right turn onto Las Vegas Boulevard and I ask again, "Which hotel are you staying at?"

Jonas laughs some more. It's getting later by the minute and he is really a big pain in the ass! I begin to think that the way to go would be to just take him down to Laughlin with me for tonight, it's not like he's going to get much accomplished here. Plus somebody should really keep an eye on him. The problem with this plan is that I really don't want to show up, late as it will be, with an intoxicated therapist on my arm. Not to mention that he's already getting under my skin and I don't want to have him rooming with me for the night. There's also the fact that I would have to drive him all the way back here tomorrow and then back down to Laughlin. I've had enough traveling today thank you. Another problem would be that if he doesn't show up at his hotel tonight they will cancel his reservation and I could be stuck with him all week.

It's time to get tough, this time with authority, "Which hotel are you going to be staying at?"

"One in Las Vegas," he answers.

Right now I'm ready to kill him! I really don't have time to deal with this. Of course I could just pull over and throw him out of the car at the next gas station. It wouldn't be nice of me but it's an option if he doesn't give up the name of the hotel in the next minute or so.

"Look, I'm trying to be nice here. I don't know if you remember this but I have to drive all the way down to Laughlin and do a show after I drop you off. The only problem is that you won't tell me where I'm taking you. Now, if you don't tell me I'm going to have to just pull over and drop you off and then you'll be on your own."

"You're a good man." Is all that he says.

I've pretty much reached my boiling point now, "WHAT HOTEL? THAT'S ALL THAT I'M ASKING YOU, WHAT FUCKING HOTEL ARE YOU STAYING AT?"

"Doen remember." He answers.

YOU DON'T REMEMBER! HOW COULD YOU NOT REMEMBER? HOW WERE YOU PLANNING ON GETTING THERE IF YOU DON'T REMEMBER WHERE IT IS?"

"Izzon the paper." He answers.

I try to calm down. I don't want to lose my voice.

"What paper?" I ask.

"The one in ma brief case." He slurs.

"And where is your brief case?" I already know the answer as I ask the question so I am able to answer along with him.

"IN THE TRUNK!"

"FUCK!"

There's an AM/PM mini-mart up ahead on the right and I pull the car into the parking lot and screech to a halt. I leave the car running and release the trunk from the key chain. I get out of the car and run back to the trunk. I retrieve the brief case and get back into the car. To save time I try to open it myself but find that it's locked. It's got one of those combination systems on the top.

"Do you want to tell me the combination or would you rather open it yourself?"

"I'll do' it. He slurs.

I hand him the brief case and he stares at it.

"What's the problem, why aren't you opening it?"

"Doen rumumber da cominashion."

I don't think that there is a jury in the world that would convict me right now if I beat this man to death with his own brief case and the thought is crossing my mind.

"How could you not remember the combination? You probably open this everyday."

"doen know." He answers.

"Well think, it's probably a number that you could remember easily, one of your kid's birthdays, maybe."

"Ur Darlene Jessup's measurements." He says.

"Who is Darlene Jessup?" I ask.

"A gurl I day-ed when I wuz in collage. Ohh baby."

"Is that what it is?" I ask.

"No, it's sumthin else." He answers as he begins to fumble with the lock.

The brief case pops open and he pulls out a paper on top. "Here it iz." He hands me the paper and I see his confirmation letter for the Luxor.

The Luxor is across the boulevard from where we are now but

not far. I pull the car through the AM/PM parking lot and make a left. At the traffic light I make another left and the Luxor is now on the right side of the car. I pull up in front of the hotel and decide that this is as far as I'm going to be able to take Jonas if there is any hope of making it down to Laughlin in time for the show. I look over and he's starting to doze off again which could cause a problem but not for me. I flag down a bellman and pull Jonas' bag from the trunk. The bellman comes up to the car and grabs the bag and puts it onto a luggage cart. That's when I decide to explain my situation to him.

"I hate to do this but I'm in a real hurry here. Our flight was really late getting in. I have to get down to Laughlin by eight o'clock."

The bellman looks at his watch. It's now six-thirty.

"Good luck with that." He says.

"Tell me about it. The thing is, my friend in the car is staying here and he's not in the best condition right now. I was hoping that you could make sure that he gets checked in and up to his room OK. After that he's on his own, I won't hold you responsible."

I slip a twenty into his hand. I'm hoping that's enough, I'm not really familiar with what would be considered a proper tip in a situation like this.

"No problem." He says.

Of course he hasn't seen Jonas yet but this can't be the first time that he's had to deal with something like this.

I open the passenger door and find Jonas snoring loudly. I shake him awake and he tries to fight me off. He doesn't want to move and I don't have time to deal with this.

"Come on, this is the end of the road." I say.

"I'lll ahhhh...."

And he goes right back to sleep. I unbuckle his seat belt and try to pull him from the car.

"Lemme alone." He slurs.

"LET'S GO!"

Again we are drawing a crowd and I have to be careful not to get too physical with him. I shake him awake again. This time he seems to come to and looks around at his surroundings.

"This is your hotel." I say.

"Oh, oh."

He seems to be coming around.

"Can you make it out of the car?" I ask.

He takes a step out of the car and stumbles forward. I stop him before he falls flat on his face and get him upright.

"Is there room for him on that luggage cart?" I ask the bellman, only half joking.

"Oh, I think we'll be all right." He says as he takes Jonas by the arm.

"Who's this?" Jonas asks.

"This gentleman is going to help you get checked in and up to your room. Then you can get a nice nap." I say.

"Come on sir." The bellman says as he leads Jonas toward the entrance of the hotel.

"Thank you so much." I say.

"No problem." The bellman responds.

I was going to ask him if twenty was enough, but you don't want to give anyone an opening like that. Of course it's not enough if you're willing to offer more you idiot. I feel kind of bad leaving Jonas all alone in this condition as I watch him stumble into the hotel, but what can I do? The person that is really responsible for this is the one that suggested that he have a couple of drinks in the first place. Oh yeah, that would be me.

The Luxor fades into the distance in the rear view mirror as I make my way back to the freeway. As I enter the freeway traffic is kind of heavy, but at least we're moving. My cell phone rings and I remember that I was supposed to call my wife back. Of course I really haven't had a free hand up until now.

"Hello."

"John, what's going on?"

"I just started on my way down to Laughlin."

"You're just leaving now? What took so long?"

"Oh, it's a long story. Dr. Jonas got drunk on the plane and he was in really bad shape and I didn't think that I could just throw him into a cab, so I took him to his hotel."

"He got drunk, why did he get so drunk?"

"He was trying to relieve the pain."

"What pain?

"The pain in his back, from where the flight attendant hit him."

"The flight attendant hit him! Why would the flight attendant hit him?"

"She was kind of a psycho."

"Still, he must have done something." She says.

"He was trying to help a woman that was losing it."

"And the flight attendant hit him for that? That's no reason to hit somebody."

What my wife is saying makes perfect sense and looking back on the whole incident it becomes even more bizarre. The only problem is that I've really got to concentrate on getting to where I'm going and I shouldn't be on a phone.

"I'll tell you the whole story tomorrow. Right now I need to pay attention to where I'm driving."

I know that it's not the kind of story to tell and then just leave a person hanging, but I'm hoping that she will understand.

"All right, call me when you get there." She says.

"It will be fast, I'm going to be cutting it really close."

"OK, be careful, love you."

"Love you too."

Once you leave the city limits of Vegas, headed for Laughlin, you are really out in the middle of nowhere. It's nothing but desert until you hit Searchlight. Searchlight is a small town in the middle of nowhere that probably wouldn't even exist if there wasn't traffic going between Las Vegas and Laughlin. It's got one stop light, a couple of gas stations, a post office and a McDonald's. Oh and of course a couple of small Casinos. There is no place in the state of Nevada where you can't throw away your hard earned money for a shot at the big time.

There's no way that I'm going to be able to shower before my show. I'm not even going to be able to check into my room until later. I hate to have to wear the same clothes that I've had on all day but the shirts in my luggage have got to be extremely wrinkled after all the time that they've spent packed away. I remember that there is an iron and an ironing board backstage and I come up with a plan. I'll grab a shirt out of my luggage and iron it backstage while the opening act is on. At least that way I won't be too disgusting. Well, I won't feel as disgusting anyway.

I pull into the parking lot of the hotel at five after eight and park. I grab a shirt and don't even bother to close my luggage. There will be time for that later. As I rush into the show room I realize that I probably should have called to let them know that I was running late because the entertainment director is in a panic.

"We've been trying to call your room and they said you hadn't checked in." He says.

"That's because I haven't checked in yet. I'm just getting in. My flight was really late getting into Las Vegas."

He leads me back stage and lets out a sigh of relief.

"You should have called." He says.

"I know, I'm sorry," I say as I begin to iron my shirt.

Although I haven't even had time to even think about doing a show tonight, when I hit the stage I kick right in. Anytime I have a frustrating day like this I usually have a great show and tonight is no different. The stage is a great place to let go of aggravation. I feel bad for people that aren't able to do a show to release their stress. They have to take it out on their friends and family and all of those around them. Some days that's the only release that I have myself, luckily today is not one of those days. When I finish the show there is almost a sense of euphoria that overcomes me. I made it, all that happened today is behind me and I made it. I got here in time and did the show and it's over. Now I can relax.

My original plan was to check in, get up to my room get un-packed, jump in for a quick shower and then go back downstairs to get something to eat and maybe a couple of beers to unwind. That was the original plan. It's just that after I get out of the shower and about to dress to go downstairs I see the bed and it looks so tempt-ing. It's been such a long day and although I usually have trouble falling asleep I'm out not long after my head hits the pillow.

FIFTEEN

Riiiing...riiiiing....What the hell? After a day like yesterday you have a tendency to fall into an extremely deep sleep which I am now being rudely awakened from. When you travel as much as I do sometimes the first night takes some adjusting, waking up and getting your bearings. Where am I? Oh, that's right Laughlin. What's that ringing? Phone, which phone? Cell phone. What time is it? I look at the clock and see that it's seven AM. I normally turn off my cell phone when I'm on west coast time to avoid people back east, who are three hours ahead, from calling and waking me up. I guess I was so exhausted last night that I forgot. Still nobody usually calls this early.

"Hello."

"John, its doctor Jonas."

"Yeah..." I respond.

"I don't know where I am." He tells me.

Now I'm starting to come around and remember the events of the previous day. This statement by Jonas has given me reason for concern. The last time I saw him he was being led into the Luxor by the bellman and now he doesn't know where he is. The bellman didn't know us. What if the son of a bitch robbed Jonas and left him for dead in some alley. And to think that I gave him a big tip!

"What's around you, what does it look like" I ask.

"Well, it looks like a very nice room. I have a hot tub in the center and the bed is extremely comfortable. It's just that somebody threw my clothes all over the room."

The idiot's in his hotel room, a nice one at that, and he's calling me and waking me up to find out where he is. What about just opening the drapes and looking out? As for the clothes all over the room I don't think it would be too hard to find the culprit responsible for that, just look in the mirror.

"You're in your hotel room in Las Vegas." I tell him.

"I was hoping I was it's just that I don't remember how I got here." He tells me.

"That's understandable. You were bombed on your ass." I say.

"Wow, I don't remember any of that. Who would let me get so drunk?" He asks

"Let's not go looking for people to blame here." I respond.

"It's just that I don't even remember landing or anything. How did I get to the hotel?" He asks.

"I drove you."

"You drove? Where did you get a car?"

"I rented it. Don't you remember taking the shuttle to the rental car terminal?"

"No."

"What's the last thing that you do remember?"

"I remember being stuck in Pittsburgh because of the snow."

Now for the important question, "Do you remember the flight attendant pounding you?" I ask.

There's a long pause on the other end, then a groan. I think he remembers.

"Yeah, that's right. I was thinking maybe I dreamed that." He says.

"I'm afraid it wasn't a dream my friend." I say.

"It's just that after that I can't remember a thing." There's another pause on the other end and then, "Oh God! I didn't do anything to embarrass myself did I?"

There it is, the inevitable question that every drunk wants to know the answer to after drinking themselves into a black out. You already know the answer so why bother asking it. The question will be answered sooner or later when you run into somebody that either wants to fight or avoid you altogether. Of course you made a complete ass out of yourself. Jonas is in luck in this regard. The chances of him running into somebody that saw him last night is remote at best. In this way it becomes like the old tree falling in the woods question, if you didn't make an ass out of yourself in front of anybody you're ever going to see again, does it count?

"No, of course not," I tell him.

"That's good." He says.

"So how do you feel?" I ask.

"Not too good. My head feels like it's made of concrete and my eyes are throbbing, oh and my mouth feels like it's full of sand. Aside from that I feel like hell! "

"That's because you just woke up, you'll feel better in an hour or so." I tell him knowing I'm completely full of shit.

What he's about to find out is that there's no worse hangover than a desert hangover. One of the main reasons for a hangover is dehydration which means out here it's ten times worse. In the desert you are constantly dry to begin with. You need to put fluids into your body constantly and not the kind that come out of a Jack Daniel's bottle. No, Jonas is screwed and the only way that he would feel better right now would be to die.

"Why don't you go back to sleep, it's early yet." I say.

"I don't know, I'm feeling kind of empty. I think I need to eat something." He responds.

Of course he feels empty. What little that was inside of him was left at the airport and the car rental agency.

"Why don't you go downstairs and get something?" I ask.

"I'm still feeling kind of woozy." He tells me.

"You're in a hotel. Get yourself some room service. Get some toast and coffee and lots of juice, juice will help." I suggest.

"Yeah, that sounds good. I think that's what I'll do." He says.

"All right, you order yourself some food and I think I'm going to go back to sleep for an hour or two." I tell him.

"Oh, I'm sorry. All right, go on." He says

"OK, I'll give you a call later and see how you're doing." I say as I hang up the phone and make sure that it's shut off.

Now as I think about it I haven't had anything to eat for more than twenty-four hours, I'm kind of hungry myself. Then again there will still be food in an hour or two.

It's Ten AM when I finally open my eyes and decide to crawl out of bed. I could probably roll over and sleep another two or three hours if it weren't for the fact that my empty stomach is telling me it needs some food and fast. I splash some water on my face, run a quick comb through my hair, throw on some clothes and I'm on my way down the elevator to the coffee shop. I grab a newspaper at the gift shop before heading into the restaurant. I want to see if there's anything in there about the hell the airline put us through yesterday. Of course I know deep down there won't be since we didn't riot. Probably due to the fact that the one person that would have led the revolution, me, is lucky to be flying at all right now and I have to be extremely careful. Still, I'm proud of the control I showed yesterday.

Around noon I decide to give Jonas a call and see if he's doing any better.

"Hello."

"Hey, Doctor Jonas, it's John, called to see if you were feeling any better yet."

"I took your advice and had some coffee and a lot of juice."

"Did that help?"

"Not a bit." He laughs and continues. "Right now my head feels like it weighs five hundred pounds. I think I've drank two gallons of water and the only result is that I've visited the men's room at least a dozen times and my back feels like it was hit by a truck."

"Aside from that how do you like Vegas so far?" I ask.

He laughs before he answers, "I have to admit the place is spectacular, it's changed quite a bit since I was here last."

"Do you have any plans for the rest of the day?" I ask.

"I'm supposed to meet an old friend for dinner, somebody that I went to college with lives out here." He tells me.

"Man or woman?" I ask thinking that Jonas might be hooking up with an old flame.

"Man." He answers sternly.

I should have known better.

"I might take a couple of Tylenol and try to grab a nap this afternoon before we hook up." He says.

"That should help." I tell him

"Listen John, I thought you did a wonderful job of controlling your emotions yesterday, after all that was quite an ordeal we went through." He tells me.

"Yes it was and thanks for noticing." I say.

"Maybe our sessions are finally starting to pay off." He says.

"Yeah and maybe it was just the fear of losing my flying privileges all together." I respond.

"Listen, fear can be quite the motivator." He says.

"Either way I made it through." I tell him.

"Yes you did and that's important. I also want you to know that I appreciate all you did for me yesterday." He says.

"No problem." I respond.

"OK, enjoy your time in Laughlin."

"I'll do the best that I can. Enjoy yourself in Vegas and try not to give them all of your money."

"OK, heh heh..."

As he hung up the phone I couldn't help but notice that it seemed like a nervous kind of laugh he let out there in the end, as if he was trying not to tell me something. I'm probably just imagining it. He is extremely hung over after all.

It's Sunday, my last show was Saturday night and I'm driving back to the airport in Las Vegas. The problem is I haven't heard from Jonas since Tuesday. I've been calling all week. I've left countless messages for him at his hotel, the voice mail for his cell phone has been full since Thursday and I've come to the conclusion that he's dead. There can be no other explanation. A guy like Dr. Jonas just wasn't able to handle a town like Las Vegas on his own. He probably ended up getting conned and then robbed, beaten and left for dead by a group he trusted because that's just the kind of guy he was. For a while I thought maybe he could have hooked up with some cocktail waitress and decided to leave his wife and family and the two of them ran off to Mexico or somewhere together. But come on, this is Jonas we're talking about. Nah, he's dead.

The problem with all of this is that I'm still unable to fly on my own. Dr. Jonas is my escort home, without him I don't know what I'm going to do. I've decided to make the drive over to Las Vegas and throw myself at the mercy of the airline. I'll just explain to them that my psychiatrist, the one that was supposed to fly home with me and keep me under control is now missing and presumed dead. You would think they would let me go just out of sympathy. I just wish it wasn't this airport since I do have some history here.

After I return the rental car, I'm back on the shuttle and unlike the last time I was here I'm wishing that Jonas was at my side right now, hiccups and all. Every time I ride this damn thing it's stressful. The last time I was worried I wouldn't make it to Laughlin on time, now I'm afraid I won't make it home at all.

The lines to check in at the Las Vegas airport are long, but seem to be moving swiftly. That's because of the new system where everybody checks themselves in at a computer kiosk. The computer kiosk, the perfect employee, they'll never demand a raise or better hours or more benefits and they never need a day off. In the event they break down, you only need one person to repair the whole lot of them. There are drawbacks of course; number one being that it is up to the general public to figure out how to work the thing. It's fairly simple really. You can either insert the credit card that you purchased the ticket with or type in your frequent flyer number or a simple code that is on your reservation sheet. It's easy enough that any five year old could figure it out. Unfortunately we're dealing with adults here, not five year olds. There's always a bunch of blank faced yokels standing around at the kiosk without a clue and usually only one airline employee available for every ten or fifteen idiots, to hold their hands and walk them through the process.

All of this is meaningless to me anyway. I can't check myself in since I'm on the no-fly list. I'm going to have to go up to an airline employee and hopefully get one that's either in a good mood or who is so fed up with the way they've been treated by the corporation that they just don't give a shit anymore. The problem is going to be finding either one. I look at my watch and see that I still have a lot of time. I made sure to arrive early to cover this from all angles. I decide to give Jonas another shot.

Outside the airport I find a place along the curb away from everybody and pull a small cigar from my bag. I light up and take a drag and then fish my cell phone out of my shirt pocket. I know it's probably useless but I attempt to get through to Dr. Jonas cell phone. It's been a few hours since I tried last and it's been futile the last few days. It's just that I don't know what else to do right now.

The voice mail comes on, "Hello this is Doctor Amile Jonas, please leave a message."

Then the bad news, "The mail box is currently full."

Son of a bitch! I can't believe that Jonas would leave me stranded like this. I guess I should be used to it by now I mean after the parking ticket, giving me the flu for Christmas and getting drunk and holding me up last week when I had to baby sit him I should be use to getting screwed over by this guy. It's just that of all I've had to deal with from him this is the worst. Here I am stranded at the airport with no way to get on a flight without his help and I can't even get in touch with him. The bastard had better be dead!

"Hello," my wife answers the phone back home.

"Hi, it's me. I've got a problem here." I tell her.

"What's wrong?" She asks.

"I'm at the airport and I don't know where the hell Dr. Jonas is. I haven't been able to get in touch with him since Tuesday, his voice mail is full and I can't get on the plane to come home without him." I explain.

"Why don't you try his answering service?" She suggests.

"It's a Sunday. I doubt there's anyway to get in touch with him." I say.

"Surely if there's an emergency there's a way to get in touch with him." She says.

"Yeah, I guess this is kind of an emergency."

"I would say so."

"All right, let me see if I can get a hold of him."

"Let me know what happens." She says.

"I will."

I have to dig through my bag for my phone book and find the number. I guess I should have the office number programmed into my phone by now but I'm just not ready to make that commitment yet. I have his business card in my book and dial the number to the office, which is not what I want but I hope it will give me the number for his answering service. I have a pen ready, I can write down the number on the back of this card.

"Hello, you have reached the office of Doctor Amile Jonas. Nobody is in at this time. If this is an emergency you can call our answering service at...."

I drop my pen, shit. I probably shouldn't be trying to make a phone call, write down a number and smoke at the same time, but hey we're in the age of multi-tasking aren't we? All right I'll just call back. The second time I get the number and write it down.

"Uhlo, dees is da anzuring suvice foh Doctah Amile Johnas."

Fuck, it's India! Even the emergency answering service for a doctor is in another country! Can't anybody in the United States answer the phone anymore?

Here we go, "Yes, hi. This is John Knight. I'm a patient of Dr. Jonas. It's very important that he get in touch with me."

"Yaas, what numbah can he reash you?"

I give my cell number and say, "It's extremely important."

"Yaas, vedy good."

I don't have much hope at this point.

I finish my cigar and look at my watch. It's now three-forty, about ten minutes since I called. I call back.

"Uhlo, dees is da anzuring suvice foh Doctah Amile Johnas."

"Yes, this is John Knight. I called a while ago. I was wondering if you were able to get in touch with Doctor Jonas yet."

"Yezzir, He not anzuring."

"He's not answering?" I say.

"Dat's right."

"Is there another way to get in touch with him?" I ask.

"Not if he not anzuring."

"Thank you, you've been a tremendous help." I say sarcastically.

"You wulcum."

I'm thinking that maybe if I were to just start screaming his name at the top of my lungs, wherever he may be he might hear me and call me back. Right now I'm just about ready to give it a shot. I'm sure if I were to start screaming out Jonas name as loudly as I could I would at least get some doctor to help me.

Walking back into the airport I realize I don't have any idea what I'm going to do. It would make no sense to stand in line just to get rejected. Maybe I could ask them to ship me as cargo. Maybe they could do that since I would be out of harms way. It might be a little cold but I bet I would have a lot more leg room.

Over the loud speaker I hear, "Paging John Knight, John Knight pick up the nearest courtesy phone to reach your party."

Did I just hear that?

Again, "Paging John Knight, John Knight please pick up the nearest courtesy phone to reach your party."

I did hear it, but who could be calling me? If it's Jonas why didn't he call me on my cell? Where's the nearest courtesy phone? I'm asking too many questions. I look around but I don't know where a courtesy phone would be. I flag down a security guard as he passes.

"Excuse me, where is a courtesy phone."

He doesn't say a word, just points to a wall across from where I'm standing.

"Thank you." I say and walk over to the phone, dragging my luggage behind me.

I pick up the phone and hear a woman's voice, "Page service."

At least she's speaking English that I can understand.

"Yes, this is John Knight, I was just being paged."

"Hang on for your party sir."

There's a pause and then a familiar voice, "John, its Doctor Jonas."

"Where are you? I've been trying to get in touch with you." I tell him.

"I'm at the airport." He responds.

"Here in Las Vegas?"

"Yes."

"I've been trying to get in touch with you since Wednesday. I'm really panicked here, where the hell have you been?" I ask."

"It's a long story. Why don't I tell it to you in person?" He responds.

"Yeah, why don't you." I shoot back.

When I see Jonas walking toward me, he's a mess. He looks like he hasn't shaved in a couple of days. His clothes are wrinkled and his hair, or what's left of it, is sticking out in all directions. Not only that but I can smell the alcohol on him when he gets within a few feet of me.

"Looks like you had a rough week." I say.

"You have no idea." He replies.

"Why didn't you call me back?" I ask.

"I'm sorry about that. I lost my cell phone." He says.

"You lost your cell phone? Where did you lose it?"

"If I knew where I lost it I could have probably found it. I had people calling it hoping that I would hear the ring. That alas went for not and it remains unaccounted for. Fortunately I was able to stop the account so nobody was able to use it."

"I left you voice mail." I say.

"Yes, my voice mail is still going through. I'm just unable to retrieve it until I get my new phone." He says.

"It's not going through anymore. Your mailbox is full." I tell him.

"Oh dear, this can't be good. I hope there were no emergencies. Oh, I guess they'll just have to fend for themselves until I can get in touch with them. I'm tired of everybody coming to me with their problems anyway. I have problems too you know!"

This was a completely different man than the one that I had dropped in front of the Luxor last week. At least he was different than the one that had boarded the flight out of Pittsburgh with me. The thing is I can't get on the flight without being escorted by this wreck of a man that is standing before me right now.

"So what the hell happened to you?" I ask.

He's somewhat hesitant, as if he really doesn't want to tell me but just has to tell somebody.

"Do you remember the other day, the last time that we spoke?" He asks.

"Yes, I remember." I reply.

"Do you remember you said something like don't lose all of your money?"

"I remember." I answer.

He begins to look down at his shoes. I can tell that he's embarrassed about what he's about to tell me.

"The thing is, when we talked…see what happened is that I went down to the casino and there was some room at a blackjack table and I hadn't been to Las Vegas in awhile, so I sat down and the next thing I know I lost five hundred dollars."

Five hundred dollars, I think to myself. This guy can make that in one morning of sociopaths and manic depressants.

"Yeah that's a lot, but you can make that back in no time." I tell him.

"I tried to." He says.

And there it is, Dr. Jonas, a man that should know better, a man that spends his time helping others with their emotional problems got caught up in the scam that keeps Las Vegas in business. Chasing the money that you lost, just trying to get back to even.

"How much?" I ask.

"By Wednesday night I was down five thousand dollars. Do you know they give you free drinks when you're gambling?" He says.

"Yeah, they're free. They only cost you five thousand dollars." I say.

"I was going to check out on Thursday and drive down to Laughlin to see you and just to get away from here, but then they offered to give me a free room through Saturday. I guess this is a slow time of year out here and they had rooms available. Anyway, I remembered that you said there isn't much to do in Laughlin and since the room was complimentary…so I stayed. I thought I was bound to get on a hot streak at some point and get back most of the money." He says.

"How much?" I ask again.

"Somewhere around thirty-five thousand." He says quietly.

"Holy shit! Thirty-five thousand? Does your wife know?"

"She does not." He answers.

The way he's standing there, humbled, nervous, not knowing what awaits him when he tells his wife the terrible news I feel sorry for him. He has that kind of teddy bear quality that makes you want to give him a big hug and tell him it will be all right. Of course I'm sure his wife won't have that reaction when he tells her what he did. She'll probably smack him across the side of the head right before she throws his ass out into the street. But, that's his problem. I've got a flight to catch.

I look him over and say, "We've got to get you cleaned up before we try to check in. Nobody is going to believe that you're a doctor looking the way that you do. We also better get some strong mints to stop you from smelling like a distillery."

It took some doing but we were able to make Jonas presentable enough to get me onto the flight. There were no problems everything was right on time, we left the gate right at five-forty-five, our scheduled departure time. Not only that but we had a much friendlier flight crew. It was dark the whole flight and most of the people were either sleeping or extremely quiet. I got lucky and the seat next to me was empty so I was able to sit in my full seat with a little room left over if I needed it. I picked up the Sunday LA Times and spent most of the flight reading. Jonas was very quiet. He looked like he was trying to doze but the stress from what he was facing at home wouldn't let him. No alcohol for him on this flight, he actually ordered milk to drink. It was close to one AM when we landed and I was anxious to get home. I could tell by looking at him that Jonas wasn't sharing my feelings. This is one flight that he wouldn't have minded being delayed. I really felt bad for him as we parted company.

"OK, I'll see you on Thursday then." He said.

"Yeah, see you on Thursday." I replied.

As he walked away I got the feeling that we wouldn't be spending a lot of time dealing with my problems at our next session.

SIXTEEN

Leaving the warmth of my car and going out into the wintry air takes some doing. It's like a punch in the face, brutal cold just shooting right through me. According to the weather report this is the coldest day of what has already been a long cruel winter. The high today is only supposed to reach about five degrees Fahrenheit and with factoring in wind chills and all, well it's really fucking cold. The last thing I wanted to do this morning was crawl out of bed for my session with Jonas but here I am. I think I had more than enough of him last week. I should get at least a month off after that whole ordeal. There's a strong wind blowing and even though I'm walking as fast as I can from the parking lot up the steps of the building it feels like I'm moving in slow motion.

Even with freezing temperature and the fact that the last place on earth that I wanted to go was for my weekly session, I was very calm on the drive here. I hit some traffic at the first tunnel and it didn't really faze me. I don't know if maybe I was just tired and numb or if this is actually starting to pay off. Whatever the reason I was feeling very relaxed.

That was until I got through the tunnel and the jackass in the BMW cut me off! The son of a bitch was on the phone, probably because nobody ever took the time to explain to him that he wasn't intelligent enough to try and do two things, like talking and driving, at the same time. The thing that really got under my skin was the fact that after he cut me off I don't think he even saw me as I drove up right behind him and started flashing my high beams. He just kept on talking on the phone and going along like nothing was wrong. That's when I considered driving up along side him and steering him off the road. He's just lucky that I'm able to control my anger now.

Once inside the lobby I decide against using the stairway. My body just doesn't feel like it wants to move today. I hit the button and wait for the ancient elevator. It's taking longer than usual this morning. I hit the button again and wait. This time I hold the button in and then hit it a second and third time. I don't know why Jonas keeps his office in such a rickety old building. He should move into a newer, more modern building. Of course that would cost more money and he's thirty five thousand in the hole right now. We may end up having these sessions in his car or maybe have to meet in the back of a church or a Denny's. The hell with it, I'll take the stairs. I'm at the top of the first landing when I hear the elevator door open in the lobby. Son of a Bitch!

As I enter the reception area of the office I wave and say hello to Lisa, the receptionist.

"Hi Lisa, how are you?"

She just stares at me and doesn't say a word. Man, I thought it was cold outside but she just chilled me. What did I do to her? Maybe she's depressed by the weather, or somebody died or she's premenstrual. Whatever it is I'm not going to pry, you just sit there in your misery and I'll sit here in mine. As a matter of fact it's not really all that warm in here, maybe I'll stand. Those wooden chairs in the waiting area are not looking all that inviting today. The door to the office opens slowly and Jonas pops his head out. He looks at me solemnly and says.

"Come on in John."

I knew that I should have called in sick. He looks like he's in worse shape than I thought.

I take my seat in the big comfortable leather chair and even though it feels warmer in here than in the waiting area, I leave my coat on. I still haven't gotten the chill out of my body.

"Are you planning on staying?" He asks grimly.

"Not if you're going to have that attitude." I say kidding.

"Whatever."

He says as he sits in the chair across from me. He buries his face in his hands and lets out a long sigh. I look around the room and notice a suitcase in the corner as well as various items of clothing scattered around the office.

"Are you having a rough week doctor?" I ask.

He lifts his head long enough to give me the news.

"My wife threw me out. She wants a divorce."

I wasn't expecting that. I knew that she'd be pissed and rightly so, but I never would have imagined that she would divorce him over it.

"I lost the down payment on the house that we were about to buy. It was my wife's dream house and now we can't get it and she doesn't ever want to see me again and none of this would have ever happened if I never met you!"

What? What was that last part? It sounds like he's trying to blame this on me somehow.

"What did you just say?" I ask.

"That's right, none of this would have ever happened if it wasn't for you. I would have never had to escort you on the flight to Las Vegas and you would have never gotten me drunk and I wouldn't have started gambling and my wife would be getting her dream house and my life wouldn't be a big pile of shit!"

"You can't be serious. There is no way you can possibly hold me responsible for this." I say.

"I have to blame somebody." He shoots back.

What kind of logic is that? I have to blame somebody. The thing is we all do it. Life's not going so well? That can't possibly be my fault can it? Blame somebody else. I know I do it myself. It's just that I never do it to anybody's face. Its one thing to do it behind a person's back but this guy just did it right to my face! That's not right, blaming me because he couldn't control his impulses. So you lost thirty five grand, most people right now wish that they had thirty five thousand in the bank they could lose. This guy has life by the balls and fucks it up and now he wants to pin it on me. You know I've really had it between struggling financially with what I've had to do because of my little incident on the plane and the economy going to shit and then there's the cold and gray weather everyday and on top of it all that idiot cut me off on the way here and then the elevator didn't work and now Jonas is blaming me because he can't control his drinking and gambling and...sometimes it's a combination of things stirring inside of you, simmering slowly, not quite yet reaching the boiling point, just simmering and then finally that last item is added and "You have to blame somebody? Is that what you're saying?"

I notice that I'm talking very loudly, yelling really. I'm now out of the chair and standing over Jonas, looking down at him as I shout. I can feel my teeth grinding as I gaze down at him. He looks very frail and hopeless right now and maybe a little frightened. I know I should just shut it down but I don't. That's my problem a lot of the time, even though I know I am behaving badly and maybe frightening some people, I need to release my anger somehow. It's the only thing important to me at that moment and that seems to be the case right now.

"Do you know what you put me through the day we flew into

Vegas? I had to baby sit you like you were a small child. I took you right up to the door of your hotel, even though I was running extremely late and I'm sorry that I didn't stick around and hold your hand the rest of the week to make sure you didn't lose the down payment for your house but I had someplace else that I had to be!"

As I look down I notice that Jonas is weeping uncontrollably and I begin to feel terrible.

Watching a grown man cry like a baby can have quite a calming effect on you. I sit back down across from him and pat his shoulder.

"Hey, I'm really sorry." I say.

"No, don't be sorry, you're right. If anybody should be apologizing it's me."

His speech is interrupted by gasps from the crying and it reminds me of how annoying he was when he had the hiccups. I walk over and grab the box of tissue from his desk and hand them to him.

"Thank you." He says as the crying begins to subside. "Please forgive me for becoming so emotional. I'm the doctor. I'm not the one that's supposed to become emotional."

"Don't worry about it. You've had a tough week." I say.

"I'm also sorry that I said it was your fault, I guess I was just looking to avoid placing the blame where it belongs, on me." He says.

"Hey we all do it. Blame somebody else for our own mistakes. It's like when people blame somebody else's kids for the way their child behaves. It's hard to accept that maybe we've screwed up ourselves." I say.

"It shouldn't be that way for me!" He shouts.

"Why not, you're human like the rest of us aren't you?" I ask.

"But I'm a doctor. A doctor of psychology, I'm supposed to know better."

I have no answer for him here because the thing is he really is supposed to know better.

"Do you know the amazing part of it John? While I was doing it I was having the time of my life. I didn't care about the money. It just seemed so meaningless to me. I spend all of my time trying to be a good husband and father when I'm at home. Then when I come here I'm listening to and trying to help others with their problems. I guess I just really needed a release. I'm constantly telling other people to find a way to free themselves, let go of that emotional baggage, involve yourself in an activity that gives you great pleasure."

He takes a pause, he's not crying anymore. He leans back in his chair and folds his hands behind his head. He looks like he's had a revelation of some sort and looks very content right now.

"When I was at the tables and I would get on a good roll and the people were cheering, I have to tell you it was one hell of a high. Then when I would get down it didn't bother me. I just figured I'd get it back and if not, well then so what. It's only money. Do you know when I came down off of that high?" He asks.

"When our flight took off to come home?" I answer.

"You're very good." He says.

Jonas seems to be calming down now and I've done the same myself. We both had a different way of releasing our emotions. I went about raving like a lunatic and he cried like a little girl, either way it wasn't pretty.

"What are you going to do?" I ask.

"I really don't know right now." He replies.

"You know when things look the worst they always turn around. Things will get better for you."

I say this even though I think it's a real crock.

"I know, I know that I will recover from this, in time." He says.

Well he bought it anyway and maybe there is some truth to positive thinking will lead to positive things happening in your life. I've just never tried it.

"I really appreciate you taking the time to listen to my problems. Here we are supposed to be dealing with you and we're spending the whole session on me." He says.

"Don't worry about it. You can pay me this week." I say.

"Don't worry this session is on the house." He says.

Didn't he hear what I just said? I wasn't looking for a free session; I told him that he could pay me! Maybe he thinks that I went into this psychology thing because of my love of people, but hey, I'm in it for the money!

"Actually you're the only patient that I've seen this week. I've canceled all of my other appointments. I feel really bad about it actually. I didn't see anybody last week when I was off having what I thought was a good time and then I blow them off again this week. These people depend on me. They need my help and I've let them down. Just like I let my wife down and I suppose most of all I've let myself down."

He looks like he's ready to start bawling again and I really don't have the stomach to listen to it so I had better say something.

"It's easy to know better after the fact," is the best that I can come up with.

"You're right." He says.

He bought this too. I'm getting really good at this psychology stuff. Maybe I can open up a little office on the side. "Dr. John's House of Pain and Suffering," It has a nice ring to it.

Jonas stands and walks over to his desk. He begins to shuffle through some papers as if he's looking for something then he stops.

He looks confused and I can see that what he is really looking for are some answers or maybe a shot at going back in time and reversing the events of the week before. That's not going to happen. I know because I've wished for it enough times in my own life. No you're just going to have to live through this and hope that it's not going to get any worse.

"We're really not going to accomplish anything here today. Why don't we just pick it up next week? I should be in better shape by then." He says.

Next week? I was really hoping that there wouldn't be a next week or any more weeks for that matter. I really think that I proved that I could control my anger when I fly when we were trapped on that torture chamber last week and I didn't kill anybody. Hell we should have all been given medals for that. We didn't even get vouchers toward a future flight. Of course the big drawback for those would be that we would have to fly on the same airline.

"I was really thinking, hoping actually that I wouldn't have to come here anymore. I thought I showed how well I was able to control myself during our flight from hell last week. Wouldn't you agree?"

He looks like he is searching for the right way to tell me this, which usually means that it isn't going to be good news.

"Yes, I agree that you were quite well behaved. Especially under what could only be classified as excruciating circumstances. I was quite proud of you, the part that I remember anyway. Do I think that you still have anger issues? Yes, you just went off the handle a few minutes ago. I will agree to sign off on you flying alone, but only under the condition that you continue to come in here and we work to get you to the point where you will no longer go into an uncontrollable rage without thinking things through first. I think the airlines will accept that you are undergoing counseling for your anger issues. Then again they may not. I don't know but we can give it a shot. I'm just not ready to release you all together right now. The thing is you've only been coming in here for a short time and I'm not a miracle worker. I wish I was. It would be nice if patients came in to see me once and walked out with all of their problems solved. Unfortunately therapy doesn't work that way. It can be a long drawn out process. Sometimes it takes years. In some cases the patient never gets better. I believe in you, I've seen you deal with the worst and come through it. It's my job to make sure that you are able to do that every time. I'm afraid that if you stop coming in here now you will just revert to the way you were. We've made some progress here in the short time you've been coming. I just think we can go further. I also should remind you that the reason you were sent to me in the first place was because a judge in Las Vegas felt that you had anger management problems, which as you remember led to an incident in which the authorities had to be called in. My reputation is on the line here. If I were to release you as a patient now they would probably think that something unscrupulous was going on. That's why I'm unable to do it. You understand don't you?"

"Yes." I reply but that really wasn't the answer I wanted to hear.

There is a long awkward silence and I can see that Jonas is aware I was hoping for him to tell me something different.

"You do realize that this is necessary don't you?" He asks.

"I can see where you are coming from. It's just that this is getting to be kind of expensive, not only that but I have a lot of work coming up and I won't be able to get in here quite as often." I say.

"That's quite all right. Why don't we just work around your schedule? You can come in when you're in town and always feel free to call if you are having any issues when you are out on the road.

This way it won't be quite as costly for you and by the way if that ever becomes a concern just let me know and we can work out some kind of a payment plan." He tells me.

"I appreciate that." I say.

"I would like to see this through. I think that in time we can get you to the point where you see how minor something is that in the past you would have, pardon my French, gone ape shit over." He says.

His terminology makes me laugh, "Pardon my French? Do people still say that?" I ask.

He lets out an embarrassed laugh.

"I'm just trying to get my point across." He says.

He walks over to his desk and opens his calendar book.

"So when will you be able to come in again? And I also should add that it doesn't necessarily have to be on Thursday. If you are in town for a few days and want to come in we can work around your schedule." He says.

"I'm usually really busy when I'm only in for a short time." I say.

"That's understandable. Just know that I'm here if you need me." He says.

"OK." I reply. "You can just make an appointment with Lisa on your way out." He says.

"I think that she's kind of pissed at me. You must have told her that I was responsible for you losing all of that money." I say.

"I never mentioned a thing about it to her. She's just in one of her moods." He assures me.

I stand to leave and Jonas walks me to the door. When we get to the door Jonas holds out his hand to shake mine but I feel that after a session like the one we've just been through we need more than that. I put my arms around him and give him a hug.

"Good luck to you Doc." I say.

"Same to you." He says.

We stop embracing and he says, "Remember I'm here if you need me. And we're not done. Just because I'm willing to give you some flexibility with our sessions does not mean that you are going to stop coming here altogether."

"Yes, I know, and also if you need somebody to talk to feel free to call. I know that you're going through a tough time." I say.

"Thank you." He says.

"You'll be all right." I say as I exit.

Jonas closes the door behind me and I have a good feeling. He really is helping me and I think I did the same for him today. He needed to unload his problems today and I was there for him. I wonder what hours I should keep when I open up my office.

As I walk down the three flights of stairs I notice a strange feeling has overcome me. I guess the best way to describe it would be some kind of euphoria. I don't know what it is specifically, whether it was helping Dr. Jonas with his problems in there or the fact that I may be able to get my flying privileges back, but I'm feeling really good about myself. There is a sense of calmness and optimism that I can't remember experiencing in a very long time if ever.

The thing with Jonas, as bad as things look for him at this moment, it's going to get better. He probably has a nice settlement coming from the airline for the way he was abused that will more than make up for what he lost in Las Vegas. That's the way it is for people with money, even when they get down it's not for too long. Under normal circumstances this would really piss me off but Jonas is a good guy and I can only wish him the best. Once he's able to afford the down payment on the house again I'm sure his wife will be happy to take him back. Hell, she'll probably take him back anyway. They've been together a long time and I'm sure that once the incident is far enough behind them she will be able to forgive him. Of course he's going to have to do a lot of ass kissing for a long time but that's all part of the deal.

Walking outside into the chill doesn't even faze me. I have such a warm feeling inside of me right now. I'm thinking to myself that if things can work out for the doctor, why not for me? It looks like I will be able to fly again soon, which means I can work. I took a bit of a hit financially but it wasn't as bad as I thought it would be. It never is. I always set myself up for total devastation, go through constant worry and stress and for no reason. It's just something that I do over and over and never learn. But no more. All this time that Dr. Jonas has been telling me this about myself I just let it go in one ear and out the other but now that he has set himself up as a shining example of somebody that is in a bad situation I'm finally able to see that it's all meaningless. It's stupid to constantly dwell on the negative when in the end things always work themselves out. I've spent years allowing myself to get angry over little things that I have no control over and it doesn't help the situation at all and if anything only makes it worse.

From this day on I'm going to look at life with a different attitude, a positive attitude. I've been at what was probably my lowest point and I've made it through. Better days lie ahead for me now. This is like a moment of revelation for me and I'm tempted to run up the stairs and share this with Dr. Jonas. I'm about to turn around toward the office when I see it. The left rear tire on my car is completely flat and there is a nail sticking into the side. Son of a bitch! I'm really getting sick and tired of this cold, gray weather.

CPSIA information can be obtained
at www.ICGtesting.com
Printed in the USA
BVHW040725110719
553135BV00009BA/99/P